A Brief Guide to Philo

Other books by Kenneth Schenck
from Westminster John Knox Press

Understanding the Book of Hebrews: The Story behind the Sermon

A BRIEF GUIDE TO PHILO

Kenneth Schenck

WESTMINSTER
JOHN KNOX PRESS
LOUISVILLE • KENTUCKY

Unless otherwise indicated, all translations are the author's. Scripture quotations marked NRSV are from the New Revised Standard Version of the Bible, copyright © 1989 by the Division of Christian Education of the National Council of the Churches of Christ in the U.S.A., and are used by permission. Scripture quotations marked RSV are from the Revised Standard Version of the Bible, copyright © 1946, 1952, 1971, and 1973 by the Division of Christian Education of the National Council of the Churches of Christ in the U.S.A., and are used by permission.

Book design by Sharon Adams
Cover design by Mark Abrams

First edition
Published by Westminster John Knox Press
Louisville, Kentucky

This book is printed on acid-free paper that meets the American National Standards Institute Z39.48 standard. ♾

PRINTED IN THE UNITED STATES OF AMERICA

05 06 07 08 09 10 11 12 13 14 15 — 10 9 8 7 6 5 4 3 2 1

Library of Congress Cataloging-in-Publication Data

Schenck, Kenneth
    A brief guide to Philo / Kenneth Schenck.— 1st ed.
        p. cm.
    Includes bibliographical references and index.
    ISBN 0-664-22735-X (alk. paper)
    1. Philo, of Alexandria. I. Title.

B689.Z7S34 2005
181'.06—dc22
                                    2004057199

To Stefanie, Stacy, Tommy, Sophie, and Papous,
in memory of our time in Germany,
and, most of all, to my magnificent wife,
whose mind reaches the heavens and whose virtue is by nature.

Contents

Abbreviations

Abr.	*On Abraham* (*De Abrahamo*)
Aet.	*On the Eternity of the World* (*De Aeternitate Mundi*)
Agr.	*On Agriculture* (*De Agricultura*)
ALGHJ	Arbeiten zur Literatur und Geschichte des hellenistischen Judentums
Anim.	*On Animals* (*De Animalibus*)
An. Procr.	Plutarch, *De Animae Procreatione in Timaeo*
ANRW	*Aufstieg und Niedergang der römischen Welt: Geschichte und Kultur Roms in Spiegel der neueren Forschung.* Edited by H. Temporini and W. Haase. Berlin, 1972– .
Ant.	Josephus, *Jewish Antiquities*
Aristeas	*Letter of Aristeas*
BEATAJ	Beiträge zur Erforschung des Alten Testaments und des antiken Judentum
BZNW	Beihefte zur Zeitschrift für die neutestamentliche Wissenschaft
CBQ	*Catholic Biblical Quarterly*

CBQMS	Catholic Biblical Quarterly Monograph Series
Cher.	On the Cherubim (De Cherubim)
Conf.	On the Confusion of Tongues (De Confusione Linguarum)
Congr.	On Mating with the Preliminary Studies (De Congressu Eruditionis Gratia)
Contempl.	On the Contemplative Life (De Vita Contemplativa)
CPJ	Corpus papyrorum judaicorum. Edited by V. Tcherikover. 3 vols. Cambridge, 1957–1964.
CQ	Classical Quarterly
Decal.	On the Decalogue (De Decalogo)
Deo	On God (De Deo)
Det.	That the Worse Attacks the Better (Quod Deterius Potiori Insidiari Soleat)
Deus	On the Unchangeableness of God (Quod Deus Sit Immutabilis)
Ebr.	On Drunkenness (De Ebrietate)
I En.	1 Enoch
Flacc.	Against Flaccus (In Flaccum)
fr.	fragment
FRLANT	Forschungen zur Religion und Literatur des Alten und Neuen Testaments
Fug.	On Flight and Finding (De Fuga et Inventione)
Gig.	On the Giants (De Gigantibus)
H.E.	Eusebius, Historia Ecclesiastica
Her.	Who Is the Heir of Divine Things? (Quis Rerum Divinarum Heres Sit)
HTR	Harvard Theological Review
HUCA	Hebrew Union College Annual
Hypoth.	Hypothetica
In Phys.	In Physica
Ios.	On Joseph (De Iosepho)
JBL	Journal of Biblical Literature
JSNT	Journal for the Study of the New Testament
Jub.	Jubilees
Leg.	The Allegorical Laws (Legum Allegoriarum)
Legat.	Embassy to Gaius (Legatio ad Gaium)
Mig.	On the Migration of Abraham (De Migratione Abrahami)
Mos.	On the Life of Moses (De Vita Mosis)
Mut.	On the Changing of Names (De Mutatione Nominum)
NovT	Novum Testamentum
Opif.	On the Creation of the World (De Opificio Mundi)
P.E.	Eusebius, Praeparatio Evangelica
PhilAnt	Philosophia antiqua
Plant.	On Planting (De Plantatione)
Post.	On the Posterity and Exile of Cain (De Posteritate Caini)

Praem.	*On Rewards and Punishments* (*De Praemiis et Poenis*)
Prob.	*That Every Good Person Is Free* (*Quod Omnis Probus Liber Sit*)
Prov.	*On Providence* (*De Providentia*)
QE	*Questions and Answers on Exodus* (*Quaestiones et Solutiones in Exodum*)
QG	*Questions and Answers on Genesis* (*Quaestiones et Solutiones in Genesim*)
1QS	Rules of the Community
Sacr.	*On the Sacrifices of Abel and Cain* (*De Sacrificiis Abelis et Caini*)
SBLDS	Society of Biblical Literature Dissertation Series
ScEs	*Science et esprit*
SJLA	Studies in Judaism in Late Antiquity
SNT	Studien zum Neuen Testament
SNTSMS	Society for New Testament Studies Monograph Series
Sobr.	*On Sobriety* (*De Sobrietate*)
Somn.	*On Dreams* (*De Somniis*)
Spec.	*On the Special Laws* (*De Specialibus Legibus*)
SPhA	*Studia Philonica Annual*
SPhilo	*Studia Philonica*
Str.	Clement of Alexandria, *Stromata*
TSAJ	Texte und Studien zum antiken Judentum
TU	Texte und Untersuchungen
VChrS	Vigiliae Christianae, Supplements
Virt.	*On Virtues* (*De Virtutibus*)
WMANT	Wissenschaftliche Monographien zum Alten und Neuen Testament
WUNT	Wissenschaftliche Untersuchungen zum Neuen Testament

Chapter 1

Philo's Piece of the Puzzle

1.1 PHILO'S PLACE IN THE HELLENISTIC WORLD

It is frustrating to work on a puzzle and suddenly realize some of the pieces are missing. Yet despite our irritation, we usually have enough left to tell what the picture was supposed to be. Perhaps we might miss a spot here or there, but the overall depiction is normally clear enough.

Now imagine that the puzzle has millions of pieces and the overwhelming majority is lost and unrecoverable. Vast portions of an entire landscape are absent, and it is unclear whether the ones in your possession are central to the picture as a whole. Fragments give you clues about what might have been there, but in the end your reconstruction is far from certain.

This scenario is quite similar to the situation in which we find ourselves when we explore the distant past. We have a host of inscriptions and ruins from structures long since deteriorated. We have a number of writings that later generations have copied and preserved. But these puzzle pieces amount to a tiny portion of the whole picture.

In some cases it is only the accidents of history that have allowed certain bits

1

of data to survive. It is thus unclear how significant those pieces originally were in their own time. In other instances people have copied and preserved documents because they found something noteworthy in them. Sometimes they have altered such texts to their liking or discarded those with opposing viewpoints. In these cases we cannot be certain how objective or representative our sources are, particularly in what they tell us about groups who opposed their ideas and practices. In the end, the vast majority of poor, illiterate, ancient people, the ones who did most of the living and dying, have left us nothing to know of their specific joys and struggles.

Any fragment is significant in such a dearth of evidence, even things like purchase agreements and lists of Scripture verses. But an entire collection of documents is a treasure of immense value. The Dead Sea Scrolls made such a contribution in 1947 when they were discovered. Suddenly our picture of Palestinian Judaism at the time of Christ came into better focus. The Oxyrhynchus papyri had a similar effect in the late 1800s. This assortment of mostly ordinary, almost trivial documents suddenly allowed us to peer into the everyday lives and language of the ancient Mediterranean world.

Against this backdrop we can better appreciate the significance of yet another large collection of writings that has survived from the ancient world. These documents are not a recent discovery—Christians preserved them throughout the centuries. Yet they are often neglected despite the immense light they shed on a number of distinct disciplines. I refer to the writings of Philo, a Jew from the Egyptian city of Alexandria who lived at about the same time as Christ.

On the one hand, Philo was no typical ancient. He was extremely wealthy and literate. He enjoyed a privileged life known to very few in his world. Even among the elite he was atypical. While he frequented social events such as athletic contests and the theater, he preferred contemplation. More than anything else, he enjoyed reflecting deeply about ultimate reality as he believed the Jewish Scriptures presented it. Nevertheless, near the end of his life the political climate of Alexandria would force him to get involved in society in a more urgent way.

Yet despite the fact that he was atypical in his world, Philo has left us numerous pieces to the ancient puzzle. This man stood at a corner by which several important traditions were passing at the time. He was a ***Diaspora*** Jew, a Jew who lived outside Palestine. As such he provides us with important information about the boundaries of Judaism, the similarities and dissimilarities of Diaspora Jews to those who lived in Israel. Apart from Josephus, Philo's writings provide us with the largest body of material by a ***Hellenistic*** Jew of the Diaspora.

Diaspora Jews: Jews who lived outside of Palestine; Jews who had "dispersed."

Hellenistic Jews: Jews for whom Greek was a first language.

For this reason, Philo also provides us with an excellent point of reference for interpret-

ing the New Testament, since it was largely written by Hellenistic Jews. The apostle Paul himself was a Greek-speaking Jew from the city of Tarsus, located in what
is now Turkey. It is thus no surprise that Philo's writings furnish us with some
very interesting parallels to New Testament thought at various points. Later
Christian thinkers would significantly draw from Philo as they attempted to for-
mulate the essence of Christian faith.

Finally, Philo stood at the crossroads of a number of ancient philosophical
movements. He consistently drew on Stoic, Platonic, and Pythagorean traditions
in order to interpret the Jewish Scriptures. Thus he provides us with an "archae-
ological dig" from which we can probe the development of ancient philosophy.
Not only do his writings preserve valuable philosophical traditions prior to him,
but they also give us a peek at the seeds from which Neoplatonism sprang in the
third century CE.

In short, Philo's writings have far too many historical, philosophical, and cultural pieces to the ancient puzzle for us to neglect them. Without him, it is not
only our appreciation of the breadth of ancient Judaism that would suffer
immensely. Our knowledge of Roman culture and politics would also diminish.
Our interpretation of the New Testament can only gain from the perspectives his
writings provide on key terms and ideas. And he provides us with the answers to
a host of questions about the development of Hellenistic philosophy that would
otherwise remain unanswered.

1.2 THE MANY PORTRAITS OF PHILO

Although scholars have painted countless portraits of Philo (see Figure 1), we can
capture his essence by way of three titles.[1] Philo was an exegete of the Jewish
Scriptures, a philosopher, and a contemplative "mystic." Each aspect of Philo's
persona has enjoyed a period of dominance, and each contributes to us an important element of his identity.

1.2.1 Philo the Exegete

The work of Valentin Nikiprowetzky turned the focus of Philonic research decisively toward Philo's identity as a biblical interpreter.[2] A little math makes the
basic point. Of the forty-eight treatises that have survived in some form, no fewer
than thirty-nine are exegetical in orientation. Thus, while Philo could and did
write treatises that did not engage the Scriptures directly, most of his work aimed
at appropriating the biblical text.

Identifying Philo's focus on biblical interpretation helps us look for the right
things in his writings. We are bound to be disappointed if we come to them looking for some systematic presentation of philosophical thought. Those who have
come to the Philonic corpus in search of such a coherent system either have
imposed their own systems on him[3] or have come away rather disgruntled.[4]

Figure 1. Portraits of Philo

Philo the Brainless: A number of scholars have claimed that Philo's voluminous writings have no original thoughts or have emphasized their incoherence. Thus A. J. Festugière believed you could read all of Philo's writings "without encountering a single original reflection that points to some personal experience" (see n. 3).

Philo, Founder of Medieval Philosophy: Harry Wolfson's two-volume *Philo: Foundations of Religious Philosophy in Judaism, Christianity, and Islam* went to the other extreme and saw Philo as the founder of medieval religious philosophy for Judaism, Christianity, and Islam (see n. 2). Philo became a systematic thinker par excellence. Unfortunately, this approach (like the one before) comes to Philo with the wrong expectations.

Philo the Mystic: Several early twentieth-century scholars turned to pagan mystery cults as the key to understanding Philo, Hellenistic Judaism, and early Christianity. For example, Erwin Goodenough believed that Philo was part of a broader tendency in Hellenistic Judaism to see itself as a mystery religion. Goodenough's celebrated *By Light, Light* almost certainly went too far in its claims (see n. 5), but we can still consider Philo a mystic in a limited sense.

Philo the Gnostic: Similar to the trend toward interpreting Philo in mystical terms, mid-twentieth-century scholarship often used Philo's writings to construct a hypothetical gnostic background that provided the key to understanding Philo and early Christianity. Hans Jonas would be a key figure who interpreted Philo in this way (e.g., *Gnosis und spätantiker Geist: Von der Mythologie zur mystischen Philosophie* [Göttingen: Vandenhoeck & Ruprecht, 1954], 70–121). This approach is now rightly seen as anachronistic: Gnosticism did not exist as a distinct entity at this point in time.

Philo the Middle Platonic Philosopher: Philo's writings are frequently philosophical in orientation. Hence scholars have often discussed Philo as a philosopher, particularly as a Middle Platonist. John Dillon's classic *The Middle Platonists: 80 B.C. to A.D. 220* (Ithaca, NY: Cornell University, 1977) devotes some forty-five pages to Philo's place in this philosophical stream. While the philosophical hat was not the primary one Philo wore, his thought frequently represents Middle Platonism, as best we can tell.

Philo the Jewish Exegete: Valentin Nikiprowetzky's classic work *Le commentaire de l'écriture chez Philon d'Alexandrie* (see n. 1) decisively turned Philonic scholarship toward the idea that Philo was more a biblical interpreter than a philosopher. This turn was an important corrective, even if Nikiprowetzky sometimes made Philo's writings more ordered than they in the end actually are.

Philo the Faithful Jew: Recent years have seen a movement across several disciplines to reclaim ancient individuals such as Jesus, Paul, and even Philo for "mainstream" Judaism. Peder Borgen and Naomi Cohen, among others, have pointed to connections between Philo's interpretations and those of later rabbinic midrash. They would claim to varying degrees that Philo's exegesis has more in common with mainstream Jewish tradition than scholars have often believed. These studies help provide balance to the picture of Philo as the consummate Hellenistic Jew, although we must be careful not to go too far in the other direction.

Of Philo's three commentary series, the series called The Exposition of the Law clearly follows the order of material in the Pentateuch in a general and selective way. The same is true in more detail with regard to his other two series as well. His Questions and Answers on Genesis and Exodus follows the biblical text unit by unit, perhaps even following the weekly readings of the synagogue. His Allegorical Commentary also proceeds through the Genesis text passage by passage, although Philo frequently digresses in it to other parts of Scripture. Yet there is usually a textual basis for his wanderings, perhaps some catchword in the text, and he customarily returns to the original passage when he is done roaming.

Nikiprowetzky and many other contemporary scholars have come to see Philo's commentaries as a reflection of the expository activity of the ancient synagogue.[5] This observation certainly does not imply that Philo simply collected and reproduced various interpretations haphazardly. But at the same time we can only imagine the depth of tradition we could potentially unearth from Philo's writings if we could only more clearly distinguish the various strata from one another.

1.2.2 Philo the Philosopher

Nikiprowetzky contended strongly that Philo's thought was not meant to be discussed in removal from the biblical text. He argued that Philo equated philosophy with the law of Moses and therefore that Greek philosophy supplied only the rational language by which Philo examined its allegorical meanings. To abstract his philosophy without due regard for the texts in question was to skew his thought. Thus we should see Philo as exegete rather than philosopher.

This analysis provided a helpful corrective to portraits of Philo that interpreted him almost exclusively as a philosopher. Yet Nikiprowetzky almost certainly erred on the other side of the equation. We must therefore in the end reverse Nikiprowetzky's argument to some extent. It was not that the law of Moses was philosophy for Philo but that the biblical text served as a window on the ideal philosophy for those who do not live it by nature (cf. *Abr.* 3–5). The biblical text was, more often than not, the focal point of Philo's attention and the catalyst for his individual ideas. But ultimately he was looking to a truth beyond the text, and such truth was frequently philosophical in nature.

Further, Philo fits his own description of a philosopher, even if he does not always satisfy modern expectations. Philo takes several paragraphs in *Special Laws* 3 to discuss how the eyes mediate philosophy's entrance into the human mind (3.185–94). After a fascinating discussion of the cosmos and how it leads us to contemplate God and the substance of the world, Philo declares the person who looks into these things a philosopher (3.191). Since Philo himself was the one leading his reader through the topic, he must certainly have thought of himself in those terms (cf. also *Cher.* 85).

1.2.3 Philo the Mystic

The word *mystic* is unfortunately a somewhat ambiguous term at present. It suggests different things to different people. To complicate matters further, those scholars who originally spoke of Philo in these terms had ancient mystery religions in view, a feature of the ancient world that does not neatly correspond to anything in our frame of reference. When E. R. Goodenough argued that Hellenistic Judaism had come to see itself as a kind of "mystery," it was the mystery cults of the ancient world he had in mind.[6]

While Goodenough contributed greatly to our understanding of Philo, scholars have not followed him on this particular issue.[7] Nevertheless, the question of whether we can rightly consider Philo a mystic has continued to raise discussion. David Winston has argued convincingly that we can consider Philo a mystic in at least a limited sense.[8]

He concludes that we can most genuinely refer to Philo as mystical when we look at the experiential language he sometimes uses.[9] Philo can speak of contemplation as a kind of intoxication or frenzy (e.g., *Opif.* 71) and of being possessed by divine love (e.g., *Somn.* 2.232). He can speak of illumination through God, "by light, light" (*Praem.* 46), and of leaving one's body to unite with God (*Fug.* 92).

Yet Winston carefully observes that none of this experiential language appears in the context of Philo's quest for a *vision* of God. Indeed, even in the passage in which Philo speaks of intoxication and frenzy (an image from the Dionysian mysteries), he speaks of *sober* intoxication, an intellectual "intoxication." Further, Winston notes that mystical experiences are almost always of short duration, while Philo aims at a permanent vision of God.[10]

The term *mystic* thus does not perfectly describe Philo, although it seems to address an important element of who he was. Philo aimed at a state of perpetual likeness to God and a clear vision of God. Clearly he also saw contemplation as joining the company of the heavens, being inspired by God and borne beyond the earthly (*Spec.* 3.1). When he described the experience of the realm beyond the world of the senses, he frequently did employ mystical language. Yet this language must be read within the appropriate bounds. God in his essence is unknowable, and the ascent of which Philo spoke was primarily a rational one.

1.3 THIS BOOK

This book is a brief guide to Philo and his writings. It is written so that someone with only an elementary knowledge of ancient Judaism, Christianity, or philosophy can understand it. Chapter 2 presents an overview of Philo's life and writings. On the whole we do not know a great deal about the specifics of his life. But we can infer a number of things from what we know of his world, and he does occasionally make comments from which we can make educated guesses.

The chapter also provides an overview of his writings and the ways in which Philonic scholars currently group them.

Chapter 3 then discusses Philo as a Jew in a Gentile world. It principally asks how Philo balanced his loyalty to Judaism with his love of Hellenism. We will find that he valued his Jewish heritage and a literal keeping of the Jewish law. Yet he also adjusted his practice at times to work within a Diaspora context, and often processed Jewish traditions from a Hellenistic perspective.

Chapter 4 presents Philo the thinker, principally in terms of his philosophical interests. His particular brand of Platonic thinking often lay at the heart of the way he interpreted the Jewish Scriptures. This chapter lays out the philosophical paradigm by which Philo sometimes interpreted Scripture, while also drawing attention to some of the Jewish exegetical traditions he inherited at Alexandria. A final section discusses some of Philo's views of society, particularly his negative view of women.

Chapter 5 is for students of the New Testament and early Christianity. It discusses some of the more significant proposals scholars have made correlating Philo's writings to the New Testament. The main candidates are the Gospel of John, Hebrews, and Paul's writings. Beyond the New Testament, the chapter briefly mentions the influence Philo had on early Christian thought in the first few centuries of the church.

Chapter 6 presents the reader with a short summary of each of Philo's extant treatises. They are presented in an order designed for someone wishing to read through the whole Philonic corpus. The order thus generally moves from the more accessible treatises to Philo's more complex writing. In themselves these summaries give a good sense of Philo's thought and approach to life.

The book closes with a topical index to Philo's writings, a glossary, and a bibliography. The topical index references passages in Philo's writings on key topics of interest. Whether you are interested in Philo for his contribution to our knowledge of Judaism, Christianity, philosophy, or some other field, the index tries to give a person access to the potential of Philo's corpus.

This book aims to be more than an introduction to Philo. While it does present the basics of Philo's writings and thought, we are also interested in how to *use* his corpus to shed light on questions raised by other disciplines. We are thus writing for the practitioner as well as for the person interested in Philo for his own sake.

Notes

1. Of inestimable value for the student of Philo is the *Studia Philonica Annual* (Providence, RI: Brown University Press, 1989–present), which not only is filled with the most recent studies of Philo but also has taken on the gargantuan task of recording all articles and books on Philo as they appear.
2. *Le commentaire de l'écriture chez Philon d'Alexandrie* (Leiden: E. J. Brill, 1977).
3. E.g., H. A. Wolfson, *Philo: Foundations of Religious Philosophy in Judaism, Christianity, and Islam*, 2 vols. (Cambridge, MA: Harvard University Press, 1947). In a much different way, J. Cazeaux "found" an extremely intricate order in the

exegetical flow of five Philonic treatises (*La trame et la chain: ou les structures littéraires et l'exégèse dans cinq des traits de Philon d'Alexandrie* [ALGHJ 15; Leiden: E. J. Brill, 1983]). Occam's razor militates against such complexity being intended.

4. Hence the infamous remarks of E. R. Dodds, W. Theiler, and A. J. Festugière. Dodds: "Any attempt to extract a coherent system from Philo seems to me foredoomed to failure; his eclecticism is that of the jackdaw rather than the philosopher" ("The Parmenides of Plato and the Origin of the Neoplatonic 'One,'" *CQ* 22 [1928]: 132 n. 1); Theiler: "A shadow of tragedy spreads over his work. This man, incapable of understanding the sense of philosophy, blinded by their light, can of course look at no more than the creation of his popular work. At most he finds here and there a genuine expression of his own religious feeling" (my translation, *Die Vorbereitung des Neuplatonismus* [Berlin: Weidmann, 1930], 30); Festugière: "Unfortunately, one is able to read all of Philo without encountering a single original reflection that points to some personal experience. There is nothing that resembles a dialog of the spirit with itself for a vision of destiny or humanity. There is always the agreed, the banalities of the manual" (my translation, *La révélation d'Hermès trismégiste* [Paris: Gabalda, 1945–54], 2.534). With less sarcasm, R. Goulet has argued that Philo largely drew his work from a continuous allegorical commentary on the Pentateuch and thus that his work was largely unoriginal (*La philosophie de Moïse: essai de reconstitution d'un commentaire philosophique préphilonien du Pentateuque* [Paris: Université de Paris, 1987]).

5. A very selective list includes R. G. Hamerton-Kelly, "Sources and Traditions in Philo of Alexandria: Prolegomena to an Analysis of His Writings," *SPhilo* 1 (1972): 3–26; B. Mack, "Exegetical Traditions in Alexandrian Judaism: A Program for the Analysis of the Philonic Corpus," *SPhilo* 3 (1974–75): 71–112; "Philo Judaeus and Exegetical Traditions in Alexandria," *ANRW* 21.1 (1984): 227–71; P. Borgen, *Philo, John, and Paul* (Atlanta: Scholars Press, 1987), 121–29; *Philo of Alexandria: An Exegete for His Time* (Leiden: E. J. Brill, 1997), 9–13; and N. G. Cohen, *Philo Judaeus: His Universe of Discourse* (BEATAJ 24; Frankfurt am Main: Peter Lang, 1995), 14–20.

6. *By Light, Light* (New Haven, CT: Yale University Press, 1935).

7. Although see the discussion of J. J. Collins, *Between Athens and Jerusalem: Jewish Identity in the Hellenistic Diaspora*, 2d ed. (Grand Rapids: Wm. B. Eerdmans, 2000), 210–60.

8. Most recently in "Philo's Mysticism," *SPhA* 8 (1996): 74–82, although he argued for a similar conclusion in "Was Philo a Mystic?" in *Studies in Jewish Mysticism*, ed. J. Dan and F. Talmage (Cambridge, MA: Harvard University Press, 1982), 29–35. See also his *Logos and Mystical Theology in Philo of Alexandria* (Cincinnati: Hebrew Union, 1985).

9. Winston, "Philo's Mysticism," 79–80.

10. Ibid., 82.

Chapter 2

Philo's Life and Writings

2.1 PHILO'S LIFE

2.1.1 Philo's Family and Education

It is impossible to date Philo's life with absolute certainty, but he was probably born some time around 20 BCE, some fifteen years or so before Jesus.[1] By this time Augustus had been emperor of Rome for about ten years and had put an end to its devastating civil wars.[2] A time of unprecedented peace and prosperity ensued.[3] In Jerusalem, Herod the Great was just beginning to refurbish the temple, giving it a grandeur it had never known before (20/19 BCE). It was the Golden Age of Rome, a time when peace and safety made it possible for the wealthy to live out lives of extreme leisure.

Philo was born in the Egyptian city of Alexandria, a place with a prestigious history for Jew and non-Jew alike. Aside from Rome, Alexandria was the greatest city in the empire and was home to the best-known library of the ancient world. Jews had lived in Egypt for over five hundred years when Philo was born, and in Alexandria from not long after its founding some three hundred years earlier.[4]

> **Septuagint:** Properly, the Greek translation of the Pentateuch made in Alexandria in the third century BCE. Scholars also regularly use the term in reference to the translation of the entire Jewish Scriptures prevalent at the time of Christ.

Indeed, it was at Alexandria that the Jewish Law was first translated into Greek, as the **Septuagint** (abbreviated LXX). It is the first known translation of a Scripture from one language to another.[5]

Philo's family had incredible wealth. For example, we know that his brother commanded immense sums of money[6] and served in a high administrative position in Alexandria.[7] Philo was likely a Roman citizen, as well as a citizen of the city of Alexandria itself—rare status for a Jew at that time.[8] For a period, the lap of luxury allowed Philo time to think and write without the encumbrance of life's hassles and necessities.[9]

Philo mentions in *Embassy* that he had a good education (*Legat.* 182).[10] His writings themselves make this point overwhelmingly clear. Not only did he possess an intimate knowledge of the biblical text, but he quotes regularly from Greek authors as well. The fact that his family was one of the wealthiest in Alexandria must have afforded Philo the best education available.

Philo's writings imply several things about the kind of teaching he and other Jewish children received in the synagogues of Alexandria. The first is that the Alexandrian synagogues primarily, if not exclusively, used the Septuagint as a basis for instruction, rather than the Hebrew Bible. While Philo knew some standardized meanings for Hebrew words, his interpretations frequently reflect a significant ignorance of the Hebrew language. His citations from Scripture always come from a Greek translation.[11]

We might also wonder whether such biblical instruction focused primarily on the Pentateuch, since Philo himself clearly favored the Pentateuch over the rest of what we think of as the Jewish Scriptures. It is surely noteworthy that Philo calls the end of Deuteronomy the "end of the holy words" (*Mos.* 2.290). At least some synagogues in Alexandria may have given primacy to the Pentateuch over and against writings that other Jews also reverenced at this time.[12]

Philo no doubt learned a vast number of traditional interpretations as he attended synagogue. The Alexandrian prayer houses no doubt shared some of these in common with Palestinian Judaism. Yet the Alexandrian synagogues also

> **Greek gymnasium:** The center of Greek culture for the elite of society in the Hellenistic age. Here male youths received both physical and intellectual training, leading to their passage into manhood.
> **paideia:** Greek education.
> **encyclios paideia:** The general education expected of a cultured individual, a course of study involving such subjects as grammar, arithmetic, rhetoric, dialectic, geometry, music, and astronomy.

had their own unique traditions and interpretations. Philo's work clearly stands in a long tradition of allegorical exegesis at Alexandria, interpretation that looked for hidden meanings in the biblical text and its stories.

It also seems likely that Philo received at least some education in a **Greek gymnasium.**[13] At first glance, this aspect of Philo is difficult to understand. Gymnasium training for young males included a significant religious component that is hard to reconcile with what we think of as "normal" Judaism. A typical gymnasium was filled with statues of Greek gods, and much of the literature they studied interacted with this religious milieu. Further, youths in the gymnasium participated in religious processions and even in sacrifices to pagan gods.

Yet Philo speaks of the gymnasium in glowing terms, as a place where parents caringly sent children to enable them to live well (*Spec.* 2.229). He favorably mentions the athletic training that dominated gymnasium life, the creation of "good tone and good health" (*Spec.* 2.230). Even more significant to him was the training of the soul that a child received in the gymnasium.

From comments scattered throughout his writings, we know that Philo's education covered all the subjects of what became the medieval trivium (grammar, rhetoric, dialectic) and quadrivium (arithmetic, geometry, music, astronomy).[14] These seven subjects appear to have become somewhat standard by the first century BCE and constituted an **encyclios paideia,** or "general education." Philo's writings make it clear that he learned his lessons well.

Philo speaks of the *encyclios paideia* as "preliminary studies" (*propaideumata*) to philosophy, although only a few took this path.[15] Philo probably went on to study philosophy as a discipline beyond his general education. The more privileged of ancient society sometimes went beyond the *encyclios paideia* to focus on a subject such as medicine, law, rhetoric, or philosophy. The role Philo ascribes to philosophy, the "lawful wife" in his allegory, seems a strong indication of the studies in which he engaged beyond his general education.[16]

Yet Philo ultimately subordinated his affinity for the Greek world and philosophy to his Jewish identity. He defined philosophy as the pursuit of wisdom. Wisdom was thus the goal of philosophy. This wisdom was the "knowledge of things divine and human and the causes of these things" (*Congr.* 79). We can be sure the wisdom he had in mind centered on the Jewish God and the proper understanding of him through the Jewish Scriptures.

2.1.2 Philo and Alexandrian Politics

At some point Philo became involved in the politics of Alexandria. The ethnic group that held primacy in Alexandria was Greek. After Alexander the Great conquered Egypt in 332 BCE, Egypt came under Greek control. Alexander's general Ptolemy retained control of the region after Alexander's death, and his descendents ruled for the next two centuries. The aristocracy of Alexandria (the chief city of Egypt) was thus primarily Greek, a situation that continued even after Roman acquisition in 30 BCE.

> **politeuma:** A smaller political unit within a city, usually a particular ethnic group allowed limited authority to self-govern according to its own customs. Sometimes such a body was directed by an *ethnarch* (a single ethnic leader), as the Alexandrian Jews were until the time of the emperor Augustus. After Augustus, the Jews had this limited self-governance by way of a *gerousia* (a council of elders).

We can distinguish three possible types of "citizenship" an Alexandrian Jew such as Philo might have held. The most obvious was membership in the Jewish *politeuma,* or the Jewish community of the city. The Romans often allowed ethnic groups to organize into communities that partially governed themselves according to their own customs.

Two other potential forms of citizenship also existed for an inhabitant of Alexandria. One might hold membership in the city itself and be an Alexandrian citizen. Such membership was necessary for participation in the city's gymnasium and overall cultural life. Jews and even native Egyptians would not normally have held such membership.

The final form of citizenship one might have was Roman citizenship, an even greater privilege than membership in a city like Alexandria. Only the elite of the city held this status. We likely include Philo and his family among this number. He thus held triple citizenship: he belonged to the Jewish *politeuma* and held both Alexandrian and Roman citizenship.

Philo's family may have received Roman citizenship in the days of Julius Caesar's involvement with Alexandria on behalf of Cleopatra (ca. 47 BCE). The name Julius appears prominently in Philo's family, as in the name of his nephew Tiberius Julius Alexander. This nephew apostatized from Judaism and went on to become procurator of Judea from 46 to 48 CE and prefect of Egypt in 66–70 CE. These are clear indications of his family's prestige and Roman citizenship, as well as the "fine line" Philo's family must have walked between their Jewish identity and their Greco-Roman environment.

While Philo probably had always participated to some degree in the politics of Alexandria, the crisis of 38 CE no doubt took his involvement to the next level. Philo mentions in one treatise that "envy" of some sort plunged him "into the great sea of civic concerns," making it almost impossible for his soul to look toward the heavens in contemplation (*Spec.* 3.3). We cannot know for certain what specific events Philo had in mind in this passage. Nevertheless, the crisis of 38 CE remains the main candidate.[17]

Long-standing tensions between Alexandrian Jews and other groups, such as the native Egyptians, stand in the background of this crisis. However, the trigger seems to have been a visit to Alexandria by the Jewish king Agrippa I. The presence of such a prominent Jew incensed many in the city. Crowds of Alexandrian citizens murmured and mocked Agrippa at the gymnasium. They even dressed up an insane man to mimic him, parading the man around and hailing him with the Aramaic word for "lord" (*Flacc.* 36–39).

The violence escalated against the Jews. Images of the emperor Caligula were forcibly placed in most of the city's prayer houses, and a bronze statue of a charioteer with four horses was placed in the largest synagogue.[18] Jews were beaten, stabbed, dragged through the city, set on fire, and their bodies left to rot (cf. *Flacc.* 65–71). To escape the violence, Jews throughout the city crowded into areas where the Jewish population was densest. Meanwhile the Roman prefect Flaccus stood by and watched, apparently doing nothing to stop the violence.

However, the event that most directly affected Philo was when Flaccus declared the Jews of the city "foreigners and aliens," which among other things denied them entrance to the gymnasium.[19] More significantly, it did not give the Jews any legal recourse in the conflict that ensued.[20] After things settled down, Philo would lead a delegation to Rome to appeal on behalf of the Jews in the city.

Just as the apostle Paul was beginning his Christian life, Philo was heading a delegation to the Roman emperor Caligula. This delegation left Alexandria for Rome in midwinter (*Legat.* 190). We would expect that the departure took place not long after Flaccus's arrest in September 38 CE, thus in late 38/early 39 CE. Philo indicates that they first met up with Caligula in southern Italy, an encounter that apparently gave hope to most of the delegation.[21]

Caligula then left for Gaul and Germany in September 39 CE, apparently leaving the delegation in limbo for the better part of a year. At some point during this time, news reached the delegation of Caligula's plans to place a statue of himself in the Jerusalem temple. Such news caused them to lose hope (*Legat.* 184–96). Their complaints had involved only smaller images in their prayer houses, and now Gaius planned to put one in the temple itself. Philo came to see his delegation as the hope for all the Jews of the world (*Legat.* 370).

Philo's main appearance before Caligula then occurred sometime between the emperor's return in perhaps May 40 CE and his assassination in January 41 CE. Philo records the frustration of trying to make a coherent argument before a person who was preoccupied with windows and irrelevant questions such as the Jewish prohibition against eating pork (*Legat.* 361–67). In the end, Caligula seems to have considered the delegation as more peculiar than guilty.

But an official verdict would wait until after Caligula's death, when Claudius became emperor. Claudius refused to assign guilt for the events of 38 CE. He instructed the Jews not to interfere with the gymnasium and implied that they should not bring individuals like Herod into the city. He refused to assign them citizenship. Yet he also told the Alexandrians to respect the particular customs and religious practices of the Jews.

We can only speculate about the effect these events had on Philo. It is possible that Philo's sympathy for Hellenistic culture and participation in Alexandrian public life diminished somewhat. In one of Philo's treatises, he compares himself to a drunken man who had deliriously involved himself in politics. He looks to others who might help him see a more appropriate way of life (*Somn.* 2.104). He hopes to hate the political dreamer as they do and yield to their superior wisdom (*Somn.* 2.104).[22]

2.1.3 The Rest of the Story

We do not know exactly when Philo died, but he may have lived beyond 47 CE. He may mention a horse race that took place that year in honor of the Roman emperor Claudius.[23] He would have been around seventy years old, dying at about the same time the apostle Paul was entering Greece for the first time. These were years of relative calm for the Jews at Alexandria. The conflict had finally ended, even if the Jews did not obtain the status they had wanted.[24] Providence spared Philo the despair of some twenty years later, when the Romans surrounded and destroyed Jerusalem (70 CE).

We thus know very little about the concrete details of Philo's life. In addition to his trip to Rome in 39–40 CE, we know that he visited the temple in Jerusalem at least once (*Prov.* 2.64). Of his social life, we know that he participated in banquets (*Leg.* 3.155–59) and went to the theater (*Ebr.* 177; *Prob.* 141). He attended athletic events such as "pancration," a combination of wrestling and boxing (*Prob.* 26). We can conjecture that he attended a horse race in 47 CE (*Anim.* 58). Beyond scattered allusions such as these, we know very little of what Philo's daily life was like.

We do know that he spent a lot of time reflecting on the Scriptures and presenting his interpretations to others. In the course of his life, Philo would write some seventy treatises, almost fifty of which have survived either completely or in fragments.[25] He may even have run a school in Alexandria to train Jewish men to become skilled interpreters of the Scriptures, particularly the Pentateuch.[26] It is to his writings that we now turn.

2.2 PHILO'S WRITINGS

We can divide Philo's writings into three distinct categories: (1) commentaries on Scripture, (2) apologetic/historical treatises, and (3) philosophical treatises. The bulk of Philo's writings by far belong in the first category. Yet Philo also wrote several significant treatises that were not primarily concerned with Scriptural interpretation. Chapter 6, "Philo's Writings in a Nutshell," provides a brief overview of these treatises and suggests an order in which to read through them.

The Philo of Alexandria Group of the Society of Biblical Literature has recently undertaken the publication of the first commentary series on Philo's treatises. While it does not intend to cover the entire Philonic corpus, it promises to provide unprecedented access to Philo's writings. David Runia's commentary on the treatise *On the Creation* has already appeared, as has Pieter van der Horst's on the *Flaccus*.[27]

2.2.1 Philo's Three Great Commentary Series

The overwhelming majority of Philo's work consisted of three great commentary series. Philo may have worked on these simultaneously throughout his lifetime.

These are his Questions and Answers on Genesis and Exodus, his Allegorical Commentary, and his Exposition of the Law. Each has a distinct flavor of its own, and Philo likely intended each for a different audience. All three focus in one way or another on the content of the Pentateuch, and on Genesis in particular.

Since the book form was not widely used in Philo's day, we have largely inherited these commentary series as individual treatises.[28] At times it is easy to see which ones go together in which order, but in other instances we have to make educated guesses.[29] In this process, we look for (1) comments within Philo's writings that give a sense of how the treatises originally related to one another and (2) the ways in which ancient authors listed and referred to Philo's corpus. We find such lists and references primarily in the early Christian authors Eusebius and Clement of Alexandria.

Questions and Answers on Genesis and Exodus

Philo may have written Questions and Answers on Genesis and Exodus as the first of his three commentary series.[30] But Questions has not received as much attention as his other writings, at least in part because it is not as well preserved.[31] This series has mostly survived in the Armenian language and consists of Philo's answers to questions he directs at the text of Genesis and Exodus. If Philo wrote similar treatises on the rest of the Pentateuch (Leviticus, Numbers, and Deuteronomy), they have not survived. It seems more likely that he never wrote them, although he may have intended to do so.[32]

Substantial portions of Questions have been lost.[33] The text we have of *Questions and Answers on Genesis* (hereafter *QG*) covers only Genesis 2:4–28:9, and even within this section we find missing passages. We have even less of *Questions and Answers on Exodus* (hereafter *QE*). The bulk of the material that has survived covers Exodus 12:2–28:4.

QG originally consisted of six books of roughly continuous commentary.[34] The same was probably true originally of *QE*, although the surviving Armenian text has only two books. A good case has been made that Philo's questions in these treatises follow the sequence in which Scripture was read in the synagogue.[35] In other words, some scholars think that Alexandrian synagogues had set Scriptural readings for each week and that Philo's Questions followed this lectionary (cycle of set readings) unit by unit.

There is less agreement on whether the question-answer style of this series originated in the synagogue or whether Philo largely drew it from Hellenistic commentaries. Peter Borgen and Roald Skarsten have argued that the question-and-answer format was part of Alexandrian synagogue practice.[36] Others argue that the method is much more in keeping with Greek problem-solution texts such as Aristotle's *Homeric Problems* or some of the writings of Plutarch.[37]

Philo presupposes some biblical and philosophical knowledge in this commentary series. But his line of thinking is much simpler than what we find in the series known as the Allegorical Commentary. He is also less dogmatic in his interpretations than in his Allegorical Commentary, and he provides a variety of literal and allegorical interpretations of the texts. On the whole, he engages more with the literal level of meaning than the allegorical in this series. Philo also refers less often to biblical passages outside Genesis in Questions than he does in the Allegorical Commentary.[38]

Despite the differences between the two series, *QG* covers much of the same textual ground as the Allegorical Commentary. This fact has led scholars to ask what, if any, relationship might exist between the two series. Samuel Sandmel suggested the Questions might have been notes Philo made in preparation for writing the Allegorical Commentary.[39] Sandmel thus considered them of most value when they did not overlap with the other commentary series. Others have thought they were later than the Allegorical Commentary or that the two series were roughly contemporaneous with each other.[40] Still others think they were prior but had a purpose independent of the Allegorical Commentary, such as to serve as a kind of elementary catechism.[41]

The Allegorical Commentary

By far the most complicated of Philo's writings are the treatises in his commentary series known as The Allegorical Commentary.[42] E. R. Goodenough rightly suggested that the Philo beginner read them toward the end of his or her pilgrimage through the Philonic corpus. They are a rite of passage, and thereafter the victorious reader can no longer be considered a beginner.[43] From a pedagogical standpoint, their placement at the beginning of most Philo collections must be seen as unfortunate.

However, none of these observations diminishes the treatises' extreme value. Philo did not likely write them for the average Bible reader. They were written for an audience with extensive biblical and philosophical acumen. And part of our difficulty is that Philo nowhere tells us the method to his presentation. Even some scholars have experienced these treatises as a formless labyrinth from which they have no sense of how to get out. More recent days have seen a number of suggestions that help unlock the format Philo is following, showing how his analysis moves from point to point.

We are certain of at least twenty-six books in this series, although there were likely more.[44] We currently have all or part of twenty-three of these:

1. *The Allegorical Laws* 1 (*Legum Allegoriae I*; Gen. 2:1–17)
2. *The Allegorical Laws* 2 (*Legum Allegoriae II*; Gen. 2:18–3:1)
3. *The Allegorical Laws* 3 (*Legum Allegoriae III*; Gen. 3:8b–3:19)
4. Lost fourth treatise (we have a fragment)
5. *On the Cherubim* (*De Cherubim*; Gen. 3:24–4:1)
6. *On the Sacrifices of Abel and Cain* (*De Sacrificiis Abelis et Caini*; Gen. 4:2–4)
7. *That the Worse Attacks the Better* (*Quod Deterius Potiori Insidiari Soleat*; Gen. 4:8–15)
8. *On the Posterity and Exile of Cain* (*De Posteritate Caini*; Gen. 4:16–25)

9. *On the Giants* (*De Gigantibus;* Gen. 6:1–4a)
10. *On the Unchangeableness of God* (*Quod Deus Sit Immutabilis;* Gen. 6:4b–12)[45]
11. *On Agriculture* (*De Agricultura;* Gen. 9:20–21)
12. *On Noah's Work as a Planter* (*De Plantatione;* Gen. 9:20–21)
13. *On Drunkenness* (*De Ebrietate;* Gen. 9:20–21)
14. Lost second treatise on drunkenness
15. *On Sobriety* (*De Sobrietate;* Gen. 9:24–27)
16. *On the Confusion of Tongues* (*De Confusione Linguarum;* Gen. 11:1–9)
17. *On the Migration of Abraham* (*De Migratione Abrahami;* Gen. 12:1–6)
18. Lost treatise on Genesis 15:1, mentioned by Philo at *Her.* 1.
19. *Who Is the Heir of Divine Things?* (*Quis Rerum Divinarum Heres Sib;* Gen. 15:2–18)
20. *On Mating with the Preliminary Studies* (*De Congressu Quaerendae Eruditionis Gratia;* Gen. 16:1–5)
21. *On Flight and Finding* (*De Fuga et Inventione;* Gen. 16:6b–14)
22. *On the Change of Names* (*De Mutatione Nominum;* Gen. 17:1–5, 16–22)
23. *On God* (*De Deo*)—Armenian fragment
24. Lost first treatise of the subseries *On Dreams*
25. *On Dreams 1* (*De Somniis I;* Gen. 28:10–22; 31:10–13)
26. *On Dreams 2* (*De Somniis II;* Gen. 37:8–11; 40:9–11, 16–17; 41:17–24)

The treatises we have roughly cover Genesis 2:1–41:24, but there are also a number of gaps. It is therefore likely that we are missing several other treatises from this collection.

Scholars of a historical-critical bent have not always shown the greatest appreciation for Philo's Allegorical Commentary. Since modern culture prizes reading texts in context, Philo's method of interpretation has often met with disapproval among post-Enlightenment scholars.[46] His interpretations in this series lean heavily toward the allegorical and often proceed by stringing together one interpretation after another on the basis of what we might consider superficial elements in the text.

In one of the nicer critiques, F. H. Colson made a famous comment worth repeating:[47]

> These treatises, which are fairly homogeneous, do not aim at any continuous or systematic body of thought. They are expositions of what Philo conceives to be the inner and spiritual meaning of various incidents and texts in Genesis. . . . Unfortunately, perhaps—though it is a fault which is rather loveable—he is an inveterate rambler. This word does not mean that the thoughts are disconnected. In fact it is the mark of a true rambler that his points are always connected, and that he is unable to restrain himself from following up each connexion as it occurs. Philo takes his text and expounds its philosophical meaning and proceeds to illustrate it from some other text, in which he discerns the same idea. But this second text generally contains some other

words in which he finds some other idea, too valuable to be passed over. The process might, of course, go on indefinitely, but even Philo feels that there must be some limit to it and ultimately returns to his main subject.

While Colson obviously loved Philo, he could not see much of a method to the way in which the Allegorical Commentary is organized. Other scholars have, of course, found incredible order to Philo's treatises—too much, in fact.[48] Such proposals have not generally convinced other scholars.

Philo's Allegorical Commentary does have an order to it, even if it is not the kind of order modern biblical commentators prefer. The primary organization is according to the biblical text. Philo proceeds from passage to passage in a mostly sequential fashion through the book of Genesis.[49] It is true that Philo often moves from the primary text in question to other, subsidiary texts. But as even Colson acknowledged, Philo ultimately returns to the passage with which he began, resulting in a "chapter" of sorts. We can thus see the basic order of the Allegorical Commentary as a progression from chapter to chapter.[50]

Admittedly, it is not always easy to define the limits of these chapters. Philo often moves from the primary text in question to other passages by way of catchwords or similarities in (supposed) meaning. Valentin Nikiprowetzky moved the discussion of such structures forward with his suggestion that the Allegorical Commentary was structured around a finite number of questions and answers.[51] However, he probably read too much structure into the Allegorical Commentary on this point. Philo often did format his interpretations by way of a question-answer format, but not universally or without exception.

The Exposition of the Law

Of Philo's three commentary series, the most accessible is clearly the Exposition of the Law. Its treatises generally do not require a very detailed knowledge of either the Bible or philosophy. As such, Philo probably intended it for an audience that had little knowledge of either Judaism or philosophy. Ellen Birnbaum suggests several possible aims Philo may have had in mind: "to reclaim the alienated Jews, educate the less knowledgeable ones, assuage non-Jews who may be hostile, and appeal to those who might be interested."[52] It is not difficult to see the Exposition as an implicit apology to the "cultured despisers" of Judaism. Perhaps Philo wrote it for the day when he believed Gentiles would turn to the Jewish God.[53]

This commentary series originally consisted of at least twelve treatises, most of which have survived. The following list presents the most widely held view of its contents:

1. *On the Creation* (*De Opificio*)
2. *On Abraham* (*De Abrahamo*)
3. A lost treatise *On Isaac*

4. A lost treatise *On Jacob*
5. *On Joseph* (*De Iosepho*)
6. *On the Decalogue* (*De Decalogo*)
7–10. *On the Special Laws*, vols. 1–4 (*De Specialibus Legibus*)
11. *On Virtues* (*De Virtutibus*)
12. *On Rewards and Punishments* (*De Praemiis et Poenis*)

Philo himself reviews this content in *On Rewards and Punishments* (1–3), where he summarizes the series. In this passage he divides Moses' writings (i.e., the Pentateuch) into three categories: (1) material on the creation, (2) historical material, and (3) legislative material.[54] The first category most likely alludes to Philo's treatise *On the Creation*, which would thus be the first treatise of the Exposition.[55] The second category relates to the historical personages Philo discusses in his *On Abraham*, his two lost treatises on Isaac and Jacob, and his treatise *On Joseph*.

Philo then divides the third, legislative part of the Pentateuch into (1) the ten general headings under which all the laws fall and (2) the specific laws themselves. He clearly refers to the treatise *On the Decalogue* when he mentions the ten general headings of the law (*Praem.* 2). The subseries *On the Special Laws* thus covers the specific laws themselves. Philo concludes his summary with mention of a discussion on virtues (i.e., the treatise *On Virtues*) and introduces the treatise he is beginning (*On Rewards*) as the continuation of the ones he has just mentioned.

The scholarly consensus on the outline of the Exposition thus corresponds well to Philo's own summary. However, scholars sometimes differ on the relationship of these writings to Philo's two treatises called the *Life of Moses*. On the one hand, the character of *Moses* fits well with the other writings in the Exposition. The two-volume work is largely written to the "outsider" with little background knowledge of Moses—the same approach as is used in the other biographies in the Exposition. We understand the sentiment that the Exposition would have "an unaccountable gap between the life of Joseph and the Decalogue" if the treatises of Moses did not belong there.[56]

On the other hand, Philo's summary in *Rewards* does not clearly allude to *Moses*, nor does it give us the sense internally that it belongs to a larger series. The flavor of Philo's *Moses* fits with the Exposition, but the series itself may or may not include it. This tension has led scholars such as E. R. Goodenough and Peder Borgen to see the *Life of Moses* as a kind of "companion piece" to the Exposition.[57] This suggestion is reasonable, although it is difficult to conclude with certitude.

2.2.2 Philo's Historical and Apologetic Treatises

It is customary to place four of Philo's surviving works into the category of "apologetic and historical treatises," although several of Philo's lost works would also belong in this category. In one reconstruction, we would have

    I. a five-volume work showing God's protection of the Jews
        1. a lost treatise on Pilate (proposed)
        2. a lost treatise on Sejanus (alluded to in *Flacc.* 1)
        3. *Against Flaccus* (*In Flaccum*)
        4. *On the Embassy to Gaius* (*De Legatione ad Gaium*)
        5. a lost sequel on the demise of Gaius Caligula (alluded to in *Legat.* 373)
    II. a defense of the Jews
        1. at least excerpt 1 from *Hypothetica*
        2. a lost book (implied by Eusebius in *P.E.* 8.5)
    III. series discussing the Essenes and Therapeutae[58]
        1. A lost treatise describing the Essenes (alluded to in *Contempl.* 1)
        2. *On the Contemplative Life* (*De Vita Contemplativa*)

There is much to debate about this reconstruction, but it nonetheless provides a starting point for discussion.[59]

Against Flaccus and the *Embassy to Gaius*

Perhaps the most significant of Philo's treatises from our perspective are his two writings *Against Flaccus* and *On the Embassy to Gaius*. Both relate in one way or another to the persecution of Alexandrian Jews under the Roman prefect Flaccus in 38 CE, during the reign of Gaius Caligula. We have lost other treatises that originally went along with these two, works that no doubt would answer a great many questions we have.

Against Flaccus originally followed another treatise that is lost. As a whole, these volumes must have demonstrated that God always punishes those who oppress the Jews. The lost work presented the demise of Sejanus, who made accusations against the Jews during the reign of the emperor Tiberius. *Flaccus* similarly shows God's judgment on Flaccus for his part in the persecution of Alexandrian Jews during the pogrom.

The treatise *Embassy* relates to the same basic set of events as *Flaccus*, but in relation to the emperor Gaius Caligula. In it Philo tells about his appearance before Caligula as part of a Jewish delegation to plead for the rights of Alexandrian Jews. *Embassy* ends somewhat abruptly, promising a "palinode" demonstrating Caligula's demise (*Legat.* 373). As such, it would have shown that God always judges those who oppress the Jews, just as the *Flaccus* did.

We cannot know for certain whether Philo ever wrote this sequel. We have no fragments or citations from it (as far as we know), and it is not explicitly mentioned in the lists we have of Philo's works. However, many Philo scholars believe that these two treatises were part of a five-book set that the early Christian Eusebius seems to mention (cf. *H.E.* 2.5).[60] In Pieter W. van der Horst's reconstruction of this series, the first volume discussed the persecution of the Jews under Pilate in Judea, while the second treated Sejanus.[61] *Flaccus* would thus be the third treatise and *Embassy* the fourth. Its promised sequel would then have been the final volume in the series.

This suggestion is attractive and possible, although we cannot know its accuracy. For example, it is surely noteworthy that *Embassy* nowhere mentions or alludes to *Flaccus*. In fact, they contradict each other at a number of points. Goodenough believed they were written for some successor to Flaccus and Caligula, respectively, another interesting if still problematic suggestion.[62] Further, this proposal contradicts the way in which the manuscripts actually present *Embassy*.[63]

Hypothetica and *On the Contemplative Life*

These two treatises raise many questions for us in terms of where they fit in the corpus of Philo's writings. Both clearly were a part of larger works (perhaps even of the same work), but it is not entirely clear what those works were. In the case of the *Hypothetica*, we only have two quotations from Eusebius, both of which are excerpts from the larger work. We cannot even be absolutely certain that the second excerpt comes from the same treatise as the first![64]

The *Hypothetica* appears to have been an apology for the Jews in at least two volumes. The first excerpt from Eusebius engages in what we might call competitive history. It presents an account of the exodus under Moses in a way that "competes" with other negative portrayals by other historians. The second excerpt is one of two instances in Philo's writings where Philo discusses the Essenes.[65]

On the Contemplative Life implies at its beginning that it follows a treatise discussing the Essenes (*Contempl.* 1). This previous volume was either (1) the *Hypothetica* (see below), (2) the treatise *That Every Good Person Is Free*, or (3) an entirely different work that is lost. While *On the Contemplative Life* clearly deals with those who pursue a life of contemplation, the treatise that preceded it presented the Essenes as a consummate example of the active life.

The *Hypothetica* thus discusses the Essenes and is missing a second volume. Similarly, *On the Contemplative Life* follows a missing volume that discussed the Essenes. For obvious reasons, these facts have led many scholars to see these two treatises as companion pieces.[66] The existing fragments of the *Hypothetica* would thus belong to the first volume of which *On the Contemplative Life* was the second. This suggestion is intriguing, although it is not entirely clear that the content of the two treatises really fits together this well on closer examination.

We should mention one other wrinkle to the equation before leaving these two treatises. The manuscripts of Philo's writings typically mention *On the Contemplative Life* as the fourth volume in a series *On Virtues*. What is surprising is that the *Embassy* to Gaius is often mentioned as the first volume in this series. We would then have the sequence:

1. *Embassy to Gaius*
2. the lost sequel, perhaps showing the demise of Gaius

3. a lost treatise that included a discussion of the Essenes (*Hypothetica?*)
4. *On the Contemplative Life*

While scholars have often struggled with how such a sequence could have the title On Virtues, we should not dismiss the possibility without at least some consideration. We should remember that the text of *Embassy* itself has a number of points where material may be missing, and its preface could well have served as a general introduction to such a series.

2.2.3 Philo's Philosophical Treatises

A final category into which we can place a number of Philo's treatises is that of the philosophical. In this category we may have some of Philo's earliest work, as well as some of his last. We have five such treatises at least in part, and know of a few others that are lost:

   I. *On the Eternity of the World* (*De Aeternitate Mundi*)
   II. at least a two-volume work
      1. A lost work, *Every Bad Person Is a Slave*
      2. *That Every Good Person Is Free* (*Quod Omnis Probus Liber Sit*)
   III. a two-volume work *On Providence* (*De Providentia*)
      1. book 1 exists only in a mangled Armenian version
      2. book 2 exists in Armenian and in two citations from Eusebius
   IV. *On Animals* (*De Animalibus*; exists only in Armenian)
   V. a lost work *On Numbers* (mentioned in *Opif.* 15, 52)

We give a brief description of the content of the volumes that are extant in chapter 6.

Of all the treatises we have mentioned, *On the Eternity of the World* is the one whose Philonic authorship scholars have most questioned. Nevertheless, the vast majority have concluded in favor of Philonic authorship. Its distinctiveness may point to a relatively early point in Philo's writing.

We have already mentioned the treatise *That Every Good Person Is Free* as another candidate for the volume preceding *On the Contemplative Life*, although most Philonic scholars would not favor this option. It includes Philo's most extensive discussion of the Essenes and is an important source of information for the background of the Dead Sea Scrolls. It mentions a preceding volume at its beginning that treated the opposite theme, namely, that every bad person is a slave.

The two-volume *On Providence* has survived as a whole only in the Armenian language, although we have citations from the second volume in Greek from Eusebius.[67] The text of the first volume in Armenian appears to be quite mangled and includes some Christian **interpolations**. The treatise was originally addressed at Philo's nephew, Tiberius Alexander, who later apostatized from Judaism. It was thus probably written in the latter part of Philo's life, perhaps before Alexander apostatized. It aimed to convince that God's hand directed the activities of the world.

> **interpolation:** A later insertion into a text.

On Animals similarly addressed Tiberius Alexander and is also known as the *Alexander*. This treatise attempts to demonstrate that animals do not have reason. Unfortunately, it survives only in Armenian translation and is not included in the Loeb Classical Library series. Abraham Terian has helpfully provided us with a critical text and English translation.[68] The possible allusion to a horse race that occurred in 47 CE would make this treatise one of the last Philo wrote.

Notes

1. The only event in Philo's life we can date with absolute certainty is his trip to Rome in 39–40 CE. On this trip he headed a delegation that defended the Jews of Alexandria to the emperor Caligula. He calls himself an "old man" as he embarked on this delegation (*Legat.* 1; see the front of the book for the Latin abbreviations of Philo's works). Since he elsewhere defines an old man as someone over fifty-seven (*Opif.* 105), a birthdate of 20 BCE is a reasonable estimation, give or take ten years. The year of Jesus' birth is equally impossible to date with certainty, although 6 BCE is suggested.
2. Augustus ruled as emperor from 31 BCE to 14 CE.
3. The so-called *pax Romana*—the "Roman peace," also called the *pax Augusta*.
4. Alexander the Great founded the city in 331 BCE.
5. Cf. *Aristeas* 173. It is called the Septuagint because of the legend that seventy men translated it. While the *Aristeas* narrative itself is largely unhistorical, its core claim that the Septuagint was translated at Alexandria during the reign of Ptolemy II Philadelphus (284–246 BCE) seems accurate.
6. For example, he lent two hundred thousand drachmas (about a million dollars) at one point to the grandson of Herod the Great (Herod Agrippa I). See Josephus, *Ant.* 18.159–60.
7. The Jewish historian Josephus refers to Philo's brother Alexander as an "alabarch," perhaps an official who supervised the collection of certain revenues (*Ant.* 18.259; 20.100).
8. While Josephus says that Caesar granted citizenship to *all* the Jews in Alexandria at this time (*Ant.* 14.188), statements made later by the emperor Claudius make this claim highly unlikely, at least in the technical sense of Roman citizenship (*CPJ* 153). See the discussion in J. J. Collins, *Between Athens and Jerusalem: Jewish Identity in the Hellenistic Diaspora,* 2d ed. (Grand Rapids: Wm. B. Eerdmans, 2000), 113–22.
9. See his regretful reminiscence in *Special Laws* 3.1–6. Political responsibilities apparently divided his attention in later life.
10. I will use the English names for Philo's treatises in text, but the Latin abbreviations in parentheses and such. This will help us get acquainted with both ways of referring to his writings.
11. The Alexandrian community may have had some favorite variations of its own on the Septuagint. See D. T. Runia for four citations from the LXX in the book of Hebrews whose unique similarity to Philo bespeaks a common origin, such as a synagogue tradition in Alexandria (*Philo in Early Christian Literature: A Survey* [Minneapolis: Fortress Press, 1993], 76).
12. The book of Sirach already implies a threefold division of the Jewish canon in

Palestine by about 200 BCE (in its Prologue). Sirach's grandson then translated the book into Greek in Egypt in the late second century BCE (also mentioned in the Prologue). Philo's writings never allude or quote from it.

13. Greek gymnasia were much more like country clubs and sports centers than schools. Nevertheless, Philo gives us strong evidence that education also took place there (*Spec.* 2.229–30). This education was primarily for male youths about to enter manhood. The most elementary schooling likely took place elsewhere.

14. For Philo's references to these subjects, see *Congr.* 11, 16–18, 75–76, 148; *Somn.* 1.205.

15. See Philo's treatise *On Mating with the Preliminary Studies*.

16. Especially since he then subordinates philosophy to wisdom (*Congr.* 79). In other words, why would Philo lead up to philosophy as the pinnacle beyond the preparatory studies, only then to make something else the height? This presentation makes sense if philosophy was the object of his study after his preliminary studies, after which he pressed on to an even higher wisdom.

17. It is perhaps noteworthy that Philo uses the same word for the cause of his troubles in *Spec.* 3.3 (*phthonos*) that he uses in *Flaccus* for the reaction of the Alexandrians to Herod Agrippa's presence in the city (*Flacc.* 29).

18. Philo's two accounts, the one in *Flaccus* and the other in *Embassy*, differ on some of the details. For example, the images are not placed in the synagogues until much later in the crisis in *Embassy* (134).

19. *Flacc.* 53–54. It is difficult to know exactly what Philo meant by this comment. The Jews in general did not possess citizenship in the technical sense. If Philo meant *politeia* in this technical sense, he must have been referring to himself and those few Jews who had such status. The other possibility is that Philo was using the word in a somewhat less than technical sense—the presumed rights and status he believed the Jews to have even though they were not technically Alexandrian citizens.

20. *Flacc.* 54.

21. Although Philo says that he himself was more dubious about Caligula's disposition toward them (cf. *Legat.* 178–83).

22. This dreamer is of course Joseph, who is portrayed extremely negatively in *On Dreams* 2. The contrast here with the way Philo had earlier portrayed him in *On Joseph* makes us wonder if Philo had undergone somewhat of a change of heart (contrast also *Fug.* 33–35). Of course, these two treatises clearly had different audiences in mind, which might also explain the difference.

23. Mentioned in *Animals* 58, it seems to be the same race mentioned by the elder Pliny, *Historia Naturalis* 8.160–61.

24. In 41 CE the Jews did rise up against those who had persecuted them in the pogrom of 38 CE, but the Romans quickly put an end to the violence.

25. Thirty-six survive complete or nearly complete in Greek, nine in Armenian translation. The rest are in Greek and Armenian fragments.

26. We do not know for certain that Philo ran an exegetical school in Alexandria. Cf. G. E. Sterling, "Philo," in *Dictionary of New Testament Background*, ed. C. A. Evans and S. E. Porter (Downers Grove, IL: InterVarsity Press, 1992), 790.

27. D. T. Runia, *On the Creation of the Cosmos according to Moses* (Leiden: E. J. Brill, 2001); P. van der Horst, *Philo's Flaccus: The First Pogrom* (Leiden: E. J. Brill, 2003).

28. Scrolls had certain length limitations that required projects such as Philo's commentary series to use multiple scrolls. We are thus left with the task of deciding which of Philo's treatises belonged together and in what order. For a general treatment of the subject, see J. R. Royse, "Philo's Division of His Works into Books,"

In the Spirit of Faith: Studies in Philo and Early Christianity in Honor of David Hay, SPhA 8 (2001): 59–85.

29. The classic study in the classification of Philo's writings was that of M. L. Massebieau, "Le classement des oeuvres de Philon," *Bibliothèque de l'École des Hautes Études: Sciences religieuses* 1 (1889): 1–91.

30. A. Terian argues for the order (1) Questions; (2) Allegorical Commentary; and (3) Exposition, in "The Priority of *Quaestiones* among Philo's Exegetical Commentaries," in *Both Literal and Allegorical: Studies in Philo of Alexandria's* Questions and Answers on Genesis and Exodus, ed. D. M. Hay (Atlanta: Scholars Press, 1991), 29–46. While this sequence may be largely correct, Philo likely worked on more than one series simultaneously at times.

31. For a collection of articles on this series, see Hay, ed., *Both Literal and Allegorical.*

32. The early fourth-century Christian Eusebius knew only the questions on Genesis and Exodus, and the Greek fragments we have similarly seem to cover these two books.

33. For a discussion of the available texts of Questions, see E. Hilgert, "The *Quaestiones*: Texts and Translations," in Hay, ed., *Both Literal and Allegorical*, 1–15.

34. Since the current Armenian manuscripts divide Genesis into four books, R. Marcus suggested the following breakdown of the original six books: books 1–3 the same as the current books 1–3, with the current book 4 divided into 1–70 (the original book 4), 71–153 (the original book 5), and 154–245 (the original book 6). See the introduction to his translation in the Loeb Classical Library series, *Philo: Questions and Answers on Genesis* (Cambridge: Harvard University Press, 1953), xii.

35. Marcus also suggested this idea in the introduction to his translation in the Loeb Classic Library series (*Questions and Answers on Genesis*, xiii–xv). J. Royse has furthered his argument in "The Original Structure of Philo's *Quaestiones*," SPhilo 4 (1976–77): 48–63.

36. P. Borgen and R. Skarsten, "Quaestiones et Solutiones: Some Observations on the Form of Philo's Exegesis," SPhilo 4 (1976–77): 1–15. Cf. also Sze-kar Wan, "Philo's *Quaestiones et solutions in Genesim et in Exodum*: A Synoptic Approach" (Th.D. diss., Harvard University, 1992). See also P. Borgen, *Philo of Alexandria: An Exegete for His Time* (Leiden: E. J. Brill, 1997), 80–101.

37. E.g. Sterling, "Philo," 790. For a discussion of this issue, see D. T. Runia, "Further Observations on the Structure of Philo's Allegorical Treatises," in *Exegesis and Philosophy: Studies on Philo of Alexandria* (1985; reprint, Aldershot: Variorum, 1990), 114–20; and "Philo, Alexandrian and Jew," in *Exegesis*, 7, where he combines both positions.

38. So D. T. Runia, "Secondary Texts in Philo's *Quaestiones*," in Hay, ed., *Both Literal and Allegorical*, 60.

39. *Philo of Alexandria: An Introduction* (Oxford: Oxford University Press, 1979), 79. So also, in general, G. E. Sterling, "Philo's *Quaestiones*: Prolegomena or Afterthought," in Hay, ed., *Both Literal and Allegorical*, 122. However, Sterling allows for the possibility that they served a catechetical purpose.

40. E.g., Marcus: Questions is later because he thinks it alludes to the Allegorical Commentary at several points (e.g., *QG* 2.4; *QE* 2.34, 113; see *Questions*, x n. a). E. Schürer believes the works contemporaneous; *Geschichte des Jüdischen Volkes im Zeitalter Jesu Christi*, vol 3, 4th ed. (Leipzig: Hinrichs, 1909), 501.

41. Independent: Borgen and Skarsten, "Quaestiones"; Wan, "Philo's *Quaestiones*"; Borgen, *Exegete*, 80–101.

42. Although E. R. Goodenough called *On the Creation* Philo's most difficult treatise (*Philo of Alexandria: An Introduction* [1940; reprint, Oxford: Oxford University

Press, 1979], 35). *On the Creation* begins Philo's commentary series known as the Exposition of the Law.

43. Goodenough, *Introduction*, 48.

44. Sterling accounts for thirty-one; "Philo," 790. For example, two treatises *On Covenants* were probably part of this series (cf. *Mut.* 53; *QE* 2.35). It is also not clear to me that we have the treatise mentioned in *QG* 2.4.

45. Many scholars believe *On the Giants* and *On the Unchangeableness of God* were originally one treatise. E.g., D. T. Runia: "[I]t has become increasingly clear to me that the two treatises were composed as a single literary unit" ("Further Observations," 106).

46. E.g., F. H. Colson, while crediting Philo's treatises for their ingenuity, equally ascribes to them "fancifulness and even perversity, when measured by the canons of sound exegesis" (in his introduction to the first volume of the Loeb Classical Library series *Philo with an English Translation* [Cambridge, MA: Harvard University Press 1929], xii).

47. *Philo*, vol. 1, x–xi.

48. E.g., J. Cazeaux's *La trame et la chain: ou les structures littéraires et l'exégèse dans cinq des traits de Philon d'Alexandrie* (ALGHJ 15; Leiden: E. J. Brill, 1983).

49. It is, of course, possible that Philo intended to extend this series beyond the *De Somniis*, or even that he did and we have lost such treatises.

50. Runia has advocated this way of analyzing the structure of Philo's allegorical treatises. See his two articles, "The Structure of Philo's Allegorical Treatises: A Review of Two Recent Studies and Some Additional Comments" and "Further Observations," both now found in *Exegesis*, 209–56 and 105–38, respectively (the page numbers of this collection follow the page numbers of the volumes in which they first appeared).

51. "L'exégèse de Philon d'Alexandrie dans le *De Gigantibus* et le *Quod Deus sit Immutabilis*," in *Two Treatises of Philo of Alexandria: A Commentary on* De Gigantibus *and* Quod Deus Sit Immutabilis, ed. D. Winston and J. Dillon (Atlanta: Scholars Press, 1983), 5–75.

52. *The Place of Judaism in Philo's Thought: Israel, Jews, and Proselytes* (Atlanta: Scholars Press, 1996), 20.

53. Cf. *Mos.* 2.43–44; *Praem.* 93–97.

54. In his *Life of Moses* (2.46–47), Philo divides the Jewish law into two parts: (1) the historical and (2) commands and prohibitions. But he then subdivides the historical part into material on the creation of the world and material on particular persons. In other words, he sees the same ultimate divisions for the Pentateuch.

    Scholars debate whether the *Life of Moses* was part of the original sequence of the Exposition, since its flavor is similar and a biography on Moses would seem appropriate for this series. The contrast in the way Philo divides the Pentateuch in *Moses* is an argument against its inclusion in the sequence of the Exposition. I would suggest that he wrote *Moses* before he began the bulk of the Exposition.

55. The treatise *On the Creation* traditionally has appeared before the *Allegorical Laws*, as most editions of Philo's writings still place it. However, most now consider it the first treatise of the Exposition, coming right before *On Abraham*. Not only does this position fit well with the summary in *On Rewards* 1–3, but the treatise *On Abraham* seems clearly to mention it as the treatise that preceded it (*Abr.* 2–3). For a more detailed discussion, see A. Terian, "Back to Creation: The Beginning of Philo's Third Grand Commentary," in *Wisdom and Logos: Studies in Jewish Thought in Honor of David Winston*, ed. D. T. Runia and G. E. Sterling, *SPhA* 9 (1997): 19–36.

56. An earlier comment of Birnbaum, *Place*, 19 n. 39. She has since adopted a posi-

tion similar to that we take below. See "Allegorical Interpretation and Jewish Identity among Alexandrian Jewish Writers," in *Neotestamentica et Philonica: Studies in Honor of Peder Borgen*, ed. D. E. Aune, T. Seland, and J. H. Ulrichsen (Leiden: E. J. Brill, 2003), 327 n. 48.

57. E. R. Goodenough: "Philo's Exposition of the Law and His De Vita Mosis," *HTR* 26 (1933): 109–25; P. Borgen: *Exegete*, 48. G. E. Sterling has even suggested that *Moses* might have served as a kind of introduction to all three commentary series ("Philo," 790).

58. Although the surviving manuscripts suggest that these writings were part of a four-volume series On Virtues. See the subsection "*Hypothetica and On the Contemplative Life*."

59. A Christian education professor and colleague of mine at Indiana Wesleyan University, Dr. Keith Drury, has whimsically suggested that we often learn best when we start with learning schemas that are "wrong." It is thus inevitably left to later study to correct the oversimplifications that "got us in the door."

60. E.g., van der Horst, *Philo's Flaccus*, 5–6.

61. The notion that one volume or part of a volume treated Pilate's attempt to set up shields dedicated to Tiberius is based on a comment by Eusebius in the same passage. However, it is unclear to me that Eusebius did not have *Legat.* 299–305 in mind.

62. E. R. Goodenough, *The Politics of Philo Judaeus: Practice and Theory* (New Haven, CT: Yale University Press, 1938), 19.

63. Namely, as the first of a four-part series on the virtues. Eusebius similarly calls at least the latter part of *Embassy* the second of a series (*H.E.* 2.5).

64. Eusebius indicates that the first excerpt comes from the first volume of a work called *Hypothetica* (*P.E.* 8.5–7). He says that the second excerpt comes from Philo's apology (i.e., defense) for the Jews. By contrast, in *H.E.* 2.18 he lists a work called *Concerning the Jews*. Scholars usually assume these are all variations on the same work, but we cannot be absolutely certain.

65. The other place is in the treatise *That Every Good Person Is Free* (*Quod Omnis Probus Liber Sit*), 75–91.

66. Or at least the second excerpt of the *Hypothetica* as it is published today. Goodenough (*Introduction*, 31–32) and many earlier scholars favored this option.

67. *P.E.* 7.21; 8.14.

68. *Philonis Alexandrini De Animalibus: The Armenian Text with Introduction, Translation, and Commentary* (Chico, CA: Scholars Press, 1981).

Chapter 3

Philo among Jews and Gentiles

3.1 THE BACKGROUND OF HELLENISM

After Alexander the Great conquered the better part of the known world (late 300s BCE), the influence of Greek culture became pervasive. You could reject it if you were so inclined, but you had to deal with it. Even opposing something has a formative effect on you: it tends to shape the categories by which you define yourself. For these reasons, this period of history is rightly called the Hellenistic Age, the period of Greek dominance (332–30 BCE). Even after Rome conquered Greece militarily, the poet Horace could aptly say that Greece had conquered Rome culturally.[1]

Jews reacted to this Hellenistic environment in various ways. A group such as those at Qumran on the Dead Sea retreated from society in an effort to eliminate such influences as much as possible. Yet the presence of Greek fragments in the caves of the Dead Sea emphasizes the point: even these separatists could not escape Greek influence. It is surely noteworthy that 2 Maccabees is written in Greek, even though it is one of the most ardent texts promoting zeal for *Jewish particularism*—emphasis on keeping practices that distinguish Jews from other races.

It must de facto have been more difficult for Diaspora Jews to escape contact with this Hellenistic environment than it was for their counterparts in Palestine. In other words, it was easier to follow Jewish purity laws in Jerusalem than it was in Alexandria. We are not surprised to find individuals who thought they could accommodate Hellenism to one degree or another alongside their Jewish identity without contradiction—advocates of *Jewish universalism.* Nor are we shocked to find that some Jews left Judaism because they could not reconcile these two identities. We have already encountered Tiberius Julius Alexander, Philo's own nephew who eventually apostatized from Judaism.

Philo stands somewhere on this spectrum between complete embrace and complete rejection of Hellenism, although far more on the side of embracing it than on that of rejecting it. On the whole, he saw little contradiction between Judaism and Hellenism. Two of the titles Philo has borne throughout history bear out these two sides of his identity: sometimes he is called Philo Judaeus, at other times Philo Alexandrinus.[2] The one focuses on his identity as a Jew, the other on his place within the Hellenistic context of Alexandria. The purpose of this chapter is to set out the fine line Philo walked between these two aspects of his identity.

3.2 DEFINING JUDAISM

We have witnessed since the 1970s a great deal of discussion on the question of what constituted "mainstream" Judaism in Philo's day. E. P. Sanders made perhaps the best-known proposal, namely, that Palestinian Judaism operated largely on the basis of *covenantal nomism* at this time.[3] By this phrase Sanders suggested that Jewish groups in Palestine at the time of Christ emphasized remaining faithful to the particulars of a *covenant* relationship between God and Israel, a solemn and binding arrangement whose stipulations were found in the Jewish law (or *nomos*), the Pentateuch.

Other scholars have been less willing to identify a single set of ideas or practices as "normative" Judaism, some even preferring to speak of Judaism*s* (plural) rather than a single Judaism.[4] The more we move away from Palestine into the Diaspora, the more we find Jews doing things that are far from "kosher" in terms of the Jewish law. Thus we find Onias IV setting up a Jewish temple in Egypt in the early second century BCE—hardly in keeping with the laws of Deuteronomy.[5] Artapanus wrote fictions that depicted Moses as the inventor of Egyptian animal cults,[6] cults that were the object of monotheistic derision by Philo.[7] And we would

> **Jewish particularism:** An emphasis on the sole legitimacy of the Jewish way of life over and against other races and influences.
>
> **Jewish universalism:** The belief that non-Jewish races and religions are equally valid to the Jewish equivalents, that a person can have legitimate status before God outside of Jewish practices and beliefs.

not even suspect that Pseudo-Phocyclides was Jewish if his words and themes did not occasionally betray his background.[8]

John J. Collins has suggested that "there was no simple normative definition which determined

> **covenantal nomism:** The notion that normative Jewish practice is based on a solemn agreement or covenant between God and Israel as found in the Jewish law (the Pentateuch).

Jewish identity in the Hellenistic Diaspora."[9] On this point he is surely correct for the most part. Beyond ethnic descent, we cannot easily set limits to what constituted "appropriate" and "inappropriate" expressions of Jewish identity in the Diaspora. Nevertheless, we can identify a rather large area of common ground among Jews, a space of Jewish identity we can reasonably refer to as "mainstream."

It is this space that non-Jewish authors clearly identified as Jewish—and that they so frequently derided.[10] We cannot deny Artapanus his Jewish identity, but we can consider him atypical in the connection he makes between Moses and the origins of the animal cults of Egypt. We do not find this viewpoint in the other Jewish writings that have survived from that period. And all the Roman emperors were aware that the Jews kept practices different from the other ethnic groups in their kingdom. Otherwise Caligula would not have known to ask Philo's delegation why Jews did not eat pork (*Legat.* 361). And how long would a person's descendants have continued to call themselves Jews if their ancestors had long since stopped circumcising male children?

In other words, we can identify certain beliefs and practices as more or less Jewish in nature. Worship of the Jewish God above all others, valuing certain stories and traditions with their particular heroes and villains, the practice of circumcision, adherence to a specific dietary code, observance of the seventh day as a special day—we can justifiably refer to these things as mainstream elements of Jewish identity. As in all times and places, there were exceptions, but the short list of characteristics was prevalent enough to locate a person like Philo in relation to "mainstream" Jewish belief and practice.

We will find that Philo fits within these general parameters of mainstream Diaspora Judaism. In addition to his predilection for things Hellenistic, Philo had a "conservative" streak that valued his Jewish heritage even more than Greek philosophy. We have far more radical examples of departure from the "norm" than he.

3.3 PHILO AND THE LITERAL INTERPRETATION OF SCRIPTURE

Philo makes a famous comment in the treatise *On the Migration of Abraham*:

> There are some who, because they consider the literal laws to be symbols of things that pertain to the intellect, are extremely attentive to the latter but flippantly make light of the former. I for one would blame those who treat the literal meaning so lightly. For it is necessary to take care with both: both

a more accurate investigation of the unseen meanings and to be beyond reproach in the way you preserve the visible aspects of the text.

But instead such individuals act as if they live privately in a desert alone or like they have become disembodied souls. They do not recognize city or village or house or human company at all. They overlook what seems important to most people and search out the naked truth itself for its own sake.

The sacred word teaches them to concentrate on good reputation and not to abandon anything from the customs that were set down by divinely inspired men greater than those of our time. Certainly the seventh day is a teaching about the power of the one who was not created and about the passivity of that which is created. But we should not abandon those things that have been put into force as laws for the seventh day. (*Mig.* 89–91)

Philo goes on to discuss a number of other commandments in the Jewish law that he believed Jews should follow literally and not just in terms of some symbolic meaning.

Despite Philo's tendency to interpret Scripture ***allegorically*** or symbolically, he clearly valued the literal meaning of the Pentateuch as well. It is true that he ultimately considered the hidden meanings more significant. But such higher meanings did not negate keeping the Jewish law in its literal sense. Philo was thus less extreme in his Hellenism than some other Jews. This passage tells us of Jews who only interpreted the Jewish law symbolically and who ignored Jewish customs.[11] Philo was far more traditional and "mainstream" than they.

> **allegorical interpretation:** Interpretation that ascribes hidden, symbolic meanings to various elements in a text that are not the meanings of the words in their normal or plain sense.

There were no doubt other Jews who accepted both literal and figurative meanings of the biblical text. Nevertheless, we must consider Philo somewhat unique among the ancient witnesses whose writings have survived. We know of individuals who interpreted texts literally and not allegorically. Similarly, we know of individuals who interpreted texts allegorically and not literally. Philo's uniqueness is that he accepted both literal and allegorical meanings as potentially legitimate.

The practice of interpreting stories and myths allegorically did not, of course, originate with Philo. The best evidence we have indicates that the practice became prominent with a non-Jewish philosophical group called the Stoics. Allegorical interpretation—ascribing symbolic meanings to various elements in a text instead of adhering to the literal, plain meaning of the text—was a way to value the Homeric writings without accepting the literal existence of gods such as Athena or Poseidon. With the Stoics, opting for an allegorical interpretation implied a rejection of the literal meaning (i.e., the literal existence of such gods).

From the early second century BCE we find Jews adopting this same interpretive practice in order to value the biblical text without accepting elements they found problematic. The Alexandrian Jew Aristobulus used such allegorical interpretations to address how the text of Exodus could say God did something with a mighty *hand* when God clearly did not have literal hands.[12] According to Aristobulus, we should read this text not literally but allegorically: hands here represent the power of God rather than literal hands.[13]

To Philo, the relationship of the literal meaning to the allegorical was like that of the body to the soul (*Mig.* 93). We have to take care of our bodies, because our souls live in them. Similarly, observing the practices of Judaism helps us get a clearer conception of the symbolic meaning, not to mention the fact that keeping them avoids the social consequences non-observance brings among other Jews.

3.4 PHILO AND JEWISH PRACTICES

Philo identifies a number of these Jewish practices in the passage cited above from the *Migration of Abraham*, all of which we can presume he kept in at least a general way.[14] The first is Sabbath observance, setting aside the seventh day as a day of rest from work. On the one hand, Philo fully accepted the allegorical significance of the Sabbath law. The seventh day teaches us the power of God as a being who was never created, while at the same time demonstrating that the world was created (e.g., *Mig.* 91). In his treatise *On the Creation*, Philo expounds the allegorical significance of Genesis 2:2–3 at great length, extolling the glories of the number seven for some forty paragraphs (*Opif.* 89–128).[15]

On the other hand, the literal practice of keeping the Sabbath was also important to Philo.[16] He gives several examples of things Jews should not do on the seventh day in order to keep the law literally:

> To light a fire or till the ground or carry a load or call a meeting or sit in judgment or seek deposits or recover debts or to do other things also allowed in those times that are not feast days. (*Mig.* 91)

In this list Philo not only shows his attention to the literal keeping of the Sabbath law, but he may also reflect Jewish oral traditions on the specifics of *how* to keep it.

The second literal practice he mentions in *Migration* is that of keeping Jewish festivals:

> And just because the feast is a symbol of the soul's gladness and of thanksgiving to God, let us not give up the festive gatherings in their yearly seasons. (*Mig.* 92)

In *Special Laws* 2, Philo identifies ten feasts in the Jewish law. While this number in part reflects Philo's fascination with the number ten, we see in this list all the feasts we associate with distinctive Jewish custom. We have every reason to believe Philo observed them in some basic way.

The most important meaning of these festivals for Philo was certainly allegorical. Their overall import to him was that God is perfect joy and that God affords some measure of this joy to humankind (e.g., *Spec.* 2.54–55). But Philo clearly valued literal observance as well, even if his location in the Diaspora led him to make greater allowances than he might have made if he had lived in Jerusalem.[17]

Philo was thus flexible in how a Jew might celebrate the festivals. For example, he believed that Jews who did not live in Palestine could celebrate the Passover without going to Jerusalem as the law required,

> [F]or those who have become aliens or live in a different place do not do wrong such that they should be deprived of equal honor, especially if one country does not have room because the nation is so populous and has sent out colonies in every direction. (*Mos.* 2.232)

Philo's interpretation of the Passover emphasized that this festival was one in which all Jews served as priests and did not need temple priests to offer sacrifices for them.[18] This (Alexandrian?) interpretation enabled Diaspora Jews to celebrate the Passover without going to Jerusalem.

Philo showed a similar spiritual rather than sacrificial emphasis in his consideration of the Day of Atonement, or the "Fast," as he preferred to call it. The Day of Atonement had prominence to Philo for many reasons, including its focus on holiness, its disciplined orientation in contrast to human pleasure, and the fact that it took place on the tenth day of the seventh month, thus giving it a heightened sacredness (*Spec.* 1.186; 2.193–203). It was a day in which Jews were to devote themselves to prayer, asking God to forgive both their intentional and unintentional sins. Philo says of this feast that it was "diligently followed not only by those who are zealous for godliness and holiness, but also by those who do nothing pious the rest of their life" (*Spec.* 1.186).

However, at the same time he focused on the more spiritual aspect of its celebration rather than on the activities of the high priest in Jerusalem. The Day of Atonement was the one day a year when the high priest entered alone into the innermost sanctum of the Jerusalem temple in order to atone for the sins of the people. As in the case of Passover, Philo placed the locus of festival observance in the hearts of the people more than in the temple itself.

A third literal practice Philo mentions in *Migration* is circumcision.[19] Once again, the allegorical meaning of this practice had immense significance to him. Circumcision represented the elimination of pleasure and the passions, as well as any notion we might have that our minds can understand in their own power (*Mig.* 92; *Spec.* 1.8–11). Yet the literal practice was extremely important to Philo as well: "let us not abolish the law established concerning circumcision" (*Mig.* 92).

Yet circumcision in and of itself was not, for Philo, the crucial element of becoming or being a Jew. In *Questions and Answers on Exodus*, Philo says,

The proselyte is not the one who has circumcised his uncircumcision, but the one who has circumcised the pleasures and the desires and the other passions of the soul. (*QE* 2.2)

Philo refers to the fact that the Israelites were not circumcised while they were in Egypt to show that you can be a ***proselyte*** and a member of Israel without being circumcised. Here we find the fine line Philo walks between particularism and universalism. On the one hand, he rails against ethnic Jews who would stop the practice of literal circumcision. On the other hand, he could consider non-Jews to be "circumcised" without converting to Judaism if they had curbed their passions.

> **proselyte:** A convert from one religion to another.

Philo's views on intermarriage with non-Jews seem to reflect the same tension: he upholds Jewish practice while opening the door to non-Jews. The Jewish custom of marrying only within their race was a well-known feature of Judaism at this time—it makes the Roman historian Tacitus's list of peculiar Jewish practices.[20] Philo accepts this practice as important for ethnic Jews:

> But do not, he says, join together in the fellowship of marriage with someone of another race, so that at some time you do not surrender after battling with customs and becoming subjugated and lose sight of the way to godliness, wandering off the path. Perhaps you yourself will even hold your ground because you are steadied by the virtuous instructions of your earliest years, which your parents instilled as they always sounded the note of the sacred laws. But it is not a little fear for your sons and daughters, for perhaps they will be enticed by illegitimate customs over the genuine and will turn and unlearn the honor of the one God—which indeed is the beginning and end of the highest misery. (*Spec.* 3.29)

In this passage Philo may reflect the sorrows of his own family or of families with which he was well acquainted. Perhaps it is significant that this passage was probably written after the crisis of 38 CE, which may have pushed marginal Jews away from their Jewish roots.

Nevertheless, Philo does not exhibit so strong an attitude toward racial intermarriage when it actually comes to his interpretation of relevant passages in the Pentateuch. Philo depicts Hagar the Egyptian as "a slave in body, but free and noble in mind . . . an Egyptian by birth, but a Hebrew by choice" (*Abr.* 251). Unlike an earlier Alexandrian, Demetrius the historian,[21] Philo makes no point of the fact that Moses' wife Zipporah was not an Israelite. While Demetrius took pains to argue that Zipporah was really in the same race as Moses, Philo never raises the issue and treats her positively when he allegorizes her.[22] These perhaps earlier treatises do not reflect any negativity toward the marriage of Jews to virtuous foreign women.

A final Jewish practice we might consider is Philo's treatment of the dietary codes. It is interesting that he does not mention them in his list of Jewish practices in *Migration* 91–92. We can wonder if Philo found these laws particularly difficult to defend on a practical level. When he was discussing the prohibition of eating camel meat, Philo could not think of any practical meaning or benefit to the law (*Agr.* 131). He did see great significance in the symbolic meaning of these laws, which all had specific allegorical truths behind them. As a whole, they symbolized the evil of gluttony (e.g., *Spec.* 4.100).

On more than one occasion Philo railed against what he saw as the excesses of the Hellenistic banquet (e.g., *Contempl.* 48–63). We can be certain that he saw the discipline of keeping the Jewish food laws as a demonstration of Jewish superiority: such laws involved the subjugation of the passions. But when the emperor Caligula asked Philo why Jews did not eat pork, Philo did not offer some practical benefit to the practice. He merely noted that every race has its own customs (*Legat.* 361–62). By implication, the Jewish food laws were probably not the most essential aspect of Jewish identity to Philo.

3.5 PHILO AND THE TEMPLE

Philo mentions that he had visited the Jerusalem temple at one point in his life (*Prov.* 2.64). While some have questioned the authenticity of this passage, it fits well with what we know of him. We would expect that he made this pilgrimage to Jerusalem at least once. At least in theory, Philo's writings demonstrate a firm loyalty to the temple in Jerusalem.[23]

In *Special Laws*, Philo considers it appropriate that there would be only one temple on earth, since there is only one God (*Spec.* 1.67). In this passage he describes the Jerusalem temple in a general way (*Spec.* 1.71–75) and tells of the mass of individuals who made pilgrimage there for the feasts (*Spec.* 1.69–70). He also mentions the collections of money from the Diaspora that were regularly taken by envoys to Jerusalem:

> It has been arranged that each man every year should bring first fruits, beginning from the twentieth year. . . . At designated times sacred envoys of the moneys take it by hand, individuals selected as virtuous, the most proven from every city. These will securely bring along with them the hopes of everyone. (*Spec.* 1.77–78)

We can wonder if Philo himself at some point was one of these "virtuous," "most proven" of men, chosen to take these offerings to Jerusalem.[24]

In *Embassy*, Philo claims that Jews would rather die than see their temple desecrated. The most pertinent passage relates to the attempt of the emperor Caligula to place a statue of himself as Zeus in the Jerusalem temple. Philo says that Caligula's orders put the Roman governor Petronius in a hard position:

> For he knew they [the Jews] would willingly die not once but ten thousand times rather than see something done that was prohibited. For all people are

watchful of their own practices, especially the Jewish race. . . . Their dili-
gence about the temple is more intense and distinctive than all of them [i.e.,
than all of their practices]. The greatest proof is the fact that they have des-
ignated death without appeal for those who pass into the inner areas. (*Legat.*
209, 212)

Philo is certainly playing up the virtues of his own people here. But we have every
reason to believe that his pride in the temple was real, even if a little exaggerated
in this passage.

Philo's pride in the temple related much more to his Jewish heritage than to
any sense of its ultimate necessity. We already mentioned *Special Laws* 1.67, where
the existence of one temple symbolizes the fact that there is only one God. Philo
also claims in this passage that the truest temple of God is the whole universe (*Spec.*
1.66), that is, not the earthly sanctuary. Thus the earthly, "handmade" temple primarily served a symbolic purpose for Philo. It was for those who wished to use sacrifices to give thanks to God or to ask for forgiveness for sins (*Spec.* 1.67).

But Philo believed that people whose minds were set on virtue were in a holy
place with their minds even if their bodies were not (*Leg.* 1.62).[25] Your body did
not need to be in a temple for your mind to be in a holy place:

[God] turns from those who approach with an intent worthy of blame, even
if they lead up a hundred bulls every day. But he receives those of blameless
intent, even if they sacrifice nothing at all. God has delight with altars without fire, concerning which the virtues play the role of choir. (*Plant.* 108)

Indeed, God could not literally inhabit any earthly structure. "What sort of
house then would we need to prepare for the king of kings and God, the ruler of
everything?" (*Cher.* 99). Philo's answer is clearly "none." "There would not be a
place for his feet. Indeed, certainly there is a house worthy: the suitable soul"
(*Cher.* 100–101).

We can thus summarize Philo's view toward the temple and sacrifices in this
way. Philo valued the Jerusalem temple as a focal point of his Jewish heritage
and as an important symbol of monotheism. He certainly did not accept the
validity of any other temple anywhere else (*Spec.* 1.67–68). But ultimately, the
function of sacrifices was largely symbolic. They were fully acceptable for those
whom they helped approach God. But a virtuous person could find God without them.

3.6 PHILO AND THE DESTINY OF ISRAEL

It is often assumed that Philo had no ***eschatology***, no sense that history was moving toward some climactic moment.[26] It is true that Philo argued vigorously
against the early Stoic idea that the world might one day be destroyed (e.g., *Aet.*
75–76, 88). He thus differed from those Jewish ***apocalyptic*** writers who looked
for the literal destruction and reconstitution of heaven and earth.

eschatology: The field that questions whether history is moving toward a climactic moment, often the end of the world ("study of last things").
apocalyptic: relating to the revelation of events in the heavenly realm to those on earth, usually in relation to some approaching transformation or judgment of the earthly realm at a specific point in time.
corporeal: Embodied, with a body (not necessarily a physical one).
resurrection: Rising from the dead, often understood by Jews in bodily terms.

Similarly, Philo would have scoffed at the notion of bodily, *corporeal resurrection* (rising from the dead), much as the Athenians of Acts 17 do when the early Christian Paul proclaims resurrection to them. While Philo believed in an afterlife for virtuous souls, he never even mentions the concept of resurrection in all his writings. The afterlife of the good person was one "no longer bound by the constraints of the body" (*Ios.* 264). In other words, Philo leaned toward the Platonic immortality of the soul and had no concept of resurrection.

Philo's thought was clearly more "vertical" than "horizontal." That is to say, his writings are far more preoccupied with the relationship between earth and heaven, humanity and God, body and soul, than with the direction of history or with some specific destiny for Israel. His primary teachings relate to issues such as attaining a vision of God, gaining wisdom and virtue, and eliminating one's passions.

Nevertheless, Philo occasionally made comments that reflected his hopes for the destiny of the Jews as a race in the world. Although it is difficult to date Philo's writings in relation to his life, we can plausibly argue that Philo became more interested in the destiny of Israel as his life progressed, particularly after the crisis of 38 CE. He did not expect the elements to burn with heat (cf. 2 Pet. 3:12), but he did have hopes that the world would one day turn to Israel's God.

Probably the earliest hints of such a view appear in Philo's *Life of Moses*, where he makes an interesting comment in an aside:

> Thus we see that the laws are zeal-worthy and worth fighting for, both to individuals and rulers, even though our nation has not had good fortune for many years. It is natural for things that are not blossoming to be overshadowed somewhat.
> But if some opportunity for a brighter future would come about, how great a change for the better would happen! I think each of the nations would leave their own practices and throw out their own ancestral customs, greatly rejoicing as they turn to honor our laws alone. For with good fortune the shining laws of our race will darken the laws of others, just as the sun does to the stars when it rises. (*Mos.* 2.43–44)

These words are full of hope that a turn of events will happen, that one day the nations might actually turn to Israel's God and his laws.[27] Perhaps Philo wrote these words before the crisis of 38 CE. Perhaps he wrote in a time when he was optimistic about the future of Israel.

It is possible that these words give us a partial rationale for Philo's commentary series the Exposition of the Law. E. R. Goodenough suggested that these books might have been aimed at a non-Jewish audience, since they presume so little biblical and philosophical knowledge. Many Philonic scholars significantly question this idea, since it seems unlikely that non-Jews read Philo to any significant extent. However, the question of whether any non-Jews ever read this series has little to do with who Philo *hoped* would read it. Philo probably did not exclusively target non-Jews in the Exposition, but it is quite possible he hoped they would one day read it and turn to the Jewish God.

Another passage in *Moses* even hints at the expectation of a messianic figure, a king who would lead Israel as they found new prosperity.[28] Peder Borgen has pointed to a number of minor alterations Philo made to the Septuagint text of Numbers 24:7 that reflect his expectation of such a figure.[29] The LXX text itself reads:

> A man will come from his seed and will rule over many nations, and even Gog, his kingdom, will be exalted, and his kingdom will be increased.

Philo makes two changes to this text that Borgen believes indicate the expectation of a coming messianic figure.

First Philo adds the phrase "at some time" to the passage: "*At some time* a man will come" (*Mos.* 1.290). This expression places the fulfillment of this verse in Philo's future. The second change is that Philo replaces the reference to a specific nation, Gog, with a more general rule: "and the kingdom of this man will grow every day and will reach to the heights." These changes seem to reflect Philo's hope that a Jewish king would find great prosperity at some point in the future.

The most eschatological material in the Philonic corpus clearly comes from the last treatise of the Exposition, namely, *On Rewards and Punishments.* If the passage from *Special Laws* 3.1–6 refers to the persecution of 38 CE, then Philo likely wrote this treatise after the pogrom. Yet we can wonder if he wrote such seemingly militaristic comments after the Jews exacted their revenge in 41 CE, after Caligula was assassinated.[30] With Caligula out of the way, some Jews in Alexandria tried to get vengeance on those who had earlier persecuted them in the city. The Roman army had to put this uprising down.

The latter part of *Rewards* presents Philo's interpretation of the blessings and curses of Deuteronomy 28. In *Rewards* 95 he refers to Numbers 24:7 again, this time in a somewhat more militaristic way:

> "A man will come out," the oracle says. And he will increase as he goes to war and battles great and populous nations, because God has sent to him the aid appropriate to those who are holy.

It is important to remember that this part of the treatise is discussing the blessings that would come to Israel if they kept God's commandments (e.g., *Praem.* 79). In other words, Philo is presenting his understanding of "covenantal nomism" in this treatise. If Israel will keep the laws he has explained in the four preceding books,[31] these blessings will follow.

In *Rewards* 79–97, Philo is discussing the victory over their enemies that would ensue if the Jews kept God's commandments. He presents this victory in two possible ways: (1) the enemies would perceive the nature of their opponents and surrender, or (2) the enemies' lust for war would lead to their defeat in battle (*Praem.* 93–94). In the first scenario, war would not pass through the land at all. But if it did come to battle, the enemy would be defeated.[32]

Philo also suggests more than one way in which the enemy would be defeated. For example, some would turn in fear, presenting easy targets to their enemies (*Praem.* 95). God would send nature against others in the form of wasps (*Praem.* 96–97). These would bring about a "bloodless" victory over Israel's enemies.

Philo returns to this general theme at the end of the treatise. In *Rewards* 152 he speaks of the joy of the proselyte in the time of reward. Such individuals are blessed because they came over to God and received a secure place in heaven—presumably the place where Philo believed the souls of the righteous went at death. In contrast, Philo says the one of good (Jewish?) lineage who has invalidated his noble birth will descend into the darkness of Tartarus. This differentiation between the fates of the dead is more Jewish than Greek, even if the image of Tartarus is Greek. Most non-Jewish individuals at this point in time either did not believe in any afterlife at all or saw the afterlife as a shadowy, nonconscious existence in the underworld.

It is easy to see some of these statements as thinly veiled warnings to well-born Jews of Philo's day who were deserting Judaism. Philo speaks of individuals

> who disregard the righteousness and godliness of the sacred laws and are led astray by the polytheistic opinions whose end is atheism and forget the teaching of their people and fathers. They received this teaching from their earliest years about the nature of the one, the one we consider God most high, to whom alone belong those who pursue the unfabricated truth instead of invented myths. (*Praem.* 162)

The reference to instruction from childhood tells us that Philo has Jews in mind in this passage, Jews who were abandoning their heritage. Perhaps the crisis of 38 CE and the years that followed created a situation in which Jews were pushed to pick sides between Judaism and Hellenism. Philo's comments here may have targeted those who were making the wrong choice.

At the time of the great "reversal" (*Praem.* 169), Jews from all over the world would return to Jerusalem:

> Those who just a little earlier were scattered in Greece and elsewhere on islands and continents will arise and focus their attention together with one purpose from every direction to one place. (*Praem.* 165)

Philo says that cities in Palestine that lie in ruins will be rebuilt (*Praem.* 168). Enemies that mocked at the misfortunes of Israel will inherit the curses of

Deuteronomy (*Praem.* 169). Israel will return to the prosperity of its past (*Praem.* 170).

The flavor of some of these comments is not unlike that of Philo in his treatise *Against Flaccus*. This treatise seems designed to show that God judges those who persecute the Jews in the end (*Flacc.* 191). The Roman prefect Flaccus seems to have stood by idly while the Jews underwent significant violence in 38 CE. The *Flaccus* shows that justice always catches up with such individuals (*Flacc.* 146). In Philo's presentation, Flaccus recognizes the reversal of his fortunes as God's judgment: "you [God] do not disregard the nation of the Jews" (*Flacc.* 170).

The *Flaccus* is not the only writing of this sort Philo seems to have composed in this general time period. A lost treatise may have followed *Embassy* and showed a similar conclusion with regard to the emperor Caligula (*Legat.* 373). Similarly, another lost treatise seems to have preceded the *Flaccus* and shown the same with regard to Sejanus, who persecuted the Jews during the reign of Tiberius (*Flacc.* 1). In other words, the events of 38 CE seem to have led Philo to emphasize the favored status of the Jews before God, as well as their prosperous destiny.

3.7 PHILO AND RABBINIC TRADITIONS

We must await a comprehensive comparison of Philo's interpretations with other Jewish interpretive traditions.[33] It is beyond question that Philo frequently drew on traditional material, for he often tells us about the interpretations of other Jews. For example, he gives several defenses of circumcision that he has inherited from those before him: "These things came to our ears as ancient teaching from inspired men who thoroughly searched the things of Moses" (*Spec.* 1.8).

Some of the interpretations Philo inherited clearly originated among Alexandrian Jews.[34] This is particularly likely of the allegorical interpretations he passes on (e.g., *Ios.* 151). Yet Philo no doubt also inherited interpretive traditions from beyond Alexandria, including traditions from Jerusalem and broader Palestine. Our discussion of the Sabbath law above wondered if Philo drew some of his thoughts on what it meant to work on the Sabbath from "unwritten customs" such as these (cf. *Legat.* 115).

But we do not know how many of Philo's interpretations ultimately originated in Palestine and were passed along to the Diaspora. It is hard enough to decide when Philo's interpretations are his original thinking and when he is drawing on the work of others, let alone what the location of such "others" might have been. Further, the largest potential source of specific Jewish **haggadah** and **halakhah** in Palestine at this time (the interpretation of biblical stories and legal codes) dates much later, to around 200 CE when the **Mishnah** was compiled. The Mishnah is a compilation of unwritten Jewish traditions that at times stretched back centuries. Unfortunately, it is not always easy to know how far back such traditions went.

We can, of course, speak of some general aspects to Philo's interpretation that

> **haggadah:** The interpretation and appropriation of biblical stories.
> **halakhah:** Jewish ethics and practice; Jewish teaching on how to live.
> **Mishnah:** A collection of Jewish oral traditions on the meaning of the law and how to keep it, dating to about the year 200 CE.

he probably held in common with the Judaism of Palestine. For example, Philo likely inherited the division of the Ten Commandments into two types of command, one of which related to human duties toward God and the other to human duties toward other humans (e.g., *Dec.* 50–52, 121; *Spec.* 2.63).[35] The Gospel of Matthew's summation of the law as "love God and love neighbor" reflects this basic division (cf. Matt. 22:34–40), as may the similar summations of the law in the writings of the early Christian Paul (Rom. 13:8–10; Gal. 5:14) and the book of James (Jas. 2:8–11).

To infer connections on a more specific level often requires much more subtlety. Two studies give us a flavor of what such investigations might look like, that is, how we might go about identifying places where Philo is drawing on common interpretative traditions with Jews in Palestine. The first is Peder Borgen's 1965 study *Bread from Heaven*.[36] The second is that of Naomi Cohen, *Philo's Universe of Discourse*.[37]

Borgen's work painstakingly examines the details of scattered comments Philo made in his writings on Exodus 16, where God provides food for the Israelites in the desert, "bread from heaven." Borgen argues that recurring phrases in Philo's accounts, particularly phrases that are not in the biblical text, reflect the fact that Philo was drawing on traditional summaries of the Exodus story.[38] Borgen finds similar features in the Gospel of John's treatment of the story (John 6). Further, he finds these same features in later rabbinic writings such as the *Mekilta on Exodus* and *Exodus Rabbah*.

Cohen's work focuses particularly on *Special Laws* 4.132–50, from which she tries to present Philo's "universe of discourse." The most notable feature of her work is the way she tries to connect Philo's "Hellenistic" vocabulary with a rabbinic conceptual framework. For example, she argues that Philo's references to "unwritten customs" often refer to such *halakhoth* and the oral traditions of this time period.[39] She suggests that Philo's distinction between the "literal meaning" (*to rhēton*) and the symbolic sometimes reduces to the distinction between previous interpretative tradition and his allegorical interpretation.[40] And Philo's term *righteousness* often means "faithful adherence to Torah statutes."[41] In short, Cohen sees a Palestinian background behind many of Philo's "Hellenistic-sounding" terms. For her, Philo represents the fusion of a "normative" Jewish "universe of discourse" with Hellenistic vocabulary and imagery.[42]

Whether all the specific suggestions of Borgen, Cohen, and others win the day in the end, their fundamental quest seems to have validity. In the end Philo was not nearly so out of sync with mainstream Judaism as scholars have often suggested, even when he is compared with the traditions that would later become rabbinic Judaism. The comparison of Philo with later rabbinic traditions is one that merits much further investigation.

3.8 PHILO AND HELLENISM

Most of this chapter has emphasized ways in which Philo fit the mold of the mainstream Jew. He valued circumcision, Sabbath observance, Jewish festivals, and the Jerusalem temple and likely kept the food laws at least to some extent. He saw the greatest meaning to these practices on a symbolic level and hence probably admitted more flexibility in his practice than some Jews might have.

We therefore have to ask whether there were ways in which he skirted the boundaries of the "typical" Jew. What was his relationship to things non-Jewish? Did he ever appropriate his Hellenistic environment in ways that stood outside the mainstream, or at least that challenge our conception of what the mainstream was?

We can certainly say Philo demonstrated a knowledge of Greek philosophy and culture that must rarely have been surpassed by his Jewish or even non-Jewish contemporaries. He clearly loved the Hellenistic thought world and thoroughly appropriated its images and literature. While he used the biblical text as the foil for his thought, the categories of the thought itself were more often than not the categories of Greek philosophy.

His allegorical method of interpretation even allowed him to appropriate elements of Greek mythology at times. Thus he could favorably refer to those Greeks who called the earth "Demeter," implying that the earth was our mother (*Opif.* 133).[43] And he could compare understanding the Pentateuch to entrance into a pagan mystery cult (*Cher.* 48–49).

Philo's gymnasium education must have put him into some tension with his Jewish identity. Thus Aryeh Kasher has argued that the Jews of Alexandria could not have aspired to full citizenship because of their Jewish identity.[44] Participation in the gymnasium had a significant religious component, even to the point of sacrifice to the gods and participation in religious processions. Kasher seriously questions whether Jews could fully participate in gymnasium life without compromising their Jewish heritage. His position seems to assume too narrow an understanding of Judaism at this time but nevertheless depicts the tension well.

These observations lead us to what seems to be the most crucial issue: whether Philo exclusively worshiped the God of the Jews and rejected all others. Was Philo a ***monotheist,*** a person who believed in a single God? And if Philo was a monotheist, did his understanding of Israel's relationship with God stand within the "mainstream" of Jewish understanding and practice, if we can even speak of common ground on this issue?

That Philo believed in a single, supreme God is beyond question. Throughout his writings he debases those who believe in many gods,[45] as well as those

> **monotheism:** Belief in a single God, in the most literal sense of that word.

who worship such gods by way of idols.[46] He presents his "creed" about God at the end of the treatise *On the Creation*.[47] He summarizes his beliefs in five points:

1. The divine exists (against atheists).
2. God is one (against polytheists).
3. The world is created (by which Philo does not clearly mean creation out of nothing).
4. The world is one.
5. God cares for the world (belief in providence).

It would be hard to fault this list for its Jewishness. While Philo could appropriate the imagery of Greek mythology, he rejected any *literal* belief in the Greek gods (e.g., *Dec.* 54) or any sacrifice to images of wood and stone (e.g., *Spec.* 1.56).

It is true that Philo does at times use the word *god* in relation to entities other than the supreme God. He can thus refer to the stars and heavenly bodies as "visible gods perceptible to our senses" (*Opif.* 27), or even to Moses as a "god" to the Jewish people (*Mos.* 1.158). But in these instances Philo was clearly using the word in a subordinate, more limited, even figurative sense that seems to stand within the parameters of mainstream Jewish monotheism.

With regard to his view of Israel, Philo did sometimes express a "universalist" approach to God's relationship with the world, that is, a sense that people of all races could capture a true vision of God. Ellen Birnbaum has made a thorough study of Philo's use of terms such as *Israel* and *Jew*.[48] She finds that Philo uses these terms in different ways with different audiences apparently in view. In particular, while the term *Jew* always has an ethnic particularity to it, *Israel* has a more metaphorical sense that could, in theory, apply to someone of any nationality.[49]

The name Israel means "he who sees."[50] Birnbaum points to several instances in Philo's writings where it is not at all clear that "those who see" are necessarily Jews.[51] After considering several possibilities, Birnbaum concludes that "Israel" in Philo almost always refers to anyone with the appropriate mind—all truly philosophically minded people, whether they are Jews or not.[52]

Thus, in theory, the supreme God could be worshiped appropriately without reference to the Jewish Scriptures or Jewish particularity. A passage in the treatise *On Virtues* implies this conclusion. While Philo is actually emphasizing the excellence of the Jewish law in this passage, he does so by comparing it to the excellence of pagan philosophy:

> Those who follow the philosophy of the most excellent gain the same things as what is gained through the laws and customs of the Jews: knowledge of the highest and eldest cause of all things and the error of those who have believed in created gods. (*Virt.* 65)

In a similar vein, Philo viewed the written laws of the Jews as only copies of the truest law, which was followed by the patriarchs Abraham, Isaac, and Jacob before the law of Moses even existed (e.g., *Abr.* 3–5):

Someone might appropriately say that the enacted laws are nothing other than memorials to the life of the ancients. (*Abr.* 5)

In this sense, the appropriate life in relation to God is something that is more "original" than the specific laws of the Jewish covenant. It was thus possible, in theory, that a non-Jew might live out this archetypal law by nature, without any actual knowledge of the Jewish law itself.

The treatise *That Every Good Person Is Free* uses the Jewish Essenes as the supreme example of individuals who were truly free because they were virtuous. Yet Philo prefaces his treatment of them with a number of pagan examples of virtue, any of whom were presumably as good as the most virtuous Jew. Philo mentions the "seven sages" of Greece, the Magi among the Persians, and the Gymnosophists of India (*Prob.* 73–74). After his discussion of the Essenes, he goes on to mention other pagan examples such as Calanus, Zeno, Anaxarchus, and Diogenes (*Prob.* 92–124). Philo gives us no indication that these persons were any less virtuous than the most pious Jew.

Birnbaum rightly concludes that neither the term *universalist* nor the term *particularist* fully applies to Philo. The way he behaved in life and practice ultimately stands in some tension with his ideas. "The place of Judaism, then, cannot be measured in Philo's thought alone. For a complete understanding, one must also consider his life."[53] His ideology was often universalist, but his sentiments, prejudices, and practice were sometimes particularist. In theory, anyone could see God; but the Jews were at a definite practical advantage in the quest.

3.9 CONCLUSION

We started this chapter by noting that different Jews reacted to their Hellenistic environment in different ways. We can identify a spectrum of such interactions, ranging from those who withdrew from society to avoid corruption to those who favored pagan life so much that they finally abandoned their Jewish identity. We said that Philo fit more on the Hellenistic side of the spectrum because he saw no contradiction between his Jewishness and his love of the Greek world.

But we have also seen a tension in Philo. As a Jew, he had pride in his heritage and identity. As a person, Philo deeply resented those who abandoned Jewish customs or who brought shame to his community. He at least gave "lip service" to the full keeping of the Jewish Torah and to strict monotheistic belief. And apparently he expected the Jewish nation to become the focus of the world's longing at some point in the future.

Nevertheless, he believed that the highest meaning of the Torah was allegorical in nature. This perspective allowed him a great deal of flexibility in the way he appropriated the law and connected it to Hellenistic concepts. Philo could allegorize both Greek myths and Jewish stories to find a philosophical middle ground. He could say that philosophers such as Heraclitus had drawn their most profound ideas from Moses. These strategies allowed Philo to maintain a dual identity of sorts.

Yet there was also a limit to how far Philo would take such ideas. He railed against extreme Jewish allegorists who used allegory to negate the literal keeping of the law. He would never have depicted Moses as the inventor of Egyptian animal cults, as the Jewish author Artapanus did. Further, while Philo's consistent references to Exodus as "Exogogue" may reflect the influence of Ezekiel the tragedian, we can wonder whether he would have felt comfortable with Ezekiel's portrayal of Moses sitting in God's seat.[54] In other words, though we find a high degree of convergence between Judaism and Hellenism in Philo, we have far more "compromising" examples.

Notes

1. *Epigrams* 2.1.156.
2. We will briefly discuss a third hat—Philo Christianus—in chapter 5. Philo was not a Christian, but some Christians in the first few centuries used his writings extensively.
3. Cf. *Paul and Palestinian Judaism: A Comparison of Patterns of Religion* (Philadelphia: Fortress Press, 1977); and *Paul, the Law, and the Jewish People* (Philadelphia: Fortress Press, 1983).
4. E.g., A. F. Segal, *The Other Judaisms of Late Antiquity* (Atlanta: Scholars Press, 1987).
5. At Leontopolis. Onias was the rightful successor to the high priesthood in Jerusalem, but his father, Onias III, was removed from office and later murdered.
6. Artapanus, in Eusebius *P.E.* 9.27.4.
7. E.g., *Mos.* 1.23; *Dec.* 76–80; 1.79; *Spec.* 2.146; *Contempl.* 8–9; *Prov.* 2.65; *Legat.* 139, 163; *QE* 1.8.
8. Namely, admonitions that presuppose the Septuagint and apparent belief in resurrection, among other things.
9. *Between Athens and Jerusalem: Jewish Identity in the Jewish Diaspora*, 2d ed. (Grand Rapids: Wm. B. Eerdmans, 2000), 273.
10. E.g., Tacitus, *Histories*, 5.5: "Among themselves [the Jews] they are inflexibly honest and ever ready to show compassion, though they regard the rest of mankind with all the hatred of enemies. They sit apart at meals, they sleep apart, and though, as a nation, they are singularly prone to lust, they abstain from intercourse with foreign women. Among themselves nothing is unlawful. Circumcision was adopted by them as a mark of difference from other men. Those who come over to their religion adopt the practice, and have this lesson first instilled into them—to despise all gods, to disown their country, and set parents, children, and brethren at nothing."
11. Cf. also *Deus* 17, where Philo takes on a note of zealousness against such Jews.
12. Fragment 2, recorded in Eusebius, *P.E.* 8.10.5–7.
13. Of course, in this instance Philo would agree: we should not read this text literally.
14. See the excellent overview of Philo and Jewish practice in A. Mendelson, *Philo's Jewish Identity* (Atlanta: Scholars Press, 1988), 51–75.
15. See also *Leg.* 1.5–20; *Cher.* 87–90; *Her.* 170; *Mos.* 2.218–19; *Decal.* 102–5; *Spec.* 2.56–70.
16. See also *Decal.* 96–101; *Spec.* 2.60; *Somn.* 2.123; *Legat.* 158.
17. So Mendelson, *Jewish Identity*, 62.
18. E.g., *Mos.* 2.224; *Spec.* 2.145–46.

19. For a discussion of Philo's views on circumcision, see P. Borgen, "Debates on Circumcision," in *Philo, John, and Paul: New Perspectives on Judaism and Early Christianity* (Atlanta: Scholars Press, 1987), 61–71.
20. See n. 10, above.
21. See fragment 3, preserved in Eusebius, *P.E.* 9.29.1–3.
22. E.g., in *Leg.* 2.67 he considers this "Ethiopian woman" to be a symbol of intense resolution, the soul's power of vision. In *Cher.* 41 he also considers her a virtue, the contemplation of things divine and blessed in heaven.
23. Thus the temple also makes Philo's shortlist of important literal Jewish practical values in *Mig.* 92.
24. Cf. also *Legat.* 312–13.
25. In contrast, even if your body was in a consecrated spot, you were not truly there if your mind was inclined to the unworthy. The sacrifice of a person without the right intentions was not really a sacrifice (*Mos.* 2.107–8).
26. E.g., R. Williamson, "There is in Philo no eschatology" (*Philo and the Epistle to the Hebrews* [ALGHJ 4; Leiden: E. J. Brill, 1970], 556) and "There is no appreciable Messianism in Philo's works" (530), although he recognizes the eschatological element in *De Praemiis* (143–44).
27. B. L. Mack does not believe Philo took Num. 24:7 messianically in *Mos.* 1.263–99 ("Wisdom and Apocalyptic in Philo," *SPhA* 3 [1991]: 34). He believes it is a symbolic reference to Israel at best, rather than to a messianic figure.
28. Did Philo have Herod Agrippa I in mind?
29. "There Shall Come Forth a Man": Reflections on Messianic Ideas in Philo," in *The Messiah: Developments in Earliest Judaism and Christianity* (Minneapolis: Fortress Press, 1992), 341–61; and more recently in *Philo of Alexandria: An Exegete for His Time* (Leiden: E. J. Brill, 1997), 269–76.
30. Josephus, *Ant.* 19.278.
31. That is, *On the Decalogue* and *On the Special Laws* books 1–4.
32. T. Tobin believes that Philo preferred the first scenario: the nations would recognize the virtue of Israel without war. But a second option would involve a messianic leader akin to that of *Sibylline Oracles* 3 and 5 ("Philo and the Sibyl," in *Wisdom and Logos: Studies in Jewish Thought in Honor of David Winston*, ed. D. T. Runia and G. E. Sterling, *SPhA* 9 [1997]: 100).
33. Although cf. the very dated study of B. Ritter, *Philo und die* Halacha (Leipzig, 1879), as well as the more recent articles by B. J. Bamberger ("Philo and the Aggadah," *HUCA* 48 [1977]: 153–85) and L. L. Grabbe ("Philo and the Aggada: A Response to B. J. Bamberger," *SPhA* 3 [1991]: 153–66).
34. Cf. B. L. Mack, "Philo Judaeus and Exegetical Traditions in Alexandria," *ANRW* 21.1 (1984): 242–43; D. M. Hay, "References to Other Exegetes," in *Both Literal and Allegorical: Studies in Philo of Alexandria's Questions and Answers on Genesis and Exodus* (Atlanta: Scholars Press, 1991), 94–95.
35. Although Philo may be unique to include the Fifth Commandment as part of the first group (honor your parents).
36. *Bread from Heaven: An Exegetical Study of the Concept of Manna in the Gospel of John and the Writings of Philo* (SNT 10; Leiden: E. J. Brill, 1965).
37. *Philo Judaeus: His Universe of Discourse* (BEATAJ 24; Frankfurt am Main: Peter Lang, 1995).
38. Borgen, *Bread from Heaven*, 1–27.
39. E.g. Cohen, *Philo Judaeus*, 278–86.
40. Ibid., 65–71.
41. Ibid., 114. See chapter 5, "Δικαιοσύνη as Keeping the Commandments," esp. 113–18.

42. "[T]he first, and often most relevant, question to be posed when reading Philo on any issue, is not whether his frame of reference is 'philosophic' or 'Jewish', but rather how the two have been indissolubly intertwined. Of course one must be able to identify Jewish and Hellenistic elements, but it is not the isolation of the 'building blocks' but their combination which produces Philo's message" (ibid., 86–87).
43. Philo's problem was with those who took such gods literally (e.g., *Decal.* 54) rather than with the allegorical interpretation of these figures from mythology.
44. He bases this claim in part on 3 Maccabees, which he thinks reflects Alexandrian attitude toward citizenship. Aryeh Kasher, *The Jewish in Hellenistic and Roman Egypt* (Tübingen: Mohr/Siebeck, 1985), 230.
45. E.g., *Decal.* 52–65; *Spec.* 1.13–20; *Praem.* 162. But cf. also *Mos.* 2.205.
46. E.g., *Decal.* 66–81; *Spec.* 1.21–31.
47. Thus E. R. Goodenough: "the first creed of history"; in *An Introduction to Philo Judaeus*, 2d ed. (1940; reprint, New York: Barnes and Noble, 1962), 37.
48. *The Place of Judaism: Israel, Jews, and Proselytes* (Atlanta: Scholars Press, 1996).
49. Ibid., 12–16.
50. It is generally agreed that Philo did not know Hebrew but had access to some standard definitions and etymologies for Hebrew words. Philo provides this definition in numerous places (e.g., *Somn.* 1.129).
51. E.g., *Congr.* 51; *Mig.* 18; *Mut.* 189; *Praem.* 44; *QE* 1.21; 2.43.
52. Birnbaum, *Place of Judaism*, 115.
53. Ibid., 230.
54. D. T. Runia does not think Philo would have left the theater at once in disgust, but that he nevertheless would have had misgivings with the scene ("God and Man in Philo of Alexandria," in *Exegesis and Philosophy: Studies on Philo of Alexandria* [Aldershot: Variorum, 1990], 63). Yet if Philo took the throne as a representation of one of God's potencies rather than as representing God himself (who after all is not visible and does not take seats on literal thrones), Philo might not have objected as much.

Chapter 4

Philo's View of the World

4.1 THE SOURCES OF PHILO'S VIEWS

4.1.1 Jewish Interpretive Traditions

We do not know the names of the vast majority of biblical interpreters at Alexandria. But they no doubt had great influence on the weekly teaching of the Alexandrian synagogues. Indeed, a significant portion of Philo's exegesis may have grown out of the question-answer method used in these synagogues.[1] David Hay has plausibly suggested that many of the questions Philo asked of the biblical text ultimately derived from such prior Jewish interpretation.[2]

History has left us several Jewish writings from Egypt in the period just prior to Philo. Some of these share features with Philo's own writings; others do not. Those that come from Alexandria lead us to place Philo in a stream of Jewish Alexandrian interpretation that persisted there for centuries.

For example, ***Aristobulus*** was a Jewish thinker from Alexandria with a philosophical bent like Philo. Most scholars date him to the time of Ptolemy VI Philometer (181–145 BCE), but we cannot be absolutely certain.[3] Aristobulus's writings suggest that by the early second century BCE Jews at Alexandria were incorporating ideas from Greek philosophical systems such as Stoicism and Pythagoreanism into their understandings of Scripture and Jewish practice.

Philo and Aristobulus share many features in common. For example, both allegorized passages in the biblical text that portrayed God anthropomorphically, that is, with human characteristics.[4] Both reflect a Pythagorean interest in numbers.[5] And both speak of God's *logos,* or word, as the generator and maintainer of all things.[6]

> **Aristobulus:** Jewish thinker from Alexandria in the mid–second century BCE who incorporated Greek philosophy into his interpretation of Scripture and Jewish practice.

A second Jewish writing we can place in this same general Alexandrian milieu is the **Letter of Aristeas.** The *Letter of Aristeas* is a largely fictional account of the translation of the Pentateuch into Greek. However, the bulk of the letter is preoccupied with other things, such as dialogues between the Ptolemaic king Philadelphus and the Jewish translators.[7] Using the question-answer format, these honorable Jews proved they were every bit as wise as any Hellenistic philosopher.

> **Letter of Aristeas:** Pseudonymous work from the second century BCE that presents a fictional account of the Pentateuch's translation into Greek. Pseudonymity is the practice of writing under the authority of another name, usually an authority figure from the past.

Several aspects of *Aristeas* reflect the same quasi-philosophical stream of Jewish thought we saw in Aristobulus. The Jews are portrayed not only with knowledge of Greek culture and philosophy but with openness to them. Indeed, the way *Aristeas* portrays the Septuagint translators probably gives us a glimpse of the attitude Philo himself had toward Hellenism. The author claims that the translators had received an excellent education (*paideia*) and had a thorough knowledge of both Greek and Jewish literature.[8]

Like Philo, the author of *Aristeas* believed that behind the particular laws of the Torah were universal truths that were applicable to people of every race. *Aristeas* thus tended toward the universalist side of the Jewish spectrum, where in theory Gentiles could be fully acceptable to God. Of course, in practice both Philo and *Aristeas* looked down on Egyptian religion and considered the Jewish race far more enlightened than the others.

A final writing we should mention that probably originated at Alexandria is the **Wisdom of Solomon.**[9] David Winston has argued that the book belongs to the Roman period, which began with the conquest of Egypt in 30 BCE.[10] His hunch is that Wisdom is dependent on Philo, if we can really say that one knew the other.[11]

Once again we have a strong example of Jewish interpretation at Alexandria

that drew heavily on Greek philosophy. In over two pages of
cross-references between Wisdom and Philo, Winston captures the extensive similarities
between the two.[12] He presents
these common ideas as similarities in regard to wisdom, cre-

> **Wisdom of Solomon:** A book of wisdom
> reputed to come from Solomon, likely written
> in Alexandria either the first century before or
> after Christ. It reflects Platonic influence at
> various points.

ation, immortality, and ethics, not to mention other linguistic parallels.

Wisdom of Solomon portrays wisdom similarly to Philo. Wisdom is an agent
of creation in both (e.g., Wis. 9:1–2; *Her.* 199; *Det.* 54). Arguably, both see creation as God bringing order out of formless, preexistent matter (Wis. 11:17; *Mos.*
2.267; *Spec.* 4.187). Both have a sense of immortality that continues for the righteous at death (e.g., Wis. 5:15; *Ios.* 264), and the soul seems to preexist the body
(Wis. 8:19–20; *Somn.* 1.33–43).

While Wisdom does not develop its philosophical themes to the extent of
Philo, it has a generally "Platonic" flavor. Philo probably did not draw any of his
ideas from Wisdom. But it likely provides us with yet another example of a philosophically oriented interpretive tradition at Alexandria. Other traditions clearly
existed in Egyptian Judaism,[13] but the philosophical one seems best attested at
Alexandria.

4.1.2 Philosophical Traditions in Philo

The bulk of Philo's thought fits within the parameters of what we might call **Middle Platonism.**[14] Middle Platonism was not a self-proclaimed movement. The
persons we place in this category did not come up with the name and did not
consider themselves part of a new
school.[15] Yet the thought of these
individuals has enough in common for us to refer to them as a
distinct phase in the history of
Platonism.

One of the characteristics of
this period was the way in which
various individuals mixed Platonism with elements from other
philosophical traditions.[16] Of
these other traditions, the influence of Stoicism and Neo-
Pythagoreanism are the most

> **Middle Platonism:** The form Platonism took on
> in the period between the first century BCE
> and the end of the second century CE. Platon-
> ists in this period placed Plato's ideas in an
> intermediate position between a transcen-
> dent, supreme principle of which it was a copy
> and the world of sense that was a copy of it.
> Platonism in this period was highly eclectic,
> particularly in its combination of Platonism
> with Stoic and Pythagorean philosophy.

important. If we add a smidge of Aristotle, we are ready to discuss Philo's philosophical leanings.

Stoicism

Although Plato preceded **Stoicism** by a number of decades, Platonic thought was going into a period of dormancy at about the time Stoicism was born.[17] A philosopher by the name of Zeno founded the movement around 300 BCE in Athens. In the years that followed, Stoicism would become a far more dominant force in the philosophical world than Platonism. What we call Middle Platonism thus emerged against the backdrop of this more prevalent Stoic influence.

> **Stoicism:** Founded by Zeno of Citium around 300 BCE in Athens, Stoicism emphasized the rational structure and direction of the universe, urging a life in accord with nature and the elimination of the passions.
>
> **logos:** Reason or Word. In the Stoic system, the divine reason that directed and permeated the world.

Stoicism was **monist** in its view of reality, which means the Stoics believed everything in the universe was made of the same basic kind of material or "stuff." They referred to the finer form of this material as "spirit" (*pneuma*), "reason" (*logos*, also translated as "word"), or even as Zeus. We all have "seeds" of this *logos* in us, fine particles/fragments of spirit.

The collective *logos* material not only permeates the universe; it also directs and governs it. The Stoics were thus ultimately **deterministic:** we cannot change our ultimate destiny. However, they did believe you could fight against your fate, the destiny **providence** (*pronoia*) had in store for you. But such struggle was pointless. We should all follow the seeds of divine reason inside us (*logoi spermatikoi*) and love our fates. We should strive for *apatheia*, complete indifference to our lot in life.

For the Stoics, therefore, the virtuous individual aimed at a life "in accordance with nature." This was a life in accordance with reason, the *logos*. We should aim at the extermination of our passions (*pathē*), which only lead us down unfruitful and unsatisfying paths. Emotions are unnatural movements in our mind that distract us from the proper path. The only way to true happiness (*eudaimonia*) is acceptance of our fate and the elimination of these passions and emotions.

> **monism:** The belief that everything that exists consists of the same type of "stuff," whatever it might be (e.g., material, ideal).
>
> **determinism:** The belief that the course of unfolding events is already determined, destined, or fated, often accompanied by the idea that some directive force is operative behind those events.
>
> **providence:** For the Stoics, another word for the *logos*, or rational, directive force behind what happens in the world.

Neo-Pythagoreanism

A second influence in the development of Middle Platonism was the rise of Neo-Pythagoreanism in the first cen-

tury BCE. The Greek philosopher Pythagoras (early 500s
BCE) lived not only well before
the Stoics but over a century
before Plato as well. He is perhaps best known for his emphasis on numbers as ultimate reality

> **Neo-Pythagoreanism:** The revival of interest in the teachings of Pythagoras that took place in some circles in the period from the first century BCE to the second century CE.

and his belief in the continued existence of the soul after death.[18] In the first century BCE, Pythagoreanism seems to have revived largely by way of a Roman
named Nigidius Figulus (d. ca. 45 BCE), thus beginning a period of *Neo-
Pythagoreanism*.

We can almost see the birth of Middle Platonism in a comment on Pythagoras made by an Alexandrian philosopher named Eudorus.[19] Eudorus of Alexandria flourished in the mid– to late first century BCE.[20] It is thus very possible
that Philo knew of him and his work, although we do not know this for certain.[21]
In this comment, Eudorus gives credit to Pythagoras for the idea that a supreme,
transcendent principle exists alone beyond all the other things on which reality
is based. He refers to this supreme principle as "the One," or the *Monad*.

Eudorus writes:[22]

> [T]he Pythagoreans postulated on the highest level the One as a First Prin-
> ciple, and then on a secondary level two principles of existent things, the
> One and the nature opposed to this.

What is interesting about this comment is that we have no evidence of any earlier Pythagorean ever teaching the existence of such a transcendent One.[23]
Eudorus is the first known
instance of such a concept by
anyone. The Pythagoreans did
teach about the two secondary
principles he mentions, principles opposed to each other. But
they placed these on the most
fundamental level of reality, not
as secondary principles.

The Pythagoreans believed
that the two most basic principles of reality were Limit (the
"One," the "Monad") and Limitlessness (the **Dyad**). They apparently believed that the Monad
exerted limitations on the limit-

> **transcendent:** Beyond everything else that exists.
>
> **Monad:** Another name for the One; in Pythagorean and Platonic thought, the active of two supreme principles, also known as Limit. Middle Platonic thinkers could use it both in this sense and in the sense of a single, supreme, transcendent principle beyond it.
>
> **Dyad:** In Pythagorean and Platonic thought, the passive of two supreme principles, also known as Limitlessness. Middle Platonic thinkers placed it below a single, transcendent principle.

less Dyad, an action that generated the basic numbers. These numbers, in turn,
served as the basis for all other reality.

But Eudorus subordinated these two principles to a singular, supreme, and transcendent One, different from the One about which the Pythagoreans actually taught. This slight modification to the Pythagorean tradition would have a significant impact on Philo and later Platonic thought. In particular, it allowed individuals like Eudorus and Philo to think of God as the ultimate cause of the fundamental principles in the philosophies of Pythagoras and Plato.

This merging of the Pythagorean tradition with Platonism possibly explains why later writers sometimes referred to Platonists, including Plato himself, as Pythagoreans. The second-century CE philosopher Numenius referred to Plato as a Pythagorean.[24] Similarly, it is uncertain whether we should think of Eudorus as a Middle Platonist or Neo-Pythagorean. In this ambiguity we have a potential explanation for why the second-century Christian Clement of Alexandria referred twice to Philo as "the Pythagorean," even though Philo clearly drew much more heavily on Plato than on Pythagoras.[25]

> **senses:** The faculties of a person that see, hear, touch, smell, and taste—that perceive the physical, visible world around us.
> **ideas:** For Plato, the realities behind the visible world of sense-perception. The physical things around us are only shadowy copies and images of the real, ideal patterns we understand with our minds.

Platonism

Plato lived from 429 to 347 BCE. He thus came on to the scene well over a hundred years after Pythagoras and died some fifty years before Zeno founded Stoicism. For our purposes, the most important feature of Plato's teaching was his belief that the world we perceive around us with our *senses* is only a shadowy copy of certain more fundamental *ideas* that we understand with our minds.

Plato believed that the truest reality is something we cannot know through our senses, but only through our minds. The *world of ideas* we know through our minds is the real world, of which the *world of senses* gives us only a shadowy picture. Thus it is the idea of a horse in our mind that is truly real, far more than some particular horse you might see with your eyes, hear with your ears, or touch with your hands.

This idea of a horse in Platonic thought—an idea we access through our minds—relates directly to the *essence* of a horse, that without which a horse would not be a horse. It is "horseness." Plato could thus speak of the ideal horse as the general *pattern* (*paradeigma*) or *form* (*eidos*) behind all particular horses. We might call this ideal horse the *archetype* (*archetypos*) of all horses, the ideal prototype. Every specific horse was thus a *copy* (*mimēma*) or *image* (*eikōn*) of the real, ideal horse, a *shadow* (*skia*) of the real one we know through our mind.

On one level, this way of looking at things makes some sense. At least at first glance, it does seem all horses have some basic characteristics they share in common.[26] But we have not really understood Plato if we think he is only saying we can identify some essential features that all horses share.[27] For Plato, these essentials are real *apart* from any horse we can see. Plato believed that the physical horses we can see are actually not the real horses at all. Ideas have a reality independent of the visible world. These ***incorporeal*** ideas—entities without visible bodies—are the patterns behind the corporeal or embodied things we see around us.

Plato himself believed we could know a vast amount about both the visible world and the more important invisible world of ideas. But those who ran

> **essence:** That without which something would not be what it is.
>
> **patterns/forms/archetypes:** Terms Plato used for the realities in the world of ideas that stood behind the shadowy representations of them in the visible world.
>
> **copies/images/shadows:** Terms Plato used for the visible things in the world of sense, which were far less real than their ideal counterparts.
>
> **world of ideas:** The world of all the Platonic ideals and forms taken together.
>
> **world of senses:** The world of all the shadowy copies of the ideas, perceived by our senses.
>
> **incorporeal:** Not embodied.

Plato's Academy in the third and second century BCE generally took the skeptical view that we cannot have any certain knowledge of the world at all, whether visible or invisible. Plato's ideas sank into a period of dormancy less than a hundred years after he passed from the scene.

This state of affairs continued until the time of Antiochus of Ascalon (ca. 130–ca. 68 BCE). At that time Philo of Larissa headed Plato's Academy (110–88 BCE)[28] and was continuing the skeptical tradition he inherited from his predecessors. Antiochus called Philo of Larissa to task for claiming to teach the same things as Plato while teaching a skeptical perspective. This challenge may have initiated a move among other Platonists away from skepticism and back toward Plato's actual teachings. It is ironic in this regard that Antiochus himself was more of a Stoic than a Platonist: it took a non-Platonist to revive Platonism.[29]

Middle Platonism

We are now in a position to sketch the origins of Middle Platonic tradition. We start with the modified Pythagoreanism of which Eudorus writes. Here we have a supreme, transcendent principle beyond all else. Eudorus, Philo, and other Middle Platonists could refer to this principle as God. Beneath the supreme God we find the two Pythagorean principles of the Monad and the Dyad, Limit and Limitlessness. In some way, the interplay of these two principles results in the generation of all the other numbers, which in Philo and others seem to correspond to Plato's world of ideas (cf. *Her.* 190; *Decal.* 102; *Praem.* 46).

Now the Platonic tradition comes into play. Plato had basically pictured a "two-story" model of reality, with the world of ideas providing patterns for the world of the senses. In contrast, Middle Platonism now functions on a "three-story" model.

> **The Three-Tiered Reality of Middle Platonism**
>
> | | |
> |---|---|
> | Transcendent level: | Transcendent God (who is the pattern of) |
> | | The Monad |
> | Logos level: | The *Logos* |
> | | The World of Ideas (which is the pattern of) |
> | Corporeal level: | The World of Sense |

On the highest level is the supreme, transcendent One. This One, or God, serves as the pattern of the middle level of reality, which corresponds to Plato's world of ideas. This world, in turn, serves as the pattern for the world of the senses around us.

Stoicism then contributes the *logos* to this system. The *logos* becomes the image of God and the container of all the ideas that are the basis for the visible, corporeal world. A person like Philo can thus incorporate a great deal of Stoic ideology and ethics into a Platonic framework.

4.2 PHILO'S VIEW OF REALITY

4.2.1 God

In ancient philosophy, **physics** was the branch of philosophy that dealt with questions of reality, a topic philosophers call **metaphysics** today. The place of God in

> **physics:** In this context, the study of the world and of the nature of reality (i.e., **metaphysics**).

Philo's metaphysics is one of the features of his thought that distinguishes him as Middle Platonic. Individuals in this category were concerned in one way or another with a supreme, transcendent principle they called by various names, of which God, the Monad, and the One were the most common. Philo regularly refers to God in these ways.[30]

But Philo could also speak of God as *beyond* the Monad and beyond the One. Take the following passage from *On Rewards*:

> When the father and savior [God] saw his [Jacob's] genuine desire and yearning, God had mercy on him and did not begrudge him the visual power to penetrate through to a vision of himself [God], at least in so far as it was possible for someone of a created and mortal nature. The vision was thus not *what* God is but *that* he is. For that which is even better than the Good and older than the Monad and purer than the One cannot be looked upon by something else. It is right for God alone to be comprehended by himself. (*Praem.* 39–40)

Philo clearly placed God in a role of extreme transcendence. God is "better than virtue, better than knowledge, better than the Good itself and the Beautiful itself" (*Opif.* 8). God is the one who can say, "[N]o name is properly used of me" (*Mos.* 1.75).

Philo is the first known person to use phrases such as "unnameable" (*akatono-mastos*), "utterable" (*arrhētos*), and "incomprehensible by any idea" (*kata pasas ideas akatalēptou*) in reference to God (*Somn.* 1.67). God's essence is thus unknowable. Philo probably did not originate this concept, this **negative theology** in which God is primarily known for what he is *not* rather than for what he is.[31] John Dillon suggests Philo may have drawn the notion from Eudorus.[32] Nevertheless, Philo is the first known instance of such an approach.

This concept of God's transcendence appears in Philo's writings in several different ways. For example, it is reflected in Philo's preferred way of referring to God, namely, as "the one who is" (*ho ōn*), "the one who truly is" (*ho ontōs ōn*), or "that which is"

> **negative theology/via negativa:** The idea that God is known not by what he is but by what he is not. Knowledge of God is thus often conceived in mystical terms.

(*ho on*). These names reflect Philo's belief that we can know only that God exists, not what his essence is. The phrase "the one who truly is" also draws a contrast between the true God and the gods of mythmakers and idols, since these gods do not truly exist.

God's transcendent goodness implied for Philo that God in his essence could not have been directly involved in the creation of the world. He considered it absurd on the highest level to suggest that God would directly be involved with "limitless and chaotic matter."[33] Instead, God created the world by way of his "incorporeal powers," which in *Special Laws* 1.329 refers to the Platonic forms or ideas.

Elsewhere Philo applies the same principle to the judgment of evil. God is "the eldest of things that exist and the most perfect good" (*Conf.* 180). He thus cannot punish the wicked himself, because he is only the giver of good things, while the truly good has God alone as its cause.[34] Thus, while God is the power behind all things, he is not the direct agent of everything (e.g., *Leg.* 1.41).

In addition to transcendence, the goodness and graciousness of God are also key characteristics of God that appear regularly throughout Philo's writings. Philo makes it clear that no human is without sin and that favor with God is possible only through his graciousness (e.g., *Mos.* 2.147). Divine providence is a key concept for Philo as well.[35] Philo combines the Stoic sense of a directing force in the cosmos with the Jewish sense of God's goodness. The result is a God who cares for both the creation (e.g., *Opif.* 171–72) and humanity (e.g., *Abr.* 137).

We find in addition to these characteristics a host of classical divine attributes in Philo's writings. God is all powerful.[36] He has no need of anything.[37] He knows everything.[38] His essence is not in this universe (e.g., *Leg.* 1.44), although his powers are (*Mig.* 182), making him everywhere present in a sense (*Leg.* 3.4–6). He is unchangeable (e.g., *Leg.* 1.51). In Philo we thus find the same basic attributes of God that later Christians would develop.

4.2.2 The Powers and Agents of God

Middle Platonists postulated an intermediate realm between the supreme, transcendent principle and the world we observe with our senses. This realm took on different forms for different thinkers. Philo's writings are full of such intermediaries between God and the world of the senses. In Philo we find the Pythagorean Monad and Dyad, the Platonic world of ideas and forms, the Stoic *logos*, and the angels of Judaism. Philo turns to various intermediary figures as they seem relevant to the Scriptural texts in front of him.

The *Logos*

Perhaps the best-known intermediary figure in Philo is the *logos*. The word is notoriously difficult for us to translate and grasp. In various contexts, its meaning can range from a word or message to reason itself. Perhaps we best start to understand the word by noting the Stoic distinction between an unexpressed word or thought (*logos endiathetos*) and an expressed one (*logos prophorikos*).[39] When we look at *logos* from this perspective, it relates to thought on its most basic level. The distinctions in its meaning largely result from whether a thought is expressed in literal word or not.

When we combine the philosophical background of this term in Stoicism with Philo's Platonism and Jewish heritage, we have a complex situation indeed. It is no wonder that it is so difficult to pin down exactly what Philo means by the term, and that Philo can use it in so many different ways. We can identify a number of key ways in which Philo used *logos* imagery in his writings.

1. The logos *as God's directive force in the world*

At times Philo retained the Stoic idea of the *logos* as a directive force in the world. He could thus say that God had set his *logos* as shepherd of the universe (*Agr.* 51–52). He could call the *logos* the commander and pilot of the world.[40] Related to these metaphors is imagery of the *logos* as governor[41] or ruler.[42]

Like the Stoics, Philo attributed things both beneficial and detrimental to the direction of the *logos*.[43] We should thus bear whatever happens to us, because the *logos* is directing the affairs of the world (*Cher.* 35–36). The *logos* is also God's ambassador and chief messenger to the creation (e.g., *Her.* 205). It so thoroughly represents God that we can attribute the same activities to both. Philo could thus say that the *logos* piloted the universe (e.g., *Cher.* 36) or that God piloted it.[44] Perhaps even more precisely, Philo could put both together, with God as pilot and the *logos* as the rudder by which he steers everything on its course (*Mig.* 6).

2. The logos *as the image of God*

The fluidity with which Philo could interchange the roles of God and the *logos* leads us to his conception of the *logos* as the image of God.[45] Here Philo was clearly integrating Platonic imagery of pattern and copy with the Stoic sense of the rational *logos*. In good Middle Platonist fashion, a three-tiered view of reality resulted. God is the ultimate pattern of which the *logos* is a copy or image, and the corporeal world in turn is a copy of the *logos*.

We find a good expression of this view in *Allegorical Laws* 3.96:

> God's Word [*logos*] is his shadow [*skia*]. By it he made the world, using it as an instrument. And this shadow—this representation [*apeikonisma*] as it were—is an archetype of other things. For just as God is the pattern [*paradeigma*] of the image [*eikōn*] that we have just called a shadow, so this image becomes a pattern of other things.

We also find in this passage two other roles of the *logos* that we will discuss below, namely, the *logos* as an instrument of creation and the *logos* as the "location" of the Platonic ideals of which the world of sense is a copy.

3. The logos *as the instrument of creation*

Philo is the first known instance in which the *logos* is understood to be the instrument of creation. Various scholars of Philo disagree on whether this conception was an "orthodox Middle Platonic doctrine" at that time.[46] Philo himself seems to be synthesizing discussions about the *logos* in philosophical circles with Jewish traditions about God's wisdom. It is just as likely that Philo inherited such a synthesis as that he made the connection himself. In either case, he represents developments that were taking place in both philosophy and Alexandrian Judaism in his day.

As early as Proverbs in the Jewish Scriptures, Jews could personify God's wisdom and speak of it as the agent of creation:

> When he [God] established the heavens, I [wisdom] was there. When he inscribed the vault on the face of the deep, when he positioned the clouds above, when he strengthened the fountains of the deep . . . I was the master-worker beside him. (Prov. 8:27–28, 30)

God's wisdom would take on a life of its own in Jewish literature. Philo retains the sense that God used wisdom as an instrument in creation (e.g., *Fug.* 109), as does the roughly contemporaneous book of Wisdom (e.g., 9:1–2).

Yet the book of Wisdom shows us how Jews could also equate imagery of God's wisdom with the idea of his word (*logos*). It is all too easy to imagine how Jews of a Middle Platonic bent might have read Isaiah 55:11:[47]

> So will my word (*hrēma*) be: whatever goes out from my mouth will never return until it has completed whatever I willed.

Clearly, it was no stretch to consider God's directive "word," like the Stoic *logos*, as his providential will, against which it would be pointless to resist.

However, with Philo we seem to move beyond these wisdom/word traditions to what we might call Jewish wisdom *speculation*. In the earlier literature, God's wisdom and word seem to be exactly that: God's personifications of God's thinking. But Philo seems to look at God's word, or *logos,* as something truly distinct from him, as a **hypostasis** that has its own distinct existence.

Philo thus integrates Genesis 1's repeated sense of God *speaking* in creation with Middle Platonic discussions about the various causes of things, perhaps following the lead of Jewish thinkers before him.[48] The result is that Philo could see the *logos* as the instrument by which God created the world.[49] "And God *said*, 'Let light come into existence.' And light came into existence" (Gen. 1:3). This statement amounts to God using his word to create.

> **hypostasis:** A distinct entity or personality, even if also a subordinate and closely related one.

Perhaps we should relate Philo's imagery of the *logos* as a cutter or divider to the sense that it was the instrument God used to create the world. The treatise *Who Is the Heir of Divine Things?* discusses creation as a succession of divisions that ultimately resulted in the cosmos as we now know it (*Her.* 133–40). And even more generally, we can attribute logical distinctions/divisions as the distinct province of the rational *logos*.

4. The logos *as the container of the world of ideas*

Philo, or more likely one of his Jewish predecessors, integrated the Jewish sense of God's word as the instrument of creation with the Platonic sense of the world of ideas as the basis for the visible world. The result was that God's *logos* contained the world of ideas. We find this notion most clearly stated in *On the Creation* 24:

> The world discerned by the mind is nothing other than the *logos* of God already engaged in making the world. For the city discerned by the mind [an illustration Philo has made about an architect designing a city] is nothing different from the reasoning [*logismos*] of the architect already contemplating the creation of the city.

This passage is a favorite of those who argue that for Philo the *logos* in the end is only a personification, since he compares the *logos* to the reasoning of an architect.

We will consider this issue below in our discussion of the *logos* as a second god. Our point now is that for Philo the world of sense we perceive around us is a copy, shadow, or image of the ideas that constitute God's *logos*. The corporeal world thus stands in the same relationship to the *logos* as the *logos* stands to God: the *logos* is the image of God and the world of sense is the image of the *logos*.

5. The logos *as the glue/prop of creation*

In keeping with Stoic tradition, Philo can speak of the *logos* as the glue or bond that holds the creation together (e.g., *Her.* 188; *Fug.* 112) or the prop that holds it up (e.g., *Plant.* 8). Such statements basically amount to the belief that rationality stands at the very core of the world's nature. The concept is thus very similar to the Stoic belief that fine *logos* particles, *logoi spermatikoi*, permeate the world.

6. The logos *as the soul's guide to God*

Because the world is full of the *logos*, and since the *logos* is God's image, the *logos* provides an appropriate path to God. We call this function **anagogical:** the *logos* can lead our souls to God. The following passage is a good example of this function:[50]

> Those who live in knowledge of the One are rightly called "sons of God." . . .
>
> And if someone is not yet worthy to be called a son of God, let that person strive to be put in order according to his firstborn *logos*, the oldest of messengers [*angelos*], chief messenger [= archangel] as it were, who possesses many names. For it is called both "beginning" and "name of God" and "word" and "the human according to the image" and "the one who sees," "Israel." . . .
>
> **anagogical:** Leading the human soul upward to the realm of the divine.
>
> For if it is not yet appropriate to consider us children of God, we can still be children of his invisible image, his most sacred *logos*. For the oldest image of God is the *logos*. (*Conf.* 145–47)

In this passage we catch a glimpse of the various elements in a biblical text that could "cue" an interpretation involving the *logos* in Philo's mind.[51] Several aspects of the *logos* are in play here: the *logos* as the image of God, for example. Because the *logos* permeated the world, because it mirrored God, the *logos*, reason, provided a fitting path to the contemplation of God. For this reason, Philo could also call the *logos* a high priest, an intercessor between God and humanity.[52]

7. The logos: *A second god?*

Philo somewhat startlingly could refer to the *logos* as a "second God":[53]

> "I am the God who appeared to you in the place of god" [Gen. 31:13]. . . .
>
> Inquire carefully if there are *two gods* in what it says. . . . For in truth God is one, even if there are many whom people improperly call "gods."
>
> Therefore, the sacred word [*logos*] in this case has revealed who is truly God by way of the articles. It states in the one place, "I am the God." But in the other instance it indicates the one we should not call god by omitting the article: "the one who appeared to you in the place" not "of *the* God" but only "of god."
>
> Here it calls God's oldest Word [*logos*] "god." (*Somn.* 1.227–30)

In this passage, Philo speaks of how many mistake God's governor and representative, the *logos*, for him. Those without wisdom cannot understand God without some sense of him having a body and being like humans. These understand God by way of his angel or messenger, his Word (*logos*).

The distinction between God, whose essence is unknowable, and the *logos* is significant for Philo.[54] When he is speaking imprecisely, he can speak of the *logos* as if it were simply God's reason in action (e.g., *Opif.* 36). But when he is in technical philosophy mode, he draws an important distinction between God and his reason (*logos*):

> To his chief messenger [= archangel] and oldest word [*logos*] the father who gave birth to everything gave a special gift to stand on the boundary and separate what has come into existence from the one who has created. And this same *logos* is a constant suppliant to the immortal for the disturbed mortal and an ambassador of the ruler to the subject.
>
> And he rejoices in the gift and tells us the whole story with pride as he says, "I stood in the middle between the Lord and you," neither being uncreated like God nor created like you. I was between the extremes. (*Her.* 205–6)

In this passage Philo puts the *logos* on the created side of the equation.

In the end, a comparison of Philo with the philosophical traditions he utilizes points us toward seeing the *logos* as something with independent existence from God. But we probably should not understand it to be a person either. Its closest philosophical parallel would seem to be the Pythagorean/Middle Platonic Monad, or One.

God himself is, of course, beyond the Monad, and Philo regularly draws this distinction. The Monad itself, for Philo, is not actually a number but the source of numbers.[55] The incorporeal world of ideas thus derives from it (*Decal.* 102), and it is the incorporeal image of God.[56] It thus seems no coincidence that the initial creation of the world of ideas is represented by day "one," not the first day (*Opif.* 35).

If we are thus to relate the *logos* to this philosophical imagery, it corresponds best to the Monad, although Philo is not very explicit about this equation. Perhaps he comes closest in *QE* 2.68, where the *logos* is the only appropriate equivalent to the Monad.[57] Because the Monad was a distinct entity from God for Philo, it would appear that we must consider the *logos* a hypostasis, although not a personal one.

Theos and *Kyrios*

To keep God untainted with the inferior world (e.g., *Spec.* 1.328–29) and beyond human comprehension, Philo made a distinction between God in his essence and God's powers. Among these intermediary figures, the *logos* of course held primacy and probably corresponded to the Pythagorean Monad. Philo also distinguished God's goodness and sovereignty as powers subordinate to the *logos*, and at times Philo may think of them in terms of the Pythagorean Dyad (e.g., *QE* 2.68).

However, as far as the biblical text is concerned, Philo drew them from the phenomenon in Genesis and Exodus where God is sometimes referred to as "God" (in Greek, *theos*) and at other times as "Lord" (*kyrios*). For Philo, these are God's powers or potencies, intermediaries by which he relates to the world. "God" represents the creative and beneficent dimension of God's relationship with the world, while "Lord" corresponds to his royal and at times punitive interaction.[58]

Angels

Philo did not always limit the powers to the two we just mentioned. He could speak of them as numberless (e.g., *Conf.* 171)—a fact that corresponds even better to the Pythagorean Dyad, which represented infinite divisibility. Beneath these potencies, in the air (e.g., *Conf.* 174), Philo placed angels as incorporeal souls whose duties were to serve God as ministers to humans below (e.g., *Gig.* 12). Angels are thus God's ambassadors between humanity and God (e.g., *Gig.* 16).

4.2.3 The Creation

Scholars continue to debate whether Philo believed in creation *ex nihilo*—out of nothing. Harry Wolfson was perhaps the most famous proponent of the idea that Philo envisaged at least a two-stage creation: the first being the creation of chaotic matter and the second involving the ordering of that matter.[59] Others, like David Winston and Gregory Sterling, have seen in Philo a belief in *creatio aeterna*, the idea that God has eternally created order in matter, in their case matter that is an indirect product of God's creative thought.[60] Still others do not think we can resolve the issue on the basis of the evidence we have.[61]

The *logos* and God's other powers are a part of the creation. One of the most interesting accounts of their generation appears in *QE* 2.68. In this text God first creates the *logos*. He then separates the creative ("God") and royal ("Lord") potencies from it. Somewhat more unusually, in this text Philo sees two further powers (i.e., beneficent and punitive) springing from the preceding two. Finally, we have the creation of the world of ideas.

> *creatio ex nihilo:* The notion that God created the universe from no prior existing materials.
> *creatio aeterna:* The notion that God has created the world for all of eternity past.
> *creatio simultanea:* The idea that creation took place at the point when God created time.

The creation of the visible world then coincides with the creation of time (e.g., *Opif.* 26), or it may postdate it (*Leg.* 1.2). The visible, corporeal world is only a shadow and copy of the invisible, incorporeal one (e.g., *Opif.* 25). But it nevertheless draws us to contemplate the realities behind the world and God its creator. Our eyes are thus the most valuable of all our senses (*Spec.* 3.185–91).

The outer boundary of the visible world is the outermost sphere of the fixed stars.[62] Within these is an inner sphere consisting of seven circles or zones, the paths of the "wanderers" or planets.[63] These are Saturn, Jupiter, Mars, the sun in the central place of prominence, Mercury, Venus, and the moon (*Her.* 225). These planets are condensed masses of ether/fire, and the upper air around them is ether.[64] They are "corporeal souls," as opposed to the angels who inhabit the region below the moon as incorporeal souls.[65]

Beneath the Moon is the lower air and, from a "Pythagorean" perspective, the third part of the creation.[66] The elements of this realm are the standard four of the ancient world: fire, air, water, and earth (e.g., *Her.* 152–53). Philo sometimes follows Aristotle in speaking of five, considering ether a fifth substance (e.g., *QG* 4.8), while at other times ether is perhaps just a pure rather than mixed fire (e.g., *Plant.* 2–6).

Meanwhile, the earth is in the center of the universe as a whole (e.g., *Mos.* 1.212), with the stars and planets rotating around it. The universe is thus divided into an upper and a lower hemisphere (e.g., *Spec.* 1.86). On the level of earth, waters have spread out over its surface (e.g., *Aet.* 33). Meanwhile, Philo pictures the destiny of the wicked dead in a downward direction.[67]

4.3.4 Humanity

Philo operated thoroughly with a two-part conception of a human being: body and soul. He viewed the body and flesh as a hindrance to the soul (e.g., *Leg.* 3.69) but did not really view the body as evil in the way the gnostics would a century later. He could conceive of the soul in more than one way, depending on which best served the exegetical purposes of the moment.

When Philo was functioning on a Platonic plane, he spoke of the soul in terms of three parts, each of which corresponded to a part of the body.[68] The head relates to the reasoning faculty of a person, the chest to the spirited dimension, while the abdomen relates to desire. As we will mention below, a different virtue corresponded to each part.

When Philo was operating in Stoic mode, he divided the components of the soul into two categories: the rational and the irrational. The rational part of a person is the mind, which serves as the ruler of the soul (*Opif.* 30) or the soul's soul (*Opif.* 66).[69] By contrast, there were seven parts to the irrational part of the soul, namely, the five senses along with the organs of speech and generation (e.g., *Leg.* 1.11). Philo saw no contradiction between the two ways of dividing the soul.

Philo no doubt was following Alexandrian Jewish tradition when he presented Genesis 1:27 and 2:7 as the creation of two different men.[70] In this interpretation, the man created in Genesis 1:27 was an incorporeal Platonic ideal, neither male nor female, created according to God's image—that is, it was a copy of the *logos* (*Opif.* 134). The man of Genesis 2:7 is thus the corporeal, "molded" man, the copy of the ideal human in 1:27 (e.g., *Leg.* 1.31). Yet Philo could also resort to the Stoic sense that the human spirit is a fragment of the divine within us, an ethereal particle.[71]

Philo's writings frequently reflect the Platonic belief in the soul's immortality (e.g., *QG* 3.11), meaning its existence both prior to entering flesh (e.g., *Somn.* 1.138–39) and after its departure from the tomb of the body (cf. *Leg.* 1.108). However, he did not believe that all souls have a blessed afterlife in store for them. In several places among his writings, a good afterlife is restricted to those who are good. These individuals can look forward to a future in the heavens.[72] In contrast, the bad look toward the depths of the underworld for their future, in Hades or Tartarus.[73]

Philo's sense of whether humans have free will is difficult to pin down.[74] Consider the two quotes that follow:

> The father who begat thought considered it alone worthy of freedom. After he had released the bonds of necessity he allowed it freedom to roam. He gave it the most suitable and fitting possession: free will. (*Deus.* 47)

> Everything is God's possession, not yours: your thoughts, your understandings, your arts, your reflections, your detailed reasoning, the perceptions of your senses, the operations of your souls both through your senses and apart from them. (*Cher.* 71)

In some way that seems fairly typical of many thinkers in his day (e.g., Paul), Philo both considered God the only active cause in the universe (e.g., *Cher.* 77) and yet regularly used language ascribing freedom to the human will. This tension allowed Philo to maintain the two ever paradoxical claims that (1) God is in sovereign control of the universe and yet (2) humans are responsible for their actions.

4.3 TRUTH AND CONTEMPLATION

Philo accepted the Stoic criterion of truth as "a perception taking hold" (*katalēptikē phantasia*), a sure and certain perception of the soul inside us (e.g., *Congr.* 141). He clearly saw the human mind as the focal point of such truth, with our senses and bodies distracting us from it more often than not. Yet the senses could also genuinely lead us to truth. Philo has a lovely passage in *Spec.* 3.185–94 where he speaks of how our sight can lead us beyond the visible heavens to contemplate the invisible realities behind them.

Philo's **epistemology**—his thoughts on how we come to know things—was basically Stoic. We find a nice presentation of it in *Leg.* 1.28–30 where Philo is interpreting the spring that waters the face of the earth in Genesis 2:6.[75] In this passage, our faculty of sense-perception stands in between our mind and the objects of sense in the world around us. The mind extends itself to the senses, while God sends the objects of sense. Philo is keen to give God the credit for this process—he is the ultimate cause of all knowledge (e.g., *Leg.* 2.46).

> epistemology: The field of philosophy devoted to the question of how we know what we know (**logic,** the ancient term).

In the end, Philo did not believe humans could know God as he truly is. We can only know that he exists, not the nature of his existence. Even Moses could not see God in his essence. And only God can make it possible for anyone to apprehend him to any degree at all (cf. *Spec.* 1.42). The true path to God is thus the path of the mystic, understood in the limited sense of one who contemplates that which is ultimately beyond human comprehension and can only be experienced.[76]

4.4 PHILO'S ETHICS

4.4.1 The Purpose of Life

The question of life's goal, or *telos,* is the question of happiness (*eudaimonia*): in what does the "good life" (*to eu zēn*) consist? Philo could speak of the ultimate purpose of life in both Stoic and Platonic terms, with the Platonic ultimately dominating. On the one hand, the goal of life for the Stoics was a life "according to nature." Philo accepted this goal as an appropriate aim in life.[77]

On the ther hand, Philo preferred the more Platonic goal of life as "likeness to God" (*homoiōsis theōi*; e.g., *Fug.* 63). Such likeness entailed becoming just and holy with wisdom. For Philo, knowledge of God was the secret to human happiness and the good life (e.g., *Det.* 86), even if God's nature was ultimately beyond human knowing.

Philo saw two principal kinds of "good life": the theoretical and the practical.[78] Virtue in general requires excellence in both, for the virtuous person both lives life appropriately and contemplates the theory behind good living (*Leg.* 1.57–58). However, some individuals live out the good life more in the manner of the Essenes, whose community demonstrated exemplary fellowship (cf. *Hypoth.* 11.1–18). Others are more like the Therapeutae, who devoted much more time to contemplation and self-discipline (cf. *Contempl.* 21–90). Philo clearly idealized the contemplative life (cf. *Spec.* 3.1) and saw it as the more profound of the two (e.g., *Fug.* 36–37).

Philo was much less consistent on the question of whether virtue alone was sufficient for happiness. In general, he seemed to favor the Stoic view that virtue alone was necessary. He could rail against the Aristotelian claim that three types of good were essential: good external circumstances, a healthy body, and a healthy soul (e.g., *Det.* 7–8). But later in the same commentary series, he openly admits the significance of all three for happiness (e.g., *Her.* 285–86). Here we find testimony to how difficult it is at times to find consistency in Philo's philosophical views, as well as the extent to which the text at hand dictated the direction of his interpretations.

4.4.2 Virtue and the Passions

Philo frequently operated with the classic sense of four cardinal virtues: prudence (*phronēsis*), courage (*andreia*), self-control (*sōphrosyne*), and justice (*dikaiosyne*).[79] Yet he did not limit himself to these.[80] His Jewish identity sometimes led him to affirm virtues such as godliness (*eusebeia*) and love of humanity (*philanthropia*) as even more important.[81] Indeed, we might subsume all the other virtues within these two.

Such virtues all come from God: their source is in his wisdom (*sophia*) and reason (*logos*) (e.g., *Leg.* 1.63–73). And when Philo was operating within Platonic categories, each of the four cardinal virtues corresponded to a part of the soul. Prudence represents the mind acting with wisdom. Courage is the appropriate working of the spirited element of a person. Self-control is the mastery of desire, and justice the harmonious and appropriate interaction of all three in concert.

Philo saw Abraham, Isaac, and Jacob as symbolic of three forms in which virtue manifests itself, although all virtuous individuals will have all three characteristics to some degree (cf. *Abr.* 53). Abraham represents the person who attains to virtue by way of teaching or instruction. Isaac is the person who is naturally virtuous, and Jacob is the person who attains to virtue through training and practice. These themes recur throughout the Philonic corpus.[82]

In contrast, Philo regularly railed against those who live for pleasure and the passions. Philo's most unique contribution to the exegetical tradition at Alexandria may well have been his interpretation of the Adam and Eve story in Genesis as an "allegory of the soul."[83] In this allegory, Adam represents the mind, Eve stands for our senses, and the serpent relates to pleasure (e.g., *Opif.* 165). Desire for pleasure plays on our senses and clouds our mind. The goal is thus to eliminate our passions (e.g., *Leg.* 3.129) and to follow reason rather than be governed by our senses.[84]

We observe a great deal of Stoic influence in Philo's thought on this subject. For example, Philo accepts the four passions of Stoicism: pleasure (*hēdonē*), desire (*epithymia*), grief (*lypē*), and fear (*phobos*).[85] Similarly, his emphasis on eliminating the passions is thoroughly Stoic,[86] although on one occasion he speaks favorably of the Aristotelian moderation of the passions (e.g., *Virt.* 195).

4.5 PHILO AND SOCIETY[87]

4.5.1 Philo and Politics

In theory Philo believed the contemplative life was the most virtuous and that a true vision of God was best found away from cities and society.[88] Joseph, who symbolizes the statesman, is always a somewhat ambiguous moral figure in Philo's treatises. While Philo's treatise *On Joseph* is at least nominally complementary toward the statesman, *On Dreams* 2 is strongly negative toward him.[89]

Philo nevertheless did involve himself in politics. In *On Flight and Finding,* he shows no affection for the Cynic idea that the philosopher should shun political life (*Fug.* 33–36). And the Jews surely would not have chosen Philo to lead a delegation to the emperor if he were not a skilled and experienced politician. Philo's regrets about the "sea of civic concerns" of *Special Laws* 3.1–6 thus did not reflect his first taste of politics, only his first really sour taste.

Philo's political thoughts may thus have had a strong connection to his own situation. It is not difficult to suppose that Philo's own involvement in the politics of Alexandria eventually left him with a bitter taste in his mouth. In *Dreams* 2 he seems to repent of his "drunken" involvement in politics and hopes to learn to "hate the political dreamer" as his friends do (*Somn.* 2.101–4).

We should also mention in this section Philo's strange conception of democracy as the best form of government. He repeatedly indicates throughout his writings that a democracy is the best-ordered and most law-oriented constitution.[90] Correspondingly, the rule of the mob is the worst form of society.

What is odd is that a democracy for him seems to mean only a *weighted* equality between participants, and that apparently over time. When Philo uses the virtuous soul as a model for democracy (e.g., *Conf.* 108), we see that equality for him did not mean that all the elements get an equal vote. Philo clearly believed the mind had a greater voice than the belly in any democracy of the soul.

Philo could also conceive of the world as a city governed by the *logos*, with the virtuous constituting its citizens.[91] In a strange passage, he considers the world's constitution a democracy because different nations get a chance to rule at different times (*Deus* 176). This "democracy" is thus under the sovereignty of the *logos*, and the nations do not have equal voice most of the time.

4.5.2 Philo and the Household

Special Laws 3.169–70 provides us with a good overview of Philo's views on the respective roles of men and women in society:[92]

> These are appropriate for males: marketplaces, council halls, law courts, gatherings, assemblies of large crowds, and life in the open air. In these settings men can discuss and act in both war and peace. But females appropriately keep the home and remain inside. Virgins should remain within the boundary of the middle door, while mature women stay within the outer door. You see there are two forms of "state": a greater and lesser one. We call the greater one a city, while we call the lesser one a household. And each is assigned leadership. The role of males relates to the greater form, government. On the other hand, females manage the lesser: the household.

It is unfortunate that while Philo leaned so much toward Plato on so many subjects, he was much more Aristotelian when it came to his estimation of women.[93] Philo consistently considered women inferior and weaker to men,[94] and we can count on his allegorical interpretations to place them in a subordinate, if not negative, light.[95]

Philo's discussions of slavery are at least more positive in theory. Philo applauds the Essenes and Therapeutae for their refusal to have slaves.[96] And Philo considers the Jewish law that set slaves free every seventh year a superb example of the law's moral excellence (*Spec.* 2.79–85). Yet, for all his pious words, in practice Philo believed that life involved any number of circumstances where slaves were a necessity (*Spec.* 2.123). He might admire the Essenes and Therapeutae, but he was clearly not ready to commit.

4.6 CONCLUSION

The previous chapter left us with a clear sense of Philo's significance for under-standing first-century Judaism. Surely this chapter also leaves no doubt of how much Philo can contribute to our knowledge of developments in philosophy and theology at the turn of the common era. We will not go far in the history of ideas after Philo before we realize the extent to which his writings serve as a kind of bridge between ancient and medieval thought.

Notes

1. E.g., see V. Nikiprowetzky, "L'exégèse de Philon d'Alexandrie dans le *De Gigantibus* et le *Quod Deus sit Immutabilis*," in *Two Treatises of Philo of Alexandria: A Commentary on* De Gigantibus *and* Quod Deus Sit Immutabilis, ed. D. Winston and J. Dillon (Chico, CA: Scholars Press, 1983), 5–75. Dissenting voices look rather to parallels in Homeric exegesis. The two influences are, of course, not mutually exclusive.
2. "References to Other Exegetes," in *Both Literal and Allegorical: Studies in Philo of Alexandria's Questions and Answers on Genesis and Exodus* (Atlanta: Scholars Press, 1991), 94–95.
3. N. Walter provides significant reasons to question this dating in *Der Thoraausleger Aristobulus* (TU 86; Berlin: Akademie, 1964), 13–26. Nevertheless, Philometer remains the best suggestion.
4. E.g., Aristobulus: fr. 2.2; Philo: *Leg.* 1.36.
5. E.g., Aristobulus: fr. 5.11–12; Philo: *Leg.* 1.5–6; *Abr.* 28–30.
6. E.g., Aristobulus: fr. 4.4–6; Philo: e.g., *Leg.* 3.96.
7. *Aristeas*, 120–300.
8. Ibid., 121.
9. Wisdom's general flavor and the amount of attention it pays to Egypt—not to mention the fervor with which it pays this attention—makes Alexandria the most likely provenance for the book.
10. *The Wisdom of Solomon: A New Translation with Introduction and Commentary* (New York: Doubleday, 1979), 20–25.
11. Ibid., 59.
12. Ibid., 59–63.
13. E.g., the author of 3 Maccabees and some of the *Sibylline Oracles*.
14. Thus the well-known proverb first mentioned by Jerome that "either Plato philonizes or Philo platonizes" (*De Viris Illustribus* 11.7).
15. Cf. J. Dillon's reaction to his critics in the afterword to his classic book *The Middle Platonists: 80 B.C. to A.D. 220*, rev. ed. (Ithaca, NY: Cornell University Press, 1996), 422–23.
16. For a recent delineation of the interaction of Stoicism and Platonism in this period, see G. J. Reydams-Schils, *Demiurge and Providence: Stoic and Platonist Readings of Plato's 'Timaeus,'* Monothéismes et Philosophie (Turnhout: Brepols Publishers, 1999).
17. With Arcesilaus (took over the Academy in 268 BCE) and Carneades (took over in 180 BCE), Plato's Academy increasingly adopted a skeptical approach to truth, in which you ask questions of everything but refrain from drawing final conclusions because of the uncertainty of all knowledge.
18. Pythagoras formulated this afterlife in terms of a "recycling" or transmigration of souls from one person to the next, a kind of reincarnation of the soul.

19. Preserved by the Neoplatonist Simplicius in *In Phys.* 1.5. We cannot say for certain that Eudorus originated the idea.
20. His *floruit*, or flourishing, was around 25 BCE.
21. W. Theiler suspected that Philo drew heavily on a commentary by Eudorus on Plato's *Timaeus* ("Philo von Alexandria und der hellenisierte *Timaeus*," in *Philomathes: Studies and Essays in the Humanities in Honour of Philip Merlan*, ed. R. B. Palmer and R. G. Hammerton-Kelly [The Hague: Martinus Nijhoff, 1971], 25–35). Cf. Plutarch, *An. Procr.* 1019e, 1020c.
22. Translation by Dillon, *Middle Platonists*, 126.
23. In fact, Alexander Polyhistor, writing forty or fifty years before Eudorus, knows nothing of this idea in his summary of Pythagorean thought.
24. Fr. 24.57, 70.
25. *Str.* 1.72.4 and 2.100.3. Cf. D. Winston, "Response to Runia and Sterling" (on the issue of whether Philo was a Middle Platonist), in *SPhA* 5 (1993): 141–46.
26. Even this perspective is overly simplistic. We cannot always identify a set of essential characteristics that all particular items in a class possess.
27. We turn to Aristotle for that perspective.
28. Philo of Larissa continued to be the putative leader of the Academy even after 88 BCE, but he was no longer in Athens after this year because the city had fallen to the army of Mithridates. From then on, Philo of Larissa taught in Rome.
29. For a more detailed treatment of Antiochus, see Dillon, *Middle Platonists*, 52–106. See also J. Glucker, *Antiochus and the Late Academy* (Göttingen: Vandenhoeck & Ruprecht, 1978).
30. E.g., *Opif.* 171–72; *Leg.* 2.1–3; *Cher.* 87; *Deus.* 11; *Her.* 187; *Decal.* 8; *Spec.* 1.28.
31. This concept of God next appears in a later philosopher known as Albinus (e.g., *Didaskalikos* 10; others consider its author to be one Alcinoos). We do not have strong evidence that Albinus knew Philo. Since Philo often drew his philosophy from earlier thinkers, it seems appropriate to think both Philo and Albinus were drawing on someone else. It does not seem as likely that Philo originated this idea and that Albinus later drew on him.
32. *Middle Platonists*, 155.
33. *Spec.* 1.329; cf. *Opif.* 75; *Conf.* 179.
34. E.g., *Opif.* 74–75; *Conf.* 181; *Abr.* 143.
35. E.g., *Ios.* 236; *Mos.* 1.12, 67; *Decal.* 58; *Spec.* 1.209; treatise *On Providence*.
36. E.g., *Abr.* 175; *Ios.* 244; *Mos.* 174.
37. E.g., *Mos.* 1.111, 157; *Decal.* 41; *Spec.* 1.152, 277.
38. E.g., *Opif.* 149; *Mos.* 2.217.
39. Cf. *Abr.* 83.
40. E.g., *Leg.* 3.80; *Cher.* 36; *Sacr.* 51.
41. *hyparchos*: e.g., *Agr.* 51; *Fug.* 111; *Somn.* 1.241.
42. *hēgemōn*: e.g., *Leg.* 3.150. Also a charioteer (e.g., *Leg.* 3.80). *Agr.* 51 couples the royal imagery of the *logos* as God's son with the idea of the *logos* as governor. Cf. also *QG* 2.110.
43. It is noteworthy that Philo did not consider God himself the cause of detrimental things (e.g., *Agr.* 129).
44. E.g., *Opif.* 46; *Conf.* 98; *Her.* 228; *Somn.* 1.157.
45. *eikōn theou*: e.g., *Leg.* 3.96; *Plant.* 20; *Conf.* 146; *Somn.* 1.239.
46. Thus Dillon, *Middle Platonists*, 161. However, David Runia rightly doubts it in *Philo of Alexandria and the* Timaeus *of Plato* (PhilAnt 44; Leiden: E. J. Brill, 1986), 174.
47. I cite the Septuagint here on the assumption that most Jews reading the Scriptures in this way would be reading this version. Philo himself never refers to this passage.

48. For a discussion, see G. E. Sterling, "Prepositional Metaphysics in Jewish Wisdom Speculation and Early Christian Liturgical Texts," in *Wisdom and* Logos: *Studies in Jewish Thought in Honor of David Winston, SPhA* 9 (1997): 219–38.
49. E.g., *Leg.* 3.96; *Sacr.* 8.
50. Cf. also *Mig.* 174.
51. Cf. also *Leg.* 1.43, where some of the same terms cue the idea of wisdom for Philo.
52. E.g., *Leg.* 3.82; *Mig.* 102; *Her.* 185; *Fug.* 108.
53. The original text of *QG* 2.62 refers explicitly to the *logos* as a "second god."
54. In *Spec.* 1.47, Philo even considers the essence of the *logos* and of God's other powers as unknowable.
55. *Her.* 190; *QG* 4.110. In turn, Philo likely equates numbers with Platonic ideals (cf. *Opif.* 102).
56. E.g., *Her.* 187; *Spec.* 2.176.
57. Cf. also *Deus* 83. Philo more frequently associates the *logos* with the numbers seven (cf. *Her.* 216) and ten (e.g., *QG* 4.110). But see *Deus* 11, 13, where the Monad is equated with the Seven.
58. E.g., *Spec.* 1.307. Perhaps the most interesting places in the biblical text where Philo finds this teaching are in his interpretation of the two cherubim and sword (*Cher.* 27–31) and in the three visitors to Abraham (*Abr.* 119–25).
59. *Philo: Foundations of Religious Philosophy in Judaism, Christianity, and Islam* (Cambridge, MA: Harvard University Press, 1947), vol. 1, 306–10.
60. E.g., David Winston, *Philo of Alexandria: The Contemplative Life, the Giants and Selections* (New York: Paulist Press, 1981), 10–12; G. E. Sterling, "*Creatio Temporalis, Aeterna, vel Continua?* An Analysis of the Thought of Philo of Alexandria," *SPhA* 4 (1992): 15–41.
61. E.g., R. Radice, *Platonismo e creazionismo in Filone di Alessandria* (Milan: Vita e Pensiero, 1989), 236; Runia, *Philo and the* Timaeus, 453–55.
62. E.g., *Cher.* 23; *Her.* 233; *Spec.* 3.189. These stars are immortal souls, mind of the purest kind (e.g., *Somn.* 1.135).
63. E.g., *Cher.* 23; *Her.* 233.
64. E.g., sun as condensed ether: *Deus* 78; sun as fire: *Conf.* 156; stars uncertain: *Somn.* 1.21; fire: *Mos.* 2.148; *QG* 3.3; ether: *Plant.* 3; *Mos.* 1.217; *QG* 4.8.
65. E.g., stars: *Gig.* 7; angels: *Plant.* 14.
66. The incorporeal and heavenly realm being the other two (cf. *QG* 4.8). See also *Her.* 224.
67. E.g., *Somn.* 1.151; *Praem.* 152.
68. E.g., *Leg.* 1.70–72; 3.115.
69. The dominating element (*hēgemonikon*; cf. *Leg.* 1.39; *Mos.* 2.82).
70. Cf. T. Tobin, *The Creation of Man: Philo and the History of Interpretation* (CBQMS 14; Washington, DC: Catholic Biblical Association, 1983).
71. E.g., *Leg.* 3.161; *Mut.* 223; *Her.* 281–83.
72. E.g., *Somn.* 1.151; *Ios.* 264; *Mos.* 2.291; *Praem.* 152; *QG* 3.11.
73. E.g., *Somn.* 1.151; *Spec.* 3.152–54; *Praem.* 69–70, 152; *Legat.* 49, 103.
74. For a discussion, see D. Winston, "Freedom and Determinism in Philo of Alexandria," in *The Ancestral Philosophy: Hellenistic Philosophy in Second Temple Judaism* (Providence, RI: Brown University Press, 2001), 135–50.
75. Cf. also *Deus* 41–44.
76. See chap. 1, "Philo the Mystic."
77. E.g., *Praem.* 11–13; cf. also *Decal.* 81.
78. E.g., *Decal.* 101; *Spec.* 2.64; *Praem.* 11; *Contempl.* 1.
79. E.g., *Leg.* 1.63; *Cher.* 6; *Agr.* 18; *Abr.* 219; *Mos.* 2.185.
80. E.g., *Cher.* 96; *Praem.* 160; and *On Virtues* in general.
81. E.g., godliness: *Abr.* 60; *Spec.* 4.135; love of humanity: *Virt.* 51. But cf. *Leg.* 1.66,

where prudence is the main virtue, and *Abr.* 27, where justice is chief of the virtues.

82. E.g., *Congr.* 35; *Abr.* 52–53; *Mos.* 1.76.
83. Cf. Tobin, *Creation*, 33–35.
84. E.g., *Leg.* 2.30; 3.49–52.
85. E.g., *Leg.* 2.8; 3.113; *Agr.* 83; *Abr.* 236; *Decal.* 142–46.
86. E.g., *Leg.* 3.129; *Agr.* 10; *Spec.* 4.79.
87. See *Fug.* 36 for the division of life into public and private: household management and statesmanship.
88. Cf. *Det.* 160; *Decal.* 2–9; *Spec.* 3.1.
89. Cf. also *Det.* 7.
90. E.g., *Deus* 176; *Agr.* 45; *Conf.* 108; *Abr.* 242; *Spec.* 4.237; *Virt.* 180.
91. E.g., *Ios.* 28–31.
92. See D. Sly, *Philo's Perception of Women* (Atlanta: Scholars Press, 1990).
93. Compare, for example, Philo's comment in *Hypoth.* 7.14 with Aristotle in *Politics* 1.3.1.
94. E.g., *Fug.* 51; *Legat.* 320.
95. E.g., Eve represents sense-perception, while Adam represents the mind (*Opif.* 165).
96. E.g., Essenes: *Prob.* 79; Therapeutae: *Contempl.* 70.

Chapter 5

Philo and Christianity

5.1 PHILO THE "CHRISTIAN"

We would not have the bulk of Philo's writings today if Christians at some point had not come to value them. In the centuries after his death neither Jews nor pagans showed much interest in Philo.[1] Yet at an early point in the history of Christianity, Christian theologians became attracted to him and "baptized" him as a Christian.[2]

Of course, Philo was not a Christian, and we have no credible evidence that he ever came into contact with early Christianity. Although his life coincided with its birth, he most likely died before a single book of the New Testament was written. While it is possible that Christianity reached Egypt within his lifetime, Philo nowhere mentions it in his writings.

Up until the 1600s, however, Christian scholars largely believed Philo *had* favorably referred to early Christianity and that he had perhaps even been a Christian. From at least the time of the church historian **Eusebius** (writing in the early 300s CE), Philo was widely drawn near or within the circle of Christianity. While Eusebius stopped short of calling Philo a Christian, he insisted that Philo had deeply admired Christians, that he had visited their community in Egypt, and that he had even met Peter in Rome during the reign of the emperor Claudius.[3] As with many later Christians, Eusebius held Philo in high regard as someone "magnificent in language and broad in his thoughts, lofty and reaching the heavens in his views of the divine Scriptures."[4]

> **Eusebius** (ca. 263–339 CE): Church historian who facilitated the use of Philo's writings in defending the intellectual respectability of the Jewish Scriptures/Old Testament.
> **Origen** (ca. 185–254 CE): The one we have most to thank for the survival of the Philonic corpus. His interest in Philo came mostly from the use of allegorical methods to interpret the Bible.

Early Christians found Philo's teaching attractive for different reasons. Some, like ***Origen*** (writing in the early 200s CE), found his methods of interpretation helpful for finding hidden, spiritual meanings in the text of the Bible. The Christians at Alexandria were particularly fond of Philo for this reason. In contrast, when someone like Eusebius wished to defend Christianity against those who despised it as uneducated and uncultured, he could use arguments Philo himself had made against pagans as a Jew.

It is much more difficult to show that Philo's writings had a direct impact on the earliest Christians. We can at least make a good case that Philo drew from some of the same traditions as certain early Christians did. For example, from the Gospel of John to Justin Martyr's *Apology*, Christian language concerning Christ as the *logos* strongly reminds us of imagery we find in Philo, language Philo himself inherited from his environment. While his claim is overstated, a statement by Henry Chadwick is still noteworthy: "[O]f all the non-Christian writers of the first century A.D. Philo is the one from whom the historian of emergent Christianity has most to learn."[5]

5.2 PHILO AND EARLY HELLENISTIC CHRISTIANITY

Philo was a Greek-speaking Jew who lived in the Diaspora. The same was also true of New Testament authors such as Paul, the author of Hebrews, and the author of John. We must be careful not to stereotype such individuals because of where they lived or what language they spoke. We find a spectrum of belief and practice among such Jews. Some were more "conservative" in the way they interpreted and kept the Jewish law (e.g., *Leg.* 3.236); others were less committed to its literal practice or to belief in its stories (e.g., *Mig.* 89–94).

Of the New Testament books, the writings of Paul, Hebrews, and John envisage the least continuity between the Jewish law and Christian life, each in their own way. For Paul, the discontinuity focused on *Gentile* converts to Christianity. It was not on his agenda to diminish the law-keeping of Jewish Christians, except when purity rules came into conflict with the oneness of the Christian body.

Yet Paul considered Christ equally available to all, regardless of one's literal law-keeping. This equality of status and insistence on fellowship tended to undermine the significance of literal law-keeping for Jewish Christians as well. Philo is in a sense more conservative than Paul in this regard (at least on paper), for he emphasizes literal law-keeping (e.g., *Mig.* 89–94).

But in the end, Philo and Paul are similar in the way their "universalism" diminished the significance of the literal law. Both Philo and Paul envisaged a more universal "law" beyond the literal law. For Paul, this was the "law of Christ" (e.g., 1 Cor. 9:21) and the commandment to love (Rom. 13:8–10). For Philo it was the law built into nature, which the patriarchs Abraham, Isaac, and Jacob embodied, and of which the written laws were only a copy (e.g., *Abr.* 5–6).

Hebrews is more systematic in the way it pits Christ against the Jewish law as the reality to which the shadowy Levitical sacrificial system pointed (e.g., Heb. 7:11–12). It has little to say about the practice of the Jewish law, but it clearly sees the importance of the law on an inner and more spiritual plane. Like Philo, it reflects a dualism of heaven and earth, body and spirit, in which significance clearly pertains to the heavenly and spiritual.

The distinction between these two realms in Hebrews is much sharper than Paul's flesh-spirit dualism. For Paul, the body was enslaved under the power of sin (e.g., Rom. 7:14, 24). But the creation and the body were redeemable, and both would one day be freed (e.g., Rom. 8:11, 19). Paul's dualism was thus ultimately apocalyptic and related directly to spiritual forces at work on the world.

However, for Hebrews and John, like Philo, the distinction between the heavenly and the earthly was much more inherent in the material of the world itself— it was much more "ontological":

> When [Scripture] says "one more time" it indicates the removal of what is shaken—*since it is created*—in order that what is not shaken remains. (Heb. 12:27)

> What is born of flesh is flesh; what is born of spirit is spirit. (John 3:6)

In Hebrews, the material world seems to have a certain innate inadequacy. Christ offers his sacrifice *through an eternal spirit* (Heb. 9:14) in part because the blood of goats and bulls can cleanse only flesh (e.g., 9:13). Christians find themselves cleansed both in body and heart (10:22: cf. conscience in 9:14, spirits in 12:23). In a striking comment, Hebrews speaks of the need for atonement "since the foundation of the world" (9:26), as if the created realm in and of itself is innately sin laden.[6]

This pervasive dualism in Hebrews relates well to Philo's dualism of body and soul. Granted, they use a slightly different vocabulary, and Philo's soul is much more of a rational entity than Hebrews' spirit. But the inherent value of each type of material[7] and its proper location in the universe is quite similar. The soul pertains to the heavens, and the souls of the heavens are good (e.g., *Somn.* 1.133–49).

John's Gospel also seems to emphasize discontinuity with literal law-keeping. Although Philo valued the literal keeping of the Jewish festivals (e.g., *Mig.* 91), both he and John saw their ultimate significance in the symbolic. John presents the story of Christ so that he reveals the true meaning of the festivals. Like God, Jesus is always working—even on the Sabbath (John 5:17; cf. *Leg.* 1.5–6). Jesus is the equivalent of the Passover (John 1:29; 2:21). He is God "tabernacling" with us (John 1:14), like the Feast of Tabernacles.

And John reflects some of the same dualistic rhetoric as Hebrews, although it seems to see more significance in embodiment than Hebrews does:

> What will you do if you see the Son of Man ascending to where he was before? The spirit is that which gives life. The flesh does not benefit at all. The words that I have spoken to you are spirit and life. (John 6:62–63)

Like Hebrews, John retains the resurrection language of early Christianity (e.g., John 5:28–29; Heb. 6:2)—language that implied some sort of continuity with one's former body. But John is more oriented toward eternal life (e.g., John 3:16) than Paul's early emphasis on embodied resurrection (e.g., 1 Cor. 15:35), just as Hebrews seems to focus more on our perfected spirits (e.g., Heb. 12:23).

What we are sketching here is a common Jewish Hellenistic milieu in which Philo and these New Testament authors moved, each in his own way. The similarities imply nothing about location or mutual acquaintance. But we can make a fair case that all these individuals represented certain tendencies in some forms of Hellenistic Judaism, particularly tendencies toward "universalism" in the sense that they were Gentile friendly. All these authors saw a universal significance to the Jewish law that surpassed its literal meaning and practice. Philo, Hebrews, and John in particular operated with a similar dualistic metaphysic that at times viewed the visible world as ontologically inferior to the invisible one. It is to the question of more specific similarity that we now turn.

5.3 PHILO AND PAUL'S WRITINGS

Few would suggest today that Philo's writings had a direct impact on Paul's thought.[8] Nevertheless, Paul seems to interact with some of the same traditions we find in Philo. In many cases, the similarities relate more to those Paul argued *against* than to Paul's own thinking. In particular, we can make a good case that Paul's opponents in Corinth had come under the influence of interpretations Philo also inherited from his environment.

5.3.1 The Corinthians

A number of scholars think that Philo's writings provide us with important keys to understanding Paul's opponents at Corinth.[9] In particular, Philo presents us with certain interpretations of Genesis that might partially explain what Paul was arguing against in 1 Corinthians. In this regard, the fact that some in Corinth favored Apollos over Paul as a teacher is conspicuous (e.g., 1 Cor. 1:12; 3:4), since Apollos apparently came from Alexandria (cf. Acts 18:24).

The text of 1 Corinthians itself tells us a great deal of what Paul's opponents were claiming. First Corinthians 4:8 indicates their attitude:

> You are already full. Already you have become rich. You have come to reign without us. And indeed I wish you did reign so that we could also reign with you.

These individuals apparently believed themselves to possess a higher wisdom than Paul and to have attained some sort of spiritual perfection.

Paul denies their claims:

> I was not able to speak to you as spiritual individuals but as fleshly ones, babies in Christ. (1 Cor. 3:1)

In two conspicuous passages (1 Cor 2:14; 15:44–46), Paul contrasts the "spiritual" (*pneumatikos*) with the "soul-ish" (*psychikos*). Since soul and spirit are more often considered broadly synonymous, this distinction is somewhat odd. A good number of commentators suggest that Paul is taking up the language of his opponents at these points, starting with their assumptions and then modifying them.

Paul goes about his argument in 1 Corinthians 15:44–46 in a somewhat curious way. He is interpreting the creation stories of Genesis, 2:7 and 1:27 in particular. Interestingly, he pits Christ as the "second" man, the heavenly man, against Adam as the first, earthly one. He calls the first man, Adam, the *psychikos*, "soul-ish" man, while Christ is the *pneumatikos*, "spiritual" man.

> But someone will say, "How are the dead raised, and with what sort of body do they come?" You fool, that which you sow does not produce life unless it dies. And with regard to what you sow, you do not sow the body it is going to have but the naked seed . . . God gives to it a body as he wants, and to each of the seeds its own body. . . .
>
> The resurrection of the dead is similar . . . it is sown a *psychikos* body; it is raised a *pneumatikos* body. So also it is written, "**The** first **man Adam came to be a living soul** [*psyche*: Gen. 2:7]," the last Adam a life giving spirit. But the spiritual [*pneumatikos*] is not first, but the soul-ish [*psychikos*] then the spiritual [*pneumatikos*]. The first man was from the earth [*choïkos*: Gen 2:7], the second man from heaven. Of the same sort as the earthly person [*choïkos*] are the earthly ones [*choïkoi*], and of the same sort as the heavenly person are the heavenly ones. And just as we have borne the image of the earthly [*choïkos*], we will also bear the image of the heavenly [Gen. 1:27]." (1 Cor. 15:35–38, 42, 44–49)

This argument probably seems peculiar to us because we are hearing only one side of the conversation. In other words, Paul is countering a competing interpretation of these passages in Genesis. It is in this regard that Philo's writings come into play, for he presents us with interpretations of Genesis 1:27 and 2:7 that go a long way toward explaining the arguments Paul was addressing.

In particular, Philo records Jewish traditions in which these two verses refer to two different individuals, a heavenly and an earthly one.[10] These traditions saw Genesis 1:27 as the creation of an ideal human, a human prototype. Genesis 2:7 then presented the creation of the physical Adam, who was a copy of the heavenly pattern. In these traditions, the heavenly human prototype came first and the earthly one second.

Philo took these traditions and developed them further into his famous allegory of the soul. Adam is the earthly man who represents the person who struggles with the pleasures (serpent) that work on his senses (Eve):

> "**And God formed the man, taking clay from the earth, and he breathed into his face the breath** [*pnoē*] **of life, and the man became a living soul**" [*psyche*: Gen. 2:7].
> There are two kinds of men. The one is a heavenly man; the other earthly. Therefore the heavenly, as he has come into existence according to the image of God [Gen. 1:27], does not partake in corruptible or earthly substance at all. But the earthly man was compounded from scattered matter, which he [Moses] has called "clay."
> Therefore he says that the heavenly man has not been molded, but impressed according to the image [Gen. 1:27]. And the earthly mold is from the creator but is not his offspring [Gen. 2:7]. (*Leg.* 1.31)

By contrast, the "heavenly man" of Genesis 1:27 symbolizes the individual who rises above the senses and the passions to contemplate the ideal realm of truth.

> The maker of all "**breathed into his face** [Adam's] **the breath of life, and the man became a living soul**" [*psyche*: Gen. 2:7], as it also says man was molded according to the image of the maker [Gen. 1:27].
> So there are two kinds of men, the one of which lives by reasoning, the divine spirit, and the other of which lives by blood and the pleasure of flesh. This [latter] kind is a mold of earth, the former a like impression of the divine image. (*Her.* 57)

Paul's Corinthian opponents may not have used this exact language and imagery, but Philo may provide us with hints of their positions. Similar to Philo, they may have related the two passages in Genesis to two different types of individual, one of which was spiritually superior to the other. Perhaps they saw themselves in terms of the heavenly person of Genesis 1:27. They were thus *pneumatikoi*, "spiritual people." In contrast, they may have seen others as only *psychikoi*, "soul-ish" individuals, basing their conception on the physical, molded Adam of Genesis 2:7.

In this context, Paul asserted that Christ became a heavenly, spiritual man at the point of his resurrection (1 Cor. 15:46). The *first* Adam, Paul asserted, was the physical Adam of Genesis. Christ was the *second* Adam who came at the end of the age (15:47). He speaks of taking on the image of Christ on the day of resurrection (15:49), not while we are still in our bodies. In contrast, the

Corinthians apparently thought they already bore the image of the heavenly man in Genesis 1:27.

5.3.2 The Colossians

The nature of the "false teaching" at Colossae has been the subject of much debate. Regardless of one's conclusion on this issue, Colossians offers some significant parallels with Philo's writings. Three are worth noting in particular.

The Colossian Hymn

The "hymn" of Colossians 1:15–20 makes a number of statements that bear a strong resemblance to things Philo says of the *logos*. The first is the depiction of Christ as the image of God (Col. 1:15). Philo's writings regularly refer to the *logos* as the "image" (*eikōn*) of God.[11] It is true that Jewish Wisdom literature could also speak of wisdom as the image of God's goodness (e.g., Wis. 7:26). But Philo's *logos* provides a closer parallel, especially in the light of the other imagery in the hymn. The cosmic Christ of the hymn is much more like the heavenly man of Philo than the physical Adam created in the image of God.

Second, the hymn tells us that Christ was the "firstborn of all creation" (Col. 1:15). Philo also considered the *logos* to be God's firstborn son and the first of God's creations. As firstborn son, the *logos* held preeminence over the universe (e.g., *Agr.* 51). Yet at the same time it was not uncreated like God himself. It stood on the boundary between God and the world, "neither uncreated like God nor created like you" (*Her.* 206).

A third similarity is Colossians' sense that everything came into existence "through" Christ (Col. 1:16). It is true that Jewish wisdom traditions occasionally spoke of wisdom (*sophia*) as God's agent in creation.[12] But no text from these traditions uses the preposition *through* to say that the world was created *through* wisdom.[13] As we will see, this language ultimately derived from the influence of philosophy on Jewish wisdom traditions.

Philo provides us with many texts where the *logos* is identified as the agent of creation, as that *through which* God created the universe. He is, in fact, the first known author to use the preposition in this way. *Special Laws* 1 gives us one such example:[14]

> And *logos* is the image of God, *through which* all the world was put together. (*Spec.* 1.81)

In contrast, the Colossian hymn also says that everything was created "in him" and "for him." This use of prepositions is less Philonic. In particular, Philo would not have said that the universe was "for" the *logos*.

A final parallel in the hymn is the statement that in Christ "all things hold together" (Col.1:17). Taken strictly in reference to Christ, the statement is somewhat odd. However, it relates directly to Philo's understanding of the *logos* as a kind of glue that holds the world together.[15]

The Law as "Shadow"

Another parallel between Colossians and Philo occurs in Colossians 2:17, where the author contrasts elements of the Jewish law with Christ. Specifically, Colossians contrasts Jewish food laws and the Jewish calendar as the "shadow" (*skia*) of things to come, with Christ constituting the "body" or "reality" (*sōma*) of those things. The contrast of shadow with reality is highly reminiscent of Platonic thought, particularly as we find it embodied in the so-called myth of the cave.[16] In that story, individuals mistake shadows they see on a cave wall for the real objects behind them outside the cave.

However, even closer parallels to this language appear in Philo's writings. In *Conf.* 190, Philo refers to literal interpretations as "shadowy" in contrast to allegorical ones, which are substantive. In this passage he uses the same terms Colossians uses.

> I would encourage [them] not to stop with these [literal interpretations] but to go on to the figurative benefit. They should consider that the letters of the oracles are like the shadows [*skia*] of bodies [*sōma*], while the values revealed are the truly underlying realities.

Philo could thus use Platonic imagery to point to symbolic meanings that were more substantial than the literal interpretations.

This parallel does not imply any direct dependence of Colossians on Philo, but it does show the reach that Alexandrian interpretation could have. As we will see, the New Testament book of Hebrews would take this line of argument to the next level. We will increasingly wonder about the degree to which subtle Alexandrian influence was present in the early church, standing behind the scenes as a silent but highly generative partner in the development of early Christian theology.[17]

A Philosophy according to the Elements of the World

Finally, some scholars believe that Philo's writings provide us with the best explanation for what Colossians means when it refers to a philosophy according to the elements of the world (Col. 2:8).[18] Richard DeMaris and Gregory Sterling have both argued that the false teaching was Middle Platonic in nature and that the phrase "elements of the cosmos" originated with the Colossians themselves.[19] Sterling in particular argues that the false teaching identified angelic forces with various heavenly zones (i.e., with "the elements of the cosmos") and that the teaching viewed these powers negatively, leading the Colossians to ascetic practices as a protection against such spirits in worship.[20]

However, this general hypothesis has not won much support among Pauline scholars. It seems more likely that the language comes from Pauline tradition than from Colossae.[21] It is true that we can find parallels in Philo's writings for the phrase "elements of the world" (*stoicheia tou kosmou*: e.g., *Aet.* 107–9). But the fact that the phrase appears in Galatians 4:3 implies strongly that Colossians is simply drawing on Pauline tradition at this point, not on the language of the

Colossian teaching. When such a close parallel exists in Paul's writings, it seems odd to suggest a hypothetical non-Christian origin for the phrase.

5.4 PHILO AND HEBREWS

The New Testament book most often identified with Philo is the so-called Letter to the Hebrews.[22] In the mid–twentieth century, many scholars believed its author was a converted Philonist, someone who not only had read Philo's writings but who at one point had deeply agreed with them. The culmination of this trajectory was the 1952 two-volume commentary of Çeslas Spicq, a work that compiled an immense number of parallels between Hebrews and Philo's writings.[23]

The following decades significantly tempered Spicq's conclusions. Discoveries such as the Dead Sea Scrolls heightened our appreciation of first-century Judaism's diversity and raised other possibilities for understanding Hebrews. Further, Spicq significantly overstated his case, obscuring the cumulative effect of his work.[24]

Nevertheless, many scholars—perhaps even the majority—still see some common ground between Philo's writings and Hebrews.[25] Both authors seem to have been Greek-speaking Jews who used the Septuagint as their Bible. Both seem to have had an extensive education, including the study of rhetoric.[26] Both seem to have leaned toward the Hellenistic end of the Jewish spectrum. We can make an excellent case that the similarities go even deeper.

5.4.1 The Cumulative Effect of Parallels

We will not find any parallel between Hebrews and Philo that demands a direct connection between the two. If anything, Ronald Williamson's classic study on Philo and Hebrews shows that most parallels are somewhat superficial.[27] Even when the two are using similar language or imagery, the conceptual framework behind the words is usually different.

But this observation does not diminish the cumulative effect of how numerous these parallels are. We can find these "superficial" parallels for every chapter of Hebrews. And their Philonic partners sometimes appear one after another in the space of a few paragraphs.[28] This phenomenon proves nothing, but it does make us wonder whether the author of Hebrews had breathed a bit of the same air that Philo did.

More concrete than this vague feeling is David Runia's observation of several Scriptural quotations that are uniquely cited in Philo and Hebrews.[29] Hebrews and Philo both quote Genesis 2:2; Exodus 25:40; Joshua 1:5; and Proverbs 3:11–14 in ways found only in their writings. By far the most striking of all these is the way Hebrews 13:5 splices together Joshua 1:5; Deuteronomy 31:8; and possibly Genesis 28:15. Philo strings these passages together in exactly the same way in *Conf.* 166. These are the only known instances of this combination in all Jewish literature.

Runia concludes that this citation is so unique we must rule out coincidence.[30] Indeed, this striking similarity even led Williamson to suggest that the author of Hebrews had come under Alexandrian influence at some point.[31] It is, of course, possible that Jews all over the world used these verses in this way. Yet when all is said and done, the weight of the evidence points toward Alexandrian influence on the author of Hebrews either directly or indirectly, even if we cannot demonstrate that he knew Philo's writings themselves.[32]

5.4.2 Angels in Hebrews and Philo

Consider the following passages on angels in Hebrews and Philo:

> Are they [angels] not all *ministering* spirits sent for service to those about to inherit salvation? (Heb. 1:14)

> [Moses] was making music with every harmony and form of accord in order that both the people and *ministering* angels might hear. (*Virt.* 73)

What is particularly interesting about this parallel is that Philo makes this comment in his interpretation of the Song of Moses in Deuteronomy 32. In that chapter, only the Septuagint of verse 43 mentions angels, so this verse must have been what triggered the comment. Hebrews quotes the same verse from the Septuagint in 1:6, in the same passage that it calls angels "ministering spirits." Add yet one more superficial parallel to the countless others between Hebrews and Philo.

In general, Hebrews and Philo have similar conceptions of how angels function in relation to the earth. On the one hand, Hebrews seems to associate their role with what it views as the obsolete Jewish law (e.g., Heb. 1:14; 2:2), a completely foreign idea to Philo.[33] On the other hand, Hebrews' general sense that angels are God's ambassadors and mediators to the earth is well attested in Philo, even if we can find similar conceptions in other Jewish literature.[34]

Yet, while apocalyptic Jewish literature could speak of both good and bad angels,[35] angels are only good beings in Philo and Hebrews. They are "ambassadors of humanity to God and of God to humanity" (*Gig.* 16). There is something about this "service" orientation, placed within the context of God as ruler of the universe, that seems to make Hebrews and Philo more similar to each other than to other Jewish contexts.

We might mention in conclusion that both Hebrews and Philo have the sense that you might encounter heavenly beings in everyday life. Hebrews 13:2 indicates that angels can go around disguised as strangers. Philo similarly mentions the belief of some that the gods go around disguised as humans to take note of wrongdoing (*Somn.* 1.233). Philo did not think we should be surprised that God might occasionally assume the likeness of an angel and appear to us (*Somn.* 1.238). This parallel is vague and superficial—but it is one more.

5.4.3 The *logos* in Hebrews and Philo

Hebrews has only one passage where God's Word, or *logos,* appears *explicitly* in any way similar to the way Philo uses the concept. Consider the following parallels:

> The word [*logos*] of God is living, active, and sharper than any two-edged sword. It can penetrate to divide even soul and spirit, bone and marrow, and it can discern the thoughts and intents of the heart. The creation is not hidden to it: everything is naked and exposed to its eyes. (Heb. 4:12–13)

> God severs by his own all-cutting word [*logos*] all those natures one by one that seem joined together and united—both of bodies and actions. (*Her.* 130)

> God sharpened the blade of his all-cutting word [*logos*] and divided the substance of everything, formless and without quality as it was. (*Her.* 140)

> It has been appointed to the priest and prophet reason [*logos*] to cause the soul "to stand before God" with uncovered head (that is, with the soul's primary doctrine naked and its intentions stripped . . .). The *logos* thus brings the soul to be judged by the most accurate eyes of uncorrupted God . . . the witness who alone is able to see the naked soul. (*Cher.* 17)

To be sure, Hebrews' comment lacks the intensely rational connotations of Philo's passages. Yet we cannot help but be struck once again by the convergence of themes in both Hebrews and Philo. Hebrews largely does not operate with the same conceptual framework as Philo, but it repeatedly dances with the same vocabulary and imagery.

Thus, while this passage is the most explicit parallel to Philo's *logos,* a number of other comments in Hebrews also may evoke its connotations. Here are some candidates:

1. Hebrews speaks of Christ as the one *through* whom God made the worlds (1:2), while at other places indicating that God was the creator (e.g., 2:10; 3:4). Philo can similarly interchange the *logos* and God as creator, and can speak of the *logos* as the instrument through which God created the world (e.g., *Cher.* 127).
2. While Hebrews 1:3 probably alludes to Wisdom 7:26, its specific vocabulary is reminiscent of Philo, for whom the *logos* is a ray (*apaugasma*: *Opif.* 146) and an impression (*charaktēr*: *Det.* 83) of God's nature.
3. Hebrews thinks of Christ as a priest after the order of Melchizedek (e.g., 5:10; 7:3). Philo thinks of the *logos* as a high priest (e.g., *Fug.* 108) and interprets Melchizedek as an allegorical representation of the *logos* (e.g., *Leg.* 3.82).
4. Imagery of God speaking, of his voice, and of his word is pervasive in Hebrews, from 1:1 to 13:17.

Some of these similarities are more substantial than others. None of them requires anything close to a direct dependence of Hebrews on Philo. Yet the case is mounting that the two moved in a very similar linguistic universe.

5.4.4 The Tabernacle in Hebrews and Philo

The greatest potential similarity between Hebrews and Philo clearly lies in Hebrews' discussion of the heavenly tabernacle. Take the Revised Standard Version's translation of Hebrews 8:5:

> [The earthly priests] serve a copy and shadow of the heavenly sanctuary; for when Moses was about to erect the tent, he was instructed by God, saying, "See that you make everything according to the pattern which was shown you on the mountain."

This translation is filled with classic Platonic vocabulary: "copy," "shadow," "pattern." Hebrews 10:1 will add "image" (*eikōn*) and "things" (*pragmata*) to this list, while 9:25 uses "antitype" (*antitypos*) in contrast to "true" (*alēthinos*).

The Platonic feel of this language is undeniable. Indeed, Hebrews' citation of Exodus 25:40 gives us one of the Scriptural parallels with Philo that we mentioned earlier. Both Hebrews and Philo add the word *all* to the quote, in effect mixing Exodus 25:40 with 25:9 (Heb. 8:5; *Leg.* 3.102). We begin to understand why a generation of scholars read Hebrews through a Platonic lens.

But in the end, the similarities are more verbal than substantial. Most translations make the verse sound more straightforwardly Platonic than it actually is. A more wooden translation of Hebrews 8:5 would be

> [The earthly priests] serve the heavenly sanctuary by example [*hypodeigma*] and shadow [*skia*], just as Moses was instructed as he was about to make the tent. "Look," he says, "you will make everything according to the type [*typos*] I showed you in the mountain."

The passage still has a vaguely Platonic feel to it, but the choice of words is much less explicitly oriented that way.

The significance of Hebrews' wording for this discussion becomes clearer when we notice that Hebrews follows the text of Exodus in using *typos* rather than *paradeigma* in its translation. Philo, who *was* thinking Platonically, uses the more explicitly Platonic *paradeigma* of Exodus 25:9 in his quotation. And the word *hypodeigma* in Hebrews 8:5 is *never* used by *any* ancient author, let alone by Philo or Plato, in reference to a Platonic copy.[36] In other words, if Hebrews was trying to be obviously Philonic or Platonic in this verse, the author botched it up.

We must then conclude that the author either (1) was veiling or modifying his Platonism,[37] (2) did not have a good grasp of Platonism,[38] or (3) was using these Platonic-sounding words without any real interaction with Platonic meanings.[39] In the end, Hebrews' imagery *does* seem to parallel Philo, but in a slightly different way than is usually suggested. For example, Philo does use the word *hypodeigma* in reference to examples in the biblical text from which he is drawing allegorical or symbolic meanings (e.g., *Her.* 256). And as we have seen in the case of Colossians, Philo could also use shadow-reality language in relation to literal-symbolic interpretations (cf. *Conf.* 190).

What we find is that Hebrews is using this Platonic language not so much ontologically, not in reference to the nature of the tabernacle's existence. Rather, Hebrews is more oriented toward whether something is more or less substantial in meaning. The sacrificial system of the Jewish law thus involved only a *shadow* of good things to come (Heb. 10:1). Its priests served the sanctuary by way of "shadowy example" (8:5).

However, such examples were not one-to-one "images" of those good things (Heb. 10:1). Christ was the high priest of those good things (9:11), the true representation (*charaktēr*) of God's substance (1:3). Hebrews contrasts an incredibly diverse number of "old covenant" sacrifices with the singular offering of Christ. In the course of its argument, we see Christ as the reality that corresponds to the Day of Atonement sacrifice (9:7), the red heifer sacrifice (9:13), the sacrifices by which Moses inaugurated the tabernacle (9:19), the scarlet wool used to clean skin diseases (9:19), sin offerings, and whole burnt offerings in general (10:8). Clearly, Christ's offering is not a Platonic ideal that corresponds to these shadowy sacrifices. The language is much less precise and is not ontologically oriented.

We find that some of the greatest similarity between Hebrews and Philo comes in their willingness to interpret the significance of the Pentateuch on a nonliteral plane. I have argued elsewhere that we cannot understand the author's use of Melchizedek in Hebrews 7 unless we realize that the author is using the *text* of Genesis 14 to interpret Psalm 110:4—he is thus not really focusing on the historical Melchizedek at all in verses such as Hebrews 7:1–3.[40] Like Philo, he uses allegory to draw out the significance of Genesis 14.

Similarly, the best interpretation of the heavenly tabernacle in Hebrews does not see it as a literal structure in heaven but largely as a metaphorical reference to heaven itself (cf. Heb. 9:24).[41] Christ's passage through the heavens is metaphorically reconceived as his entrance into a heavenly inner sanctum. Philo's writings also attest to this conception of the universe as a cosmic sanctuary.[42]

But even this line of interpretation does not exhaust Hebrews' penchant to allegorize the tabernacle's structure. Hebrews 9:6–10 uses the two-part structure of the Exodus tabernacle as an allegory of the two covenants and the two epochs of human history. Hebrews 9:23 speaks of an inaugural cleansing for the heavenly tabernacle that can make sense only if the cleansing of the sanctuary is some sort of metaphor for the cleansing of the human conscience. These are interpretative strategies we might find in Philo's corpus, even if he would not be using them to reach the same conclusions.

5.4.5 Other Parallels

Time will not permit me to narrate concerning many other superficial parallels between Hebrews and Philo. We mentioned at the beginning of this chapter that both operate with a dualistic sense of reality. We could go on to show interesting parallels in their use of perfection language,[43] parallel discussions of faith and use of example lists,[44] and parallel understandings of what makes sacrifices effective.[45] None of these parallels are so significant that they require us to believe the author of Hebrews knew Philo's works.

But the cumulative effect of this section brings us to the conclusion that they must have moved in closely related circles. On the whole, it seems likely that the author had either direct or indirect contact with Alexandrian interpretation. Philo's writings themselves drew heavily on Jewish interpretative traditions in Alexandria. In other words, any Jew attending the great synagogue of the city would likely have absorbed a vocabulary similar to that Philo used. And do we really suppose that Jews all over the world were not at least superficially aware of Philo after the reign of Caligula? As I have said elsewhere, I would not at all be surprised if the author of Hebrews had some general acquaintance with Philo's thought.[46]

5.5 PHILO AND THE GOSPEL OF JOHN

5.5.1 General Similarities in Imagery

C. H. Dodd's 1953 study, *The Interpretation of the Fourth Gospel*, provides us with the classic starting point for a discussion of the parallels between John and Philo's writings.[47] In this work Dodd suggested a number of affinities between the two. The most obvious, of course, is their common use of *logos* language.

Yet they do share other similarities in imagery. Dodd mentioned three in particular: (1) "light as a symbol of the Deity in His relation to man and the world,"[48] (2) "God as the Fountain from which life-giving water streams,"[49] and (3) God as a shepherd.[50] Philo uses all three of these images of the *logos*, just as John uses all three in relation to Christ.[51]

Dodd himself recognized that these three metaphors—God as light, fountain, and shepherd—ultimately derive from the Jewish Scriptures.[52] Further, even as Dodd was writing his work, the Dead Sea Scrolls were making it clear that some of these images, such as the play between light and darkness, were far from unique to Philo in the first century.[53] The absence of any clear, direct dependence of the Gospel of John on Philo led F.-M. Braun to conclude, "If Philo had never existed, the Fourth Gospel would most probably not have been any different from what it is."[54]

The *Logos* in John and Philo

The most obvious similarity between John and Philo's writings lies in their common use of *logos*/word imagery. *Logos* imagery pervades Philo's writings. The

Gospel of John begins with a hymn to God's *logos*/word, which we find out became flesh in the person of Jesus Christ (John 1:14). Johannine scholars have long recognized the parallel with Philo.

Also well known are the similarities between Jewish wisdom tradition and the *logos* of John's prologue.[55] John tells us that the *logos* was present with God in the beginning (John 1:1–2); Proverbs 8 tells us that wisdom was with God from the beginning, before the world began (Prov. 8:22–23; cf. also Wis. 9:9). John indicates God made everything through the *logos* (John 1:3); Proverbs 8:30 pictures wisdom as a craftsman by God's side. Wisdom of Solomon 9:1 similarly praises God: "You made everything by your word [*logos*] and by your wisdom formed humanity." This last verse connects God's wisdom with his word (cf. also Ps. 33:6).

The Johannine prologue also echoes other elements from Jewish Wisdom literature. Sirach 24 not only reinforces the characteristics of wisdom we have already seen: wisdom made the sky (24:5), God made wisdom "in the beginning" (24:9). Sirach also mentions that wisdom made its "tent" in Israel (24:8) by way of the Jewish law (24:23). John 1:14 tells us that the *logos* became flesh and "pitched its tent" on earth, apparently echoing this idea. In this light, John 1:14 probably entails an implicit contrast of Jesus with the Jewish law. Indeed, John explicitly contrasts Jesus with Moses in John 1:17–18.

However, as Thomas Tobin has pointed out, the wisdom traditions we have mentioned above do not fully account for the *logos* imagery of John 1.[56] While Jewish traditions concerning wisdom do illuminate many of the statements in John 1:1–18, they do not adequately account for the shift from God's wisdom to his *logos*. For this transference of imagery, as well as for the rest of the imagery of the prologue, we must turn to Jewish wisdom *speculation*, in particular Jewish speculation regarding the *logos*.

The concept of God's word appears several times in the Jewish Scriptures, but in these instances *logos* is not a technical term, personification, or hypostasis. Psalm 119:105 (118 LXX) says, "Your word [*logos*] is a lamp to my feet and a light to my paths."[57] Here God's word directs the paths of the psalmist, but it is not pictured as a free-standing entity or person.[58]

Similarly, Isaiah 55:11 says, "So will my word [*hrēma*] be: whatever goes out from my mouth will never return until it has completed whatever I willed." In this context, God's word relates to his directive will for the world. Yet *logos* still does not carry the conceptual weight it does in John.

Peder Borgen and others have rightly recognized that the Prologue of John is to some extent a commentary on Genesis 1:1–5.[59] In this regard, the *logos* of John 1 functions as the counterpart of "And God said . . ." in Genesis 1. God speaks throughout the process of creation in this chapter.[60]

However, John's Prologue uses *logos* imagery in a way that goes beyond all these precedents in the Jewish Scriptures. John's *logos* is more than a personified aspect of God, such as God's wisdom or word. John refers to the *logos* as something that has its own existence—it is not simply a poetic way of talking about God's will. For this level of wisdom speculation we most naturally turn to Alexandrian traditions concerning the *logos*. The closest parallels to the Johannine use of the *logos* are not to be found in the Jewish Scriptures but in the writings of Philo and his predecessors.

The Divine *Logos:* In the Beginning with God

> In [the] beginning was the *logos*, and the *logos* was with the God, and the *logos* was God. (John 1:1)

As in the Colossian hymn, the idea that Christ is the image of God, the firstborn of creation, finds its closest parallels in Philo's writings where similar things are said of the *logos* (e.g., *Conf.* 145–46). When Philo discusses Genesis 1:1, he clearly sees the beginning of creation as the creation of the patterns in God's divine reason, or *logos* (cf. *Opif.* 17–29). While John knows nothing of this Platonic element, John's *logos* is similarly present "with" God at the beginning of creation.

Very significant is the way in which Philo's writings consider the *logos* to be God, on the one hand, and yet distinct from God, on the other. John 1 makes a similar distinction when it speaks of the *logos* as God and yet distinguishes it from the God.[61] In his treatise *On Dreams*, Philo carefully notes how the LXX text of Genesis 21:13 does not say "of *the* God" but simply "of God" (*Somn.* 1.228–30). The distinction, Philo claims, is that the text is referring to the *logos*, which is not *the* God but is nevertheless God (as his image). Philo concludes that there are not really two gods in this text, but the one true God and his *logos* (or image).

The parallel with John 1:1 is striking. Both texts refer to the *logos* as God without the article. David Runia has noted that these two texts are the only instances in this period where we find a distinction of this sort.[62] Certainly, the Jewish Scriptures and Jewish wisdom traditions come nowhere close to Philo in the proximity of the parallel.

Logos: Agent of Creation

> All things through it [the *logos*] came into existence, and apart from it not even one thing came into existence. (John 1:3)

As we saw in our discussion of the Colossian hymn, no text from the Jewish wisdom tradition uses the word *through* to describe wisdom as that by which God created the world. This language ultimately derives from the influence of philosophy on Jewish wisdom traditions, particularly Stoic and Middle Platonic philosophy. In other words, speaking of the *logos* as that "through which" God made the world moves us into the domain of Jewish wisdom *speculation*.

Life and Light in the *Logos*

> In it [the *logos*] was life, and the life was the light of humanity. And the light shines in the darkness, and the darkness did not overcome it. . . . It/he was in the world . . . and the world did not know it/him. (John 1:4–5, 10)

John turns in verse 4 from the *logos* as the agent of creation to the *logos* as the source of life and light. John still has Genesis 1 in view. Genesis 1:2–3, like John 1:4, involves the topics of darkness, breath (= spirit), and light. Philo said of these verses in Genesis,

> Both the breath and the light were deemed worthy of privilege, for [Scripture] named the one "[breath] of God" because the breath is most life-giving and God is the cause of life, and it named the other "light" because it is surpassingly beautiful. (*Opif.* 30)

Philo situated both the life and light of Genesis 1:3–4, along with the entire world of ideas, *in* the *logos* (*Opif.* 36).

Certainly, John gives us no evidence of the Platonic element in Philo's interpretation of Genesis. Nevertheless, the fact that both Philo and John locate the life and light of Genesis 1:2–3 *in* the *logos* is enticing. While we can find the themes of light versus darkness in other Jewish literature of the time, Philo's writings once again provide the closest parallel.

Children of God

> But as many as received him/it, he/it gave to them the right to become children of God. (John 1:12)

The idea that many reject wisdom is not unique (e.g., *1 En.* 42:2), and the book of Wisdom refers to the righteous as "sons of God" (e.g., Wis. 2:12–18). However, only in Philo do we find that those who align themselves with the *logos* are "sons of God," and only in Philo's writings is the *logos* called God's "only-born son" (cf. *Conf.* 145–46). Such parallels do not mean that John knew Philo or that John understood the *logos* in the same way Philo did. Nevertheless, the evidence seems to bear out Tobin's claim that Jewish wisdom/*logos* speculation provides the most likely background to John's Prologue.

The *Logos* Became Flesh

> And the *logos* became flesh and tabernacled among us. . . . (John 1:14)

John's claim that the *logos* became flesh is the part of the Prologue that, at least at first glance, seems most distant from anything Philo would say. It is at this point that Tobin's suggestions are most speculative. We have seen in the previous chapter and in our discussion of 1 Corinthians that Jews at Alexandria had come to see the human of Genesis 1:27 as an ideal, prototypical human. Further, Philo equated this heavenly person with the *logos* (e.g., *Conf.* 146). Tobin wonders whether[63]

> [t]his assimilation in Hellenistic Judaism of the *logos* to the figure of the heavenly man may have served as an important step in the kind of reflection

that led to the identification of the *logos* with a particular human being, Jesus of Nazareth, in the hymn in the Prologue of John.

Beyond the Prologue

This is not the place for a thorough study of how we might see *logos* overtones in the way John portrays Christ in the remainder of the Fourth Gospel. But let me suggest a few possible connections, even if they are somewhat superficial ones.[64]

1. John's theme that Christ descended to earth from heaven (e.g., John 3:13) is similar to Philo's sense that the *logos* as God's eldest messenger can come to earth in God's place (e.g., *Somn.* 1.232).
2. The imagery of Christ as manna-like bread from heaven (John 6:32–40) is similar to Philo's sense that the manna of the Exodus text is the *logos* (*Her.* 79).
3. For John, Christ is the only one who has seen the Father. Christ is the "only-begotten God" who reveals the Father (e.g., John 1:18; 6:46). Philo also denies that God himself can be seen or comprehended (e.g., *Spec.* 1.42). The *logos* is God in the place of *the* God, who helps us become sons of God (e.g., *Conf.* 145–47).
4. While Philo never equates God at the burning bush to the *logos*, Philo does emphasize that God is the "one who is." John equates Christ with this appearance at the burning bush with a statement by Jesus that "I am" (John 8:58).

5.6 PHILO AND NEW TESTAMENT "HYMNS"

Some of the most Philo-sounding imagery in the New Testament occurs in its "hymnic" material. We have already seen this phenomenon in relation to Colossians and John. In such cases it is not always clear whether the hymns existed independently of their contexts or whether authors like Paul composed them "on the spot." But it is striking that the same themes appear repeatedly.

More often than not, these hymns use such imagery in reference to Christ. Consider the following poetic excerpts from the New Testament:

> There is one God, the father, from whom [are] all things and we for him,
> And one Lord Jesus Christ, through whom [are] all things and we *through* him. (1 Cor. 8:6)

> In him [Christ] all things were created . . . all things *through* him and for him have been created. (Col. 1:16)

> . . . in these last days [God] spoke by way of a Son, whom he placed as heir of all things, *through* whom also he made the ages. He is a reflection of [God's] glory and a representation of his substance, and he bears everything

by the word of his power. When he had made a cleansing of sins, he sat on the right hand of majesty in the heights. . . . (Heb 1:2–3)

All things came into existence *through* it [the *logos*], and apart from it not even one thing came into existence. (John 1:3)

We observe in these poetic snippets the same instrumental language we have discussed throughout this chapter. A good argument can be made that Middle Platonic imagery left its mark on Christology more than on any other aspect of early Christian thinking. The Greek-speaking church seems to have found such language particularly helpful for describing the risen and exalted Christ. We can only conjecture when and why they began to look at Christ in this way. But it is clear that the phenomenon was taking place already by the time Paul wrote 1 Corinthians in the early 50s CE.

5.7 BEYOND THE NEW TESTAMENT

It is not clear that Philo's thought had much impact on the next century of Christians. He is not mentioned by any Christian author until Clement of Alexandria late in the second century. We can find parallels with his thought in Justin Martyr (d. 168 CE), particularly in relation to Christ as *logos*, but no necessary connection.[65] The consensus is actually against Theophilus of Antioch knowing Philo (late second century).[66]

This situation changed with Clement and the foundation of a Christian school at Alexandria. Runia argues that Clement found in Philo a way to connect his theology with the biblical text.[67] In other words, Philo taught Clement how to allegorize Scripture. Origen, who succeeded Clement as head of the Alexandrian school, would continue this tradition. As we mentioned in the introduction of this chapter, we probably have Origen more than anyone else to thank for the survival of Philo's works.

From Origen at the beginning of the third century to Cyril of Alexandria in the fifth, numerous Christian thinkers would draw on concepts from Philo's writings to help them interpret the biblical text and wrestle with issues in early Christian theology. The church historian Eusebius in the early fourth century "baptized" Philo as a Christian and bequeathed us the first list of his writings. The fourth-century Cappadocian fathers, especially Gregory of Nyssa, viewed him in an immensely positive light. In the Western church, Ambrose also used Philo's writings extensively in the same century.

But the Council of Nicaea (325 CE) perhaps marks a turning point in the church's use of Philo. Those who saw in Philo's *logos* a potential explanation for Christ's divinity would soon border on heresy. Christianity had come to affirm that Christ was "of one substance with the Father," and the Philonic *logos* was far too subordinate to God to be fully acceptable.[68]

David Runia's study of the *Nachleben,* or "afterlife," of Philo in early Christian literature concludes that Philo's principal contribution to the thought of the church fathers "lies above all in his role as a mediator between the biblical and the philosophical tradition."[69] At its beginnings, it is possible that Philo had some direct impact on the New Testament authors, but we cannot be certain. At times they draw on similar traditions.

Then with Clement of Alexandria and Origen, Philo's influence would become direct for a time.[70] He would become a Christian in the minds of interpreters. Still later, his direct influence would lessen. He would now speak indirectly through the writings of Clement, Origen, and others who had drawn on him. When all is said and done, Philo's influence on Christian tradition proves to be rather significant. We can genuinely wonder how different Christianity would look if he had not existed.

Notes

1. For a discussion of Philo's "afterlife" in Judaism and non-Christian philosophy, see D. T. Runia, *Philo in Early Christian Literature: A Survey* (Minneapolis: Fortress Press, 1993), 8–16.
2. Many Byzantine manuscripts of the Bible have commentary notes in the margins called *catenae,* or "chains." These notes frequently refer to Philo as "Philo *the bishop.*"
3. Eusebius, *Ecclesiastical History* 2.16–18. The writing that Eusebius believed referred to Christians was Philo's discussion of the Therapeutae in *On the Contemplative Life,* particularly paragraphs 21–22, 25, 28–29, 34–35, and 78.
4. *H. E.* 2.18.
5. "St. Paul and Philo of Alexandria," *Bulletin of the John Rylands Library* 48 (1966): 287–88. For a more extensive treatment of Philo in relation to the New Testament, see G. E. Sterling's *The Jewish Plato: Philo of Alexandria, Greek-Speaking Judaism, and Christian Origins* (Peabody, MA: Hendrickson, forthcoming).
6. I am not thereby suggesting a gnostic dualism for Hebrews. Hebrews 9:26 is surely somewhat hyperbolic.
7. Remembering that the difference between body and soul for Philo is not that of material to immaterial but of density of material, embodiment, and visibility.
8. Although see E. Brandenberger, *Fleisch und Geist: Paulus und die dualistische Weisheit* (WMANT 29; Neukirchen-Vluyn: Neukirchener Verlag, 1968). See Chadwick (n. 5, above) and S. Sandmel (*Philo of Alexandria: An Introduction* [Oxford: Oxford University Press, 1979], 150–54) for some dated comparisons of the two.
9. E.g., B. Pearson, *The Pneumatikos-Psychikos Terminology in 1 Corinthians: A Study in the Theology of the Corinthian Opponents of Paul and Its Relation to Gnosticism* (SBLDS 12; Missoula, MT: Scholars Press, 1973); R. Horsley, "*Pneumatikos* vs. *Psychikos:* Distinctions of Spiritual Status among the Corinthians," *HTR* 69 (1976): 269–88; G. Sellin, *Die Streit um die Auferstehung der Toten: Eine religionsgeschichtliche und exegetische Untersuchung von 1 Korinther 15* (FRLANT 138; Göttingen: Vandenhoeck & Ruprecht, 1986); and G. E. Sterling, "'Wisdom among the Perfect': Creation Traditions in Alexandrian Judaism and Corinthian Christianity," *NovT* 37 (1995): 355–84.
10. E.g., *Opif.* 134; *Leg.* 1.31, 53, 88–95; 2.4; *Plant.* 44, *Her.* 57; *QG* 1.4, 8; 2.56.
11. E.g., *Leg.* 3.96; *Plant.* 20; *Conf.* 146–47; *Somn.* 1.239.

12. See the discussion of the *logos* in John and Philo, below (5.4.2).
13. For a discussion of the origins of this language, see G. E. Sterling, "Prepositional Metaphysics in Jewish Wisdom Speculation and Early Christian Liturgical Texts," in *Wisdom and* Logos: *Studies in Jewish Thought in Honor of David Winston*, *SPhA* 9 (1997): 219–38. The classic discussion of the topic appeared in W. Theiler's *Die Vorbereitung des Neuplatonismus* (Berlin: Weidmann, 1930), 29–31, where Theiler coined the phrase a "metaphysics of prepositions."
14. Philo could also use this prepositional language with regard to wisdom. Cf. *Fug.* 109: ". . . wisdom, *through which* everything came to birth."
15. Note that similar things were earlier said of wisdom (cf. Wis. 1:6–7) and of God's word (*logos*) in a nontechnical sense (e.g., Sir. 43:26).
16. Plato, *Republic* 514a–517a.
17. For a discussion of the impact of Philo's thought on the Jewish world of his day, see G. E. Sterling, "Recherché or Representative? What Is the Relationship between Philo's Treatises and Greek-speaking Judaism?" *SPhA* 11 (1999): 1–30.
18. Chiefly R. E. DeMaris, *The Colossian Controversy: Wisdom in Dispute at Colossae* (SNTSMS 96; Sheffield: JSOT, 1994); and G. E. Sterling, "A Philosophy according to the Elements of the Cosmos: Colossian Christianity and Philo of Alexandria," in *Philon d'Alexandrie et le langage de la philosophie*, ed. C. Lévy (Monothéismes et Philosophie; Turnhow: Brepols Publishers, 1999), 349–73.
19. DeMaris, *Controversy*, 55–56: "[I]f the philosophers did not use exactly this language to describe themselves, the letter writer has at least accurately approximated the position of the philosophy"; Sterling, "Philosophy," 360: "[T]he community has introduced 'the elements of the cosmos.'"
20. "Philosophy," 370.
21. My wording here reflects ongoing debates about the authorship of Colossians.
22. See my article "*Philo and the Epistle to the Hebrews*: Ronald Williamson's Study after Thirty Years," *SPhA* 14 (2002): 112–35.
23. *L'épître aux Hébreux*, 2 vols. (Paris: Gabalda, 1952).
24. R. Williamson's study *Philo and the Epistle to the Hebrews* (ALGHJ 4; Leiden: E. J. Brill, 1970) was highly critical of Spicq's work. Other studies that have turned scholarship away from Philo include C. K. Barrett's foundational article "The Eschatology of the Epistle to the Hebrews," in *The Background of the New Testament and Its Eschatology*, ed. D. Daube and W. D. Davies (Cambridge: Cambridge University Press, 1956); and L. D. Hurst's *The Epistle to the Hebrews: Its Background of Thought* (SNTSMS 65; Cambridge: Cambridge University Press, 1990).
25. E.g., H. A. Attridge, *The Epistle to the Hebrews* (Philadelphia: Fortress Press, 1989), 29; Runia, *Philo in Literature*, 78; H. Feld, "Der Hebräerbrief: Literarische Form, religionsgeschichtlicher Hintergrund, theologische Fragen," in *ANRW* II 25.4 (1987): 3550; Schenck, "Williamson after Thirty Years," 134.
26. Hebrews not only demonstrates extensive rhetorical skill; it even seems to draw upon the Greek educational model to urge its audience to move to the next level (Heb. 5:11–14).
27. See n. 24 above.
28. E.g., in *Who Is the Heir of Divine Things?* (whose title is reminiscent of Heb. 1:2) we find within the space of a few paragraphs (1) the idea of the world as a sanctuary (*Her.* 75; cf. Heb. 9:24); (2) the idea that life in the body is like sojourning in a foreign land (*Her.* 82; cf. Heb. 11:14–16); (3) faith as the most perfect virtue (*Her.* 91; cf. Hebrews 11); (4) God's promises to Abraham (*Her.* 101; cf. Heb. 6:13–20); and (5) God's word as a cutting instrument (*Her.* 140; cf. Heb. 4:12–13).
29. Runia, *Philo in Literature*, 76.

30. Ibid.
31. *Philo*, 571.
32. The masculine participle in Heb. 11:32 makes it all but certain that the author was male.
33. See my "A Celebration of the Enthroned Son: The Catena of Hebrews 1," *JBL* 120 (2001): 469–85. It is interesting that Philo thought the best person did not need angels—such a person could relate to God directly (cf. *Somn.* 1.238).
34. Cf., for example, the angels of *Jub.* 2:2.
35. E.g., *1 En.* 6:2; 1 Cor. 6:3.
36. Cf. Hurst, *Hebrews*, 13.
37. G. W. MacRae suggested that the author was using his own Platonic categories to address an audience that was more apocalyptically oriented ("Heavenly Temple and Eschatology in the Letter to the Hebrews," *Semeia* 12 [1978]: 179–99).
38. E.g., G. E. Sterling, "Ontology versus Eschatology: Tensions between Author and Community," in *In the Spirit of Faith: Studies in Philo and Early Christianity in Honor of David Hay*, ed. D. T. Runia and G. E. Sterling, *SPhA* 13 (2001): 208–10. Sterling reverses MacRae's suggestion, suggesting that the audience was Platonically oriented while the author did not have a profound understanding of Platonism.
39. Hurst and those who take the heavenly tabernacle apocalyptically would fall into this category.
40. K. L. Schenck, *Understanding the Book of Hebrews: The Story behind the Sermon* (Louisville, KY: Westminster/John Knox Press, 2003), 75–80.
41. Cf. ibid., 84–86.
42. E.g., *Somn.* 1.215; *Mos.* 2.88; *Spec.* 1.66; *QE* 2.91.
43. E.g., Heb. 5:11–6:3; *Agr.* 9, 158–68; cf. *Somn.* 1.131, 213; *Prob.* 160.
44. E.g., Hebrews 11; *Abr.* 262–74; *Virt.* 198–225.
45. E.g., Heb. 10:2–4; *Mos.* 2.107; *Spec.* 1.257–61.
46. "Williamson after Thirty Years," 134.
47. *The Interpretation of the Fourth Gospel* (Cambridge: Cambridge University Press, 1953), 54–73.
48. Ibid., 55.
49. Ibid., 56.
50. Ibid., 56–57.
51. (1) The *logos* as light: e.g., *Somn.* 1.75; Christ as light: John 9:5. (2) The *logos* as a fountain of life: e.g., *Somn.* 2.245; Christ as a fountain of life: John 4:10, 13–14. (3) The *logos* as shepherd: e.g., *Agr.* 51; Christ as good shepherd: John 10:11.
52. God as light: Ps. 27:1; God as fountain: Jer. 2:13; and God as shepherd: Ps. 23:1.
53. E.g. 1QS 1.9–10.
54. "Somme toute, à supposer que Philon n'ait point existé, le quatrième évangile ne serait le plus probablement pas autre qu'il n'est" (*Jean le théologien*, Etudes bibliques, vol. 2, *Les grandes traditions d'Israël et l'accord des écritures selon le quatrième évangile* [Paris: Gabalda, 1964], 298).
55. Cf. G. Rochais, "La formation du prologue (Jn 1:1–18)," *ScEs* 37 (1985): 173–82, for a discussion of the verbal and conceptual parallels between John's Prologue and Jewish Wisdom literature.
56. "The Prologue of John and Hellenistic Jewish Speculation," *CBQ* 52 (1990): 252–69.
57. All translations of the Jewish Scriptures in this section are made on the basis of the Septuagint (abbreviated LXX) as the Bible from which Hellenistic Jews conducted *logos* speculation.

58. Note the connection here between God's word/*logos* and light, as in John 1:4–5.
59. P. Borgen, *Philo, John, and Paul: New Perspectives on Judaism and Early Christianity* (Atlanta: Scholars Press, 1987), 76–80.
60. E.g., "God *said*, 'Let light come into existence.' And light came into existence."
61. The absence of the article on God in John 1:1 is probably more than just a matter of word placement ("Colwell's Rule" stating that when a predicate nominative appears before the verb and the subject, the article is often omitted from the predicate nominative to indicate the subject clearly). While God and the *logos* are equated in some sense in this verse, they are also distinguished.
62. *Philo in Literature*, 83.
63. "Prologue," 267.
64. For possibility 2, cf. P. Borgen, *Bread from Heaven: An Exegetical Study of the Concept of Manna in the Gospel of John and the Writings of Philo* (Leiden: E. J. Brill, 1965).
65. Cf. Runia, *Philo in Literature*, 104.
66. Cf. ibid., 112, 116.
67. Ibid., 155.
68. From the Nicene Creed affirmed at the Council of Constantinople (381 CE).
69. *Philo in Literature*, 339.
70. See Runia's funnel diagram of Philonic influence, in ibid., 341.

Chapter 6

Philo's Writings in a Nutshell

6.1 READING THROUGH PHILO

In his 1940 introduction to Philo, E. R. Goodenough helpfully suggested that the first task of the Philo beginner was simply to plow through his writings.[1] Accordingly, he went through about half of Philo's treatises, summarizing them in an order he thought was easy for a beginner to follow.[2] Over sixty years later, Goodenough's suggestion remains as good as ever.

We presented an overview of Philo's writings in chapter 2, mentioning the ways in which Philo probably grouped them. In particular, Philo undertook three great commentary series: Questions and Answers on Genesis and Exodus, The Allegorical Commentary, and The Exposition of the Law. In addition to these he wrote a number of miscellaneous treatises with possible relationships to one another. For our convenience today, scholars often divide these other treatises into "apologetic works" and "philosophical works."

However, the purpose of this chapter is not to go through Philo's treatises in the way he arranged or wrote them. Rather, we want to get acquainted with the basic content of the Philonic corpus in a way that lets us get into Philo's head.

The following pages thus present Philo's treatises in an order that will ease you into his world. If you are interested in a specific treatise, you can skip the others and go directly to its summary. Yet I encourage you to read through his writings one by one as you work through this chapter. The best English translation remains the twelve volumes of the Loeb Classical Library series.[3]

Bon appétit!

6.2 TWO APOLOGETIC TREATISES: *EMBASSY* AND *FLACCUS*

The best place to begin reading through Philo's writings is with his two most famous historical/apologetic treatises, both of which relate in one way or another to the pogrom of 38 CE in Alexandria. These are his *Against Flaccus* and *Embassy to Gaius*. Because these two treatises relate to concrete historical events, they are relatively easy for the "Philo initiate" to follow. They are also the most vivid of Philo's writings and the ones in which he talks most about himself. As E. R. Goodenough once wrote, "the reader of Philo's other works should always have in mind that they were written by a man who could write these."[4]

6.2.1 *Against Flaccus* (*In Flaccum*)

Flaccus divides nicely into two sections. The first treats the persecution of the Jews in Alexandria under Flaccus while he was prefect of the city (1–101). The second shows the consequent judgment of God on him (102–91).[5]

As Philo presents it in *Flaccus*, the trigger for the persecution in Alexandria (38 CE) was the visit of Herod Agrippa I, a Jewish king, to the city (25–42).[6] Philo believed that the presence of such a prominent Jew in Alexandria led to wholesale jealousy and envy on the part of the Alexandrians. First they made fun of Agrippa; then they dressed up a "lunatic" named Carabas to mock him in the gymnasium. In all these events Flaccus did nothing to stop the mockery of Agrippa, one of "Caesar's friends."

The opponents of the Jews then seized and desecrated some Jewish synagogues by installing images of Caligula in them.[7] Flaccus proclaimed the Jews of the city to be foreigners and aliens (54), assigning them a political status far short of their ambitions for equal status in the city. Jews throughout the city's five quarters flooded into part of one—in effect a ghetto (55).

Jewish residences and shops were raided, and violence broke out against the Jews. Some Jews were set on fire in the center of the city (68) and others crucified (72, 84–85). Flaccus flogged members of the *gerousia*, the council of elders that led the Jewish element within the city. Jewish women were even forced to eat pork (96).

The latter half of the *Flaccus* (102–91) relates Flaccus's subsequent arrest (108–15), exile (146–79), and death (180–91). Philo was convinced that all these misfortunes were God's judgment on Flaccus for the way he had treated the

Jews of Alexandria (116, 170, 191). Alexandrian individuals who had previously been subordinate to Flaccus now brought charges against him in Rome (125–27).

The last paragraphs of the treatise relate Flaccus's journey into exile in pathetic terms in which he regrets his past actions (e.g., 170) and spends his days in constant shame (166). He longs for evening in the morning and morning in the evening, dreading the visions he had at night (167). He suffers all the acts he has committed against the Jews (170). Eventually, his sense that he would be put to death comes to pass, and he dies a gruesome, bloody death (188–90).[8]

6.2.2 Embassy to Gaius (De Legatione ad Gaium)

While *Flaccus* presents the persecution of 38 CE in relation to the prefect Flaccus in Alexandria, *Embassy* relates to the emperor Gaius Caligula in the same time period. While *Flaccus* says nothing of any direct connection between Gaius and the persecution, *Embassy* claims that his attitude toward Jews encouraged the Alexandrians to take hostile action against them (119–20).

Embassy differs on several points from *Flaccus* in its account of the pogrom. For example, in *Embassy* the persecution of the Alexandrian Jews takes place *before* their synagogues are attacked, while in *Flaccus* the persecution follows. *Embassy* further recounts the burning of prayer houses (132), as well as successful resistance in some quarters (134). *Flaccus* tells of neither.

The heart of the treatise covers events outside Egypt. The most noticeable of these was Caligula's attempt to set up his statue in the Jerusalem temple, along with the protests that ensued (184–333). This event took place in either 39 or 40 CE, after Caligula began to consider himself the "new epiphany of Zeus." Philo recounts the efforts of both Petronius (the Roman governor of Syria) and Herod Agrippa I (Jewish client-king and friend of Caligula) to delay and dissuade Gaius from this course of action. Their efforts worked, although Philo insists Caligula still planned to install the statue secretly (337–38).

Only a small part of the treatise actually relates to the embassy Philo led to Gaius in order to plead for the rights of the Jews in Alexandria to be citizens. In the early part of the treatise, Philo recounts his initial arrival in Italy and the embassy's first appearance before the emperor (166–83). The last few paragraphs then record their main appearance before him (349–73). Throughout this latter hearing, Philo emphasizes Caligula's preoccupation with other things, his hostility toward them for their failure to recognize him as a god, and his musings on irrelevant questions such as why Jews do not eat pork.

6.3 ON THE LIFE OF MOSES (DE VITA MOSIS)

Scholars do not agree on exactly how Philo's two-volume *Life of Moses* relates to his three great commentary series.[9] Nevertheless, they are another great place to start reading in his corpus. They were likely written for the "beginner" of Philo's own day, the person with little knowledge of Judaism or philosophy. They present us with one of the ways Philo used biblical material, in this case the way he could "rewrite" and re-present biblical narratives.[10]

> **bios:** An ancient biography.

Philo tells us at the beginning that he is writing a ***bios,*** or biography, of Moses, the "greatest and most perfect man" (*Mos.* 1.1; cf. 2.292). He treats Moses' life by way of four aspects of Moses' identity: (1) king, (2) lawgiver, (3) high priest, and (4) prophet. His portrayal of Moses as king takes the entirety of the first volume and largely follows the biblical story line of the Pentateuch. The second volume then follows a more topical route, covering each of Moses' roles as lawgiver (8–65), high priest (66–186), and prophet (187–291) in turn.

Philo presents Moses according to the highest ideals of Greek culture. He gives him a Greek education, no doubt similar to the one Philo himself enjoyed (*Mos.* 1.21–24). He portrays him as disciplined in adolescence and philosophical in orientation (1.25–29, 48). The actions of his early life anticipate his later nobility and prophetic abilities.

From the departure of the Jews from Egypt, Philo speaks more explicitly of Moses' role as king (1.148), the role to which the first treatise as a whole is dedicated (cf. 1.334). In this role Moses is "god and king" of the nation (1.158). The first treatise ends with the Jews about to enter the land, the point at which Moses dies in the biblical narrative.

Because of the topical nature of the second book, it does not follow any particular biblical order. Philo's concern is to show in Moses a perfect combination of philosopher-king, lawgiver, high priest, and prophet (2.3–7). The first section expands on Moses' role as lawgiver (*Mos.* 2.8–65). Moses possessed all the needed virtues to be a great lawgiver: love of humanity, love of justice, love of the good, and hatred of evil (2.9). Philo ends this section with regret that the Jewish nation has not prospered for many years. He is convinced that all the nations would adopt the Jewish customs if the Jewish nation were only to enjoy prosperity (2.43–44).

Moses 2.66–186 goes on to discuss Moses' role as high priest for the Jewish nation. It presents his priestly role in the construction of a portable sanctuary in the wilderness (2.71–93), in the making of the vessels and vestures for that sanctuary (2.94–140), and in the appointment of priests and attendants to serve it (2.141–86). Philo portrays Moses as a hierophant of divine mysteries (e.g., 2.71, 153) who could see with his soul's eye the patterns behind the material forms he was making (2.74). One of the most notable passages in this section indicates that a sacrifice is effective only if the person offering it has an appropriate attitude when offering it (2.106–8).

The final section of the second treatise discusses Moses in the role of prophet (*Mos.* 2.187–291). Philo mentions three types of divine oracle a person could receive: those directly initiated and revealed by God, those given in response to questions asked God, and those discerned by an inspired human (2.187–90). He shows the greatness of Moses as he received oracles of the second and third type. The treatise concludes with Moses' prophetic vision of his own death, which he recorded before it actually happened (2.288–91).

6.4 THE EXPOSITION OF THE LAW

We are now ready to read one of Philo's commentary series, the Exposition of the Law. Like the *Life of Moses*, this series was largely written for the beginner without much knowledge of Judaism or philosophy. To be sure, some of these treatises are easier than others. But they are an excellent next step in his corpus, and they introduce us to some of the other flavors in Philo's writings.

6.4.1 *On the Creation (De Opificio)*

Although the Exposition as a whole is Philo's easiest commentary series for the beginner, its first treatise is perhaps the hardest of all Philo's treatises—at least Goodenough thought so.[11] It gives us a good taste of Philo at his most philosophical. Yet despite the foreignness of so much of its argument, Philo still follows the basic order of the biblical text, ultimately grounding his presentation in the progress of Genesis 1–3.

Apart from the introduction (1–12) and conclusion (170b–72), the bulk of the treatise follows the general story line of the creation narratives. The body of the treatise divides into two parts, which correspond broadly to the two Genesis creation stories. Roughly the first two-thirds present Philo's interpretation of Genesis 1 (13–128), while the last third draws some general inferences from the second and third chapters of Genesis (129–70a).

A number of characteristic Philonic themes and elements appear in this treatise. For example, Philo's lengthy discussion of the number seven gives us a good example of his love of number speculation and the influence of Pythagorean traditions on him (89–128). Philo's Platonism comes out in the fact that the incorporeal world of ideas is created before the "embodied" material world (e.g., 13–35). In fact, Philo passes on a Jewish tradition that the human created in Genesis 1:27 was a Platonic ideal human, while the man of Genesis 2:7 was the first physical man (134–50).

Philo considers much of the Adam and Eve story as allegorical rather than literal, and it is at this point of the treatise that he presents his "allegory of the soul." In this allegory, man represents the human mind, the serpent is pleasure, and the human senses are represented by the woman (e.g., 165). As the woman was deceived by the snake, pleasure has its hold over a person by way of our senses and threatens to ensnare our minds.

Philo concludes *On the Creation* with a list of five points we should take with us from the creation story (170b–72).[12] We know from elsewhere how important these conclusions were for Philo:

Philo's Creation Creed

1. God exists and exists eternally (directed at atheists).
2. God is one (directed at polytheists).
3. The world is created (directed at those who think the world is eternal like God).
4. The world is one (directed at those who think there is more than one world).
5. God cares for the world as a parent for a child.

Goodenough considered this list "the first creed of history."[13]

6.4.2 *On Abraham* (*De Abrahamo*)

The treatise *On Abraham* was apparently the first of three biographies Philo wrote concerning the patriarchs Abraham, Isaac, and Jacob, although only the *De Abrahamo* has survived. Philo saw the lives of the patriarchs as embodiments of the law (*Mos.* 2.45–48). They show us what the law looks like in a person. Philo actually valued the patriarchs as "originals" (*archetypoi*) over and against the written law of the Pentateuch, which were only copies of their lives (*eikones*) (*Abr.* 3).

On Abraham divides into three main sections: (1) Philo's introduction (1–6); (2) his discussion of the triad Enos, Enoch, and Noah (7–47); and (3) his discussion of Abraham himself, the namesake of the treatise (48–276).[14] While Enos, Enoch, and Noah represent *progress* toward virtue, Abraham is the first of a triad of characters who actually attained perfection (*Abr.* 52–53). Abraham represents the pursuit of virtue through teaching; Isaac, the pursuit by nature; and Jacob, pursuit through practice (52).

Philo spends the majority of the treatise discussing the literal and allegorical lessons we learn from Abraham in Genesis (60–276). The first part of his discussion relates to Abraham's godliness or piety (*eusebia*), his honor-worthy relationship with God (*Abr.* 60–207). The second half largely deals with Abraham's honorable behavior in relation to his fellow humans (*Abr.* 208–74).[15]

One interesting point in the treatise is Philo's interpretation of the three travelers who visit Abraham.[16] One visitor represents God himself (*to on*—"that which is") and points to those individuals who worship God simply because he is God (*Abr.* 121, 124–25, 128). The other two visitors represent more shadowy apprehensions (*skiai*) of God necessary for some to worship him, two "potencies" or "powers" (*dynameis*) of God. These are God's creative power, represented by the title "God" (*theos*), and his kingly power, represented by the title "Lord" (*kyrios*). Thus some serve God because he is beneficent, a father who cares for his creation and brings blessings (= God as *theos*). Others serve him because they fear God's royal power (= God as *kyrios*).

6.4.3 *On Joseph* (*De Iosepho*)

On Joseph discusses a different type of individual from those symbolized by Abraham, Isaac, and Jacob. This is the life of a statesman, or *politicus* (*Ios.* 1). The difference between Philo's generally positive portrayal of Joseph here and his extremely negative portrayal in *On Dreams* 2 is notorious. The best explanation is probably a difference in audience, although Philo may also have written them at different times in his life.

Philo proceeds through the biblical story of Joseph, alternating between the implications of the literal story and allegorical meanings he thinks the story has. The literal story provides us with several insights into ancient family values such as the authority and significance of older children (e.g., 16–21, 173, 176), the importance of keeping old customs (e.g., 202), and the heinousness of adultery (44).[17] We can add to this list distinctive Jewish ideas such as the blindness of idolatry (254) and the importance of sexual restraint (43–45).

Philo also draws a number of allegorical inferences from the story. These largely consider Joseph as an allegory for the true *politicus*. His name implies that the statesman has "added" to the laws of nature. Philo will treat these additions very negatively in *On Dreams* 2. But in *On Joseph,* Philo treats them as necessary for the *politicus* to adjust to different situations (*Ios.* 34). The statesman is a true interpreter of life's "dreams" (125), the shadowy and shifting nature of life and the world.

Some of the most interesting comments in the treatise relate to the afterlife. These statements presume a basic dualism between the human body and soul (e.g., *Ios.* 71). Philo says that no good man has really died.[18] Such a person will live the time of eternity through an immortal nature, a soul that is no longer bound by the necessities of the body (264).

6.4.4 *On the Decalogue* (*De Decalogo*)

At the beginning of *On the Decalogue*, Philo tells us he is now going to consider the written laws of the Pentateuch. He reminds us that the preceding biographies of Abraham, Isaac, Jacob, and Joseph have unfolded the "unwritten law" embodied in the lives of these patriarchs (*Decal.* 1).[19] Philo takes a little less than a third of the treatise to introduce the "ten words" and explain why the setting in which God revealed them was appropriate (1–49). Philo then divides the ten words into two sets of five, half of which relate to our relationship with God, and the other five to our duty toward humanity (50–51, 110).

Philo's presentation of the first two commandments brings him to his usual polemic ("battling argument") against polytheists and idolaters. The Third Commandment reveals Philo's sense that it is best not to swear at all (84), but certainly we must take any oath in God's name with the utmost seriousness (86). Philo briefly discusses the Sabbath as a day devoted to the study of wisdom (e.g., 98) and the importance of honoring parents as servants of God (e.g., 119).

Philo's summary of the second five "words" is somewhat briefer than that of the first five (121–53). He proclaims adultery the greatest of crimes (121) in its focus on pleasure (122), its breach of faith (126), its disgrace to the family (126–27), and the consequences for the children (128–31). Murder attacks the laws of nature and destroys the best of living creatures, humankind, those most like heaven (132–34). A thief is an enemy of the nation (135–37). And those who bear false witness not only corrupt the truth but also lead an innocent jury to bring about injustice (138–41). The last word of the ten inveighs against the most difficult passion of all to control: desire (142). The final paragraphs of *On the Decalogue* prepare for the next four treatises (154–74).

6.4.5 *On the Special Laws* 1–4 (*De Specialibus Legibus*)

On the Decalogue treats the Ten Commandments as ten "headings" under which all the specific laws of the Pentateuch fall. The treatises *On the Special Laws* then explore those specific laws in some detail. *On the Special Laws* 1 discusses the first two commandments, which relate to the monarchy of God and the prohibition of idolatry. The second treatise then covers the Third, Fourth, and Fifth Commandments of the Decalogue. *On the Special Laws* 3 discusses the sixth and seventh "words," and the final treatise with this title covers the remaining three commandments, as well as the virtue justice.

On the Special Laws 1

Philo may reflect Jewish tradition by discussing the practice of circumcision before discussing the other laws of the Pentateuch (*Spec.* 1.2–11). From this discussion he proceeds to discuss the first "word" of the Decalogue, which concerns the monarchy of God (1.12–20). The remainder of the book thus falls very roughly under the heading of the second word of the Decalogue against idolatry (1.21–345). Under this general heading Philo discusses a number of miscellaneous elements in the Pentateuch, most of which relate to aspects of Jewish temple worship, including rules for priests and sacrifices.

Philo has several interesting comments in this treatise. One is his belief that the nature of God is beyond human understanding (1.32, 36–50): we can know *that* he is (existence) but not *what* he is (essence). Philo's discussion of the temple includes the common notion that the temple is a symbolic representation of the universe itself, the truest temple of God (1.66). Philo further considers the high priest's robe to be a symbolic representation of the universe (1.82–97).

In his discussion of sacrifices, Philo makes the interesting claim that even the most perfect individual cannot escape sinning because she or he is created (1.252). All individuals thus stand in need of atonement. Philo also discusses the piety required of those who bring sacrifices (1.257–345). Philo believes that the attitude of the person offering the sacrifice is the important thing, rather than the actual sacrifice itself (e.g., 1.277, 283, 290).

The treatise ends with an allegorical interpretation of Deuteronomy 23. Philo condemns those who deny the existence of incorporeal patterns behind visible reality (*Spec.* 1.327–29), atheists (1.330), polytheists (1.331–32), and those who make either the mind or the senses into idols (1.333–43). In contrast to these, knowledge of the God who truly exists brings happiness (1.345).

On the Special Laws 2

The second treatise of this series treats the Third, Fourth, and Fifth Commandments. In Philo's numbering, these are the commandments on oath-taking (*Spec.* 2.2–38), Sabbath observance (2.39–223), and honoring one's parents (2.224–41). He ends the book with the punishments and rewards in store for those who violate the first five commandments, all of which relate to our duty toward God (2.242–62).

Philo's discussion of the Sabbath is quite lengthy. He incorporates what he considers to be the ten feasts of the Jewish law under this heading (cf. *Spec.* 2.41). These are (1) the feast of every day (2.42–55); (2) the feast of the seventh day, or Sabbath feast (2.56–139);[20] (3) the new moon feast (2.140–44); (4) the feast of Passover, or Crossing feast (2.145–49); (5) the feast of Unleavened Bread (2.150–61); (6) the feast of Sheaf, or First Fruits (2.162–75); (7) feast of Weeks, or Pentecost (2.176–87); (8) the Trumpet feast, or sacred month-day (2.188–92); (9) the Fast, or Day of Atonement (2.193–203); (10) the feast of Tabernacles (2.204–13). Besides these, he discusses the practice of the "Basket" (2.215–22) before concluding the section (2.223).

Several comments of note appear throughout this lengthy treatment. For example, more than once he mentions that the seventh day is called the Sabbath by the "Hebrews" (e.g., 2.41, 86). Such comments would be significantly out of place if Philo did not at least hope that some non-Jews might one day read the Exposition commentary series.

The treatise ends with an enumeration of the penalties (*Spec.* 2.242–56) and rewards (2.257–62) relating to the first five commandments. Philo argues backward from the Fifth to the First that the violation of all five demands the death of the lawbreaker. In contrast, the virtue of keeping the first four is its own reward, while honoring the Fifth Commandment results in long life.

On the Special Laws 3

Philo begins the third treatise of the series on a surprising autobiographical note (*Spec.* 3.1–6). His description of the change that has occurred in his life is striking in its intensity. Thus, while he may very well idealize the serenity of his earlier days, something significant surely took place at about this time in his life. The best candidate for such events is the pogrom of 38 CE and the subsequent mission Philo led to Rome.

The interruption ends as quickly as it comes. Philo briefly introduces the second half of the Decalogue (*Spec.* 3.7) and proceeds in the rest of the treatise to cover the Sixth Commandment against adultery (3.8–82) and the Seventh against murder (3.83–209). Under the prohibition of adultery Philo discusses all the pentateuchal laws relating to sexuality, while he places all the laws relating to violent actions with the command against murder.

Philo's discussion of the prohibition of adultery is full of insights into the Greco-Roman and Jewish culture of his day. It is in this section that we find Philo's famous discussion of the roles appropriate to men and women (3.169–71), where he places men in the public domain and women inside the house. He even partitions the home into zones appropriate for virgins (within inner door) and those who have reached full womanhood (within outer door). Women of innocence are said to wear veils (3.56, 60).

Perhaps the most interesting aside in his treatment of violence is the seriousness of damaging the eye of a servant. Here Philo considers the eyes the pathway to philosophy, since it is the observation of the visible world that leads us to consider the existence of the mind that created it and its underlying metaphysics (3.185–94). The person who investigates such things is a philosopher, which Philo must thus consider himself to be.

On the Special Laws 4

The final treatise of this series treats the last three commandments, namely, the prohibitions against stealing (*Spec.* 4.1–40), bearing false witness (4.41–77), and coveting (4.78–131). The remainder of the treatise then deals somewhat surprisingly with the virtue of justice (4.136–238), which Philo believes relates to all ten commandments (4.133–34).

As in the other treatises in this series, Philo demonstrates an amazing ability to place miscellaneous laws under the individual headings of the Ten Commandments. For example, he discusses the food laws under the heading of covetousness, because he relates eating to desire (4.100–118). In this sense, the food laws reflect the virtue of self-control (e.g., 4.112).

Another interesting passage presents Philo's understanding of the inspiration of Scripture (4.49). Here Philo claims that prophets do not originate their own words. Rather, their reasoning stops and the divine Spirit moves their vocal cords, dictating words to them. This sentiment is remarkably reminiscent of 2 Peter 1:20–21 in the New Testament.

6.4.6 *On Virtues* (*De Virtutibus*)

This treatise actually consists of four smaller essays, each on a different virtue. In Philo's mind, these virtues apply to the keeping of all ten commandments. The essays are "On Courage" (*peri andreias*: 1–50), "On Love of Humanity" (*peri philanthrōpias*: 51–174), "On Repentance" (*peri metanoias*: 175–86), and "On Nobility" (*peri eugeneias*: 187–227).

This sequence of virtues is curious, but Philo considers himself to have covered other virtues such as piety, wisdom, and self-control already in the series (cf. *Spec.* 4.135). To gain perspective, Philo places piety or godliness as the highest virtue, and love of humanity second (*Virt.* 51). Piety relates to a person's duty toward God, while love of humanity subsumes our duties toward each other. Together they cover the gamut of moral responsibility.

In this treatise, Philo's essay on courage completes his treatment of the four cardinal virtues, since he discussed justice at the end of *Special Laws* 4. As elsewhere, he gives the Stoic definition of courage (e.g., *Virt.* 1). Otherwise, Philo's short treatment of repentance and his longer clarification on true nobility seem odd additions to the treatise. One interesting aspect of Philo's final essay is its rejection of Aristotle's belief that a person needed a good environment, a healthy body, and a sound mind to be happy (187). Philo later speaks favorably of another Aristotelian notion he usually rejected vigorously: the "moderation of the passions" (195).

6.4.7 *On Rewards and Punishments* (*De Praemiis et Poenis*)

The final treatise of The Exposition of the Law is Philo's *On Rewards and Punishments*. Philo begins with a brief overview of the whole commentary series (1–3). He then presents the topic of this final treatise, namely, the rewards and punishments that await the good and the bad.

We can divide the treatise into two basic parts. It is actually the first of these that deals with the rewards and punishments of various individuals from the past (7–78). The second half then treats typical blessings and curses in store for those of the future.[21] A sizeable *lacuna*, or lost portion of the text, almost certainly appeared after paragraph 78, leaving us without the conclusion to Philo's discussion of punishments, as well as the beginning to his discussion of blessings.

This treatise has several significant features, including Philo's remarkable sense that we cannot know God for what he is, only that he is. *Rewards* 40 gives us one of the most succinct expressions of Philo's negative theology, his sense that God is beyond human comprehension. Goodenough found in this discussion a phrase that, for him, typified Philo's mysticism for him: "They seek truth who apprehend God by way of God and *light by way of light*" (*Praem.* 46).[22]

> **lacuna:** A lost portion of text.

But perhaps the most noteworthy feature of the treatise is its remarkable eschatology. We would scarcely think Philo had such a strong sense of Israel's national destiny if it were not for this treatise. It is one of very few places where Philo may even reveal a messianic expectation (*Praem.* 91–97). In this treatise Philo expects the future restoration of the Jews as a political force in the world, with an apparent return of Diaspora Jews to their homeland (e.g., 165–72).

6.5 TWO APOLOGETIC TREATISES

We have now read through the only one of Philo's three commentary series that he seems to have finished. This is quite an accomplishment. Before we begin his most difficult series, a break is in order to read a few of his miscellaneous treatises. They are some of his most interesting and are very readable.

6.5.1 *On the Contemplative Life* (*De Vita Contemplativa*)

Philo believed that the virtuous person lived either an active or contemplative life. Of the two, he considered the contemplative the highest form (*Fug.* 36–37). The Jewish group known as the Essenes provided him with the best example of the virtuous active life. In contrast, this treatise presents an otherwise unknown group called the Therapeutae as a superior example of the contemplative life.

Presuming that this group actually existed, they lived in an ascetic community outside Alexandria. Their life was largely devoted to prayer (e.g., *Contempl.* 25–27) and meditation (29). They lived a simple life, and Philo spends much of the treatise contrasting their abstinent meals with the excessive banquets of the Greeks (48–74). According to Philo, the focus of their banquets was nothing other than contemplation (75–82), followed by hymn singing (83–89).

6.5.2 *The Hypothetica*

We unfortunately do not have the full text of this treatise. Our excerpts come from the early Christian Eusebius, who quotes the work extensively. The first excerpt extols the Jews as it recounts their exodus from Egypt and the establishment of their law. The second excerpt provides us with valuable information on the Essenes, leading many scholars to suggest that the *Hypothetica* was the treatise that preceded *On the Contemplative Life*. Philo briefly describes their lifestyle and ends with praise for the Essene practice of celibacy. Here he makes extremely negative comments on the nature of wives (*Hypoth.* 11.14–17).

6.6 A PHILOSOPHICAL TREATISE: *THAT EVERY GOOD PERSON IS FREE* (*QUOD OMNIS PROBUS LIBER SIT*)

This treatise followed a lost one whose thesis was that every bad person is a slave (*Prob.* 1). Correspondingly, *Good Person* follows through with the Stoic idea that every good person is free. Secular references permeate the treatise, leading some in the past to think it one of Philo's earliest writings. But Philo could have written it at any point of his life.

True freedom, Philo believes, is not the freedom of our bodies but a freedom of our minds from the domination of our passions (17). You could thus be a slave in body but free in terms of your mind. Philo spends about the first third of the treatise proving this point (16–61). In the course of his argument he turns to Zeno, the most famous proponent of this Stoic idea, and interestingly claims that Zeno drew his ideas on the subject from Moses (57).

The remainder of the treatise presents examples of such "freedom" (62–136) and of the human struggle for freedom in general (137–57). His discussion of the Essenes gives us perhaps the most significant example for our purposes (75–91). This passage provides some of the most important information we have about the group. Philo proceeds from groups to give examples of truly free individuals (105–16). He even deigns to find women (whom he says in general have little sense, 117) and animals (131–35) worthy of such freedom! He ends the treatise with an exhortation to vanquish passion and move beyond "milk" and "soft food" to stronger "meat" (158–60).

6.7 THE ALLEGORICAL COMMENTARY

We are now ready to tackle Philo's most difficult commentary series, the Allegorical Commentary. In many respects it is unfortunate that this series always appears near the beginning of Philo collections. The typical edition of Philo's works begins with the treatise *On the Creation*, one of Philo's more difficult, and then follows with the Allegorical Commentary.[23] The unintended effect is to discourage the beginner before she or he even starts reading.

The structure of the series derives from a verse-by-verse analysis of the Genesis text. As he interprets the text allegorically, we find him returning to the same basic themes over and over. Once you get a sense of these basic themes, the series is not difficult to follow. Perhaps the most frequent concept to which Philo returns is his so-called allegory of the soul. Philo frequently finds some way to connect some biblical character or comment to the mind, the senses, or the passions. His conclusion is always the same: the virtuous person will eliminate his passions.

If you intend to do more serious study of Philo later, I would encourage you to read the parallel passages in Philo's Questions and Answers on Genesis and Exodus as you work through the Allegorical Commentary. Reading through the corpus in this way allows you to see more clearly the constants of Philo's interpretations, the points of flexibility, and the points at which he is drawing on previous traditions.

Length does not permit as detailed an examination of each treatise in the Allegorical Commentary as we have made for the other treatises up to this point. You will find the specific passage each treatise covers in chapter 2. And I refer you to the Scripture index in volume 10 of the Loeb series if you are interested in what Philo does with a specific biblical passage throughout his writings. Even though a particular Genesis text may provide the skeleton of each treatise, his asides to other biblical passages are frequent. My purpose here is to give you a snapshot that captures the flavor of the twenty-two extant treatises in the series.

Allegorical Laws 1–3 (*Legum Allegoriae*)

These three treatises (we have a fragment of a lost fourth) together cover the Adam and Eve story of Genesis 2–3. They are thus primary sources for Philo's allegory of the soul (especially *Leg.* 1), as well as his epistemology (especially *Leg.* 2). *Allegorical Laws* 1 has important material on Philo's view of creation, particularly the "double creation" of humankind in Genesis 1:27 and 2:7. In general, the topic of creation naturally leads Philo to Platonic themes; that of the senses and passions, to Stoic ones.

On the Cherubim (De Cherubim)

This treatise has two distinct parts: the first on the expulsion of Adam and Eve from the garden (*Cher.* 1–39), the second on Cain's birth (40–130). The treatise provides the standard reference for Philo's view of causes, particularly his use of the preposition *through* for the instrumental cause (125–26). The treatise is also noteworthy for its interpretation of the two cherubim and sword in Genesis 3 as God's two powers (creative and royal) and the *logos* (27–28).

On the Sacrifices of Abel and Cain (De Sacrificiis Abelis et Caini)

This treatise interprets three verses covering the birth of Abel and the sacrifices that Cain and Abel offered to God (Gen. 4:2–4). The course of Philo's interpretation leaves us with a number of interesting discussions. At one point he pauses to give us a list of 147 vices that characterize the lover of pleasure. We learn Philo's answer to the puzzle of Cain's faulty sacrifice—he delayed his offering (*Sacr.* 53–71) and did not bring the *first* fruits (72–87). Perhaps most interesting, Philo indicates that Abraham became like the angels at death—a disembodied and blessed soul (5). In contrast, Moses was transformed to be with God—an even higher destiny (8).

That the Worse Attacks the Better (Quod Deterius Potiori Insidiari Soleat)

We find Philo's interpretation of the murder of Abel and the "sentencing" of Cain in this book. Cain, the lover of self, does not truly kill Abel, the lover of God. True, the self-lover dispenses the thought of loving God, and the lover of God is "dead" to the life of wickedness (*Det.* 48–49). But the opposite is actually the case: the lover of self is dead to a happy life, and the lover of God is alive with the happy life in God.

The treatise has a few discussions of interest, including Philo's argument against Aristotle's three goods (external, bodily, of the soul) (*Det.* 7). Philo insists that goodness applies only to the soul (9). Also of interest is his discussion of blood as the essence of life (79–90). He believes that this comment in Leviticus 17 applies only to the irrational part of a human—the spirit is the essence of the rational soul. Finally, Philo implies that the person whom God has abandoned can never be reconciled with him (142, 149).

On the Posterity and Exile of Cain (De Posteritate Caini)

Philo proceeds to the exile of Cain and the descriptions of his offspring. Of note are this treatise's strong denunciations of literal interpretations when they conflict with Philo's understanding of God or truth (e.g., *Post.* 1–7, 33). Philo's words against sophists past and present are also of interest. He rails against Protagoras's dictum that "humanity is the measure of everything" (34–39), but also against the sophists of his own day who used rhetoric only to fight truth (101). Finally, Philo makes some interesting comments on war, indicating that it usually results from desire for bodily and external things (116–19) in contrast to attention to the soul (184–85).

On the Giants (*De Gigantibus*)

It is often suggested that *Giants* and *Unchangeableness* (see below) were originally a single treatise. *On the Giants* is an important source for Philo's view of angels. He believes that each part of the universe is filled with souls of different kinds (*Gig.* 7), and angels are incorporeal souls who serve God by ministering to humanity (12–13). He relates the story of the giants in Genesis 6 to three types of individuals (60–61): the earth-born who live for pleasure, the heaven-born who love to contemplate, and the God-born who are priests and prophets.

On the Unchangeableness of God (*Quod Deus Sit Immutabilis*)

Unchangeableness, as the name suggests, defends the idea that God cannot change his mind, even though the biblical text portrays him doing so. Moses portrays God changing his mind only to teach those who are not able to understand the truth that God is not like any kind of created thing (*Deus* 52–55). *Unchangeableness* has the passage in which Philo sounds the most like he believes in human free will (47–48), although passages elsewhere make him sound equally like a determinist (e.g., *Cher.* 41).

On Agriculture (*De Agricultura*)

We have probably lost several treatises between *Unchangeableness* and this one. The current treatise divides neatly into Philo's discussion of what it means to call someone a farmer (*Agr.* 1–123) and what it means to "begin" (124–81). Most interesting is the typology Philo creates of the process of moving toward virtue: beginning, making progress, and initial perfection (e.g., 158–68). It is not enough to believe that God created everything—a beginning toward truth. You must go further to recognize that God is the cause only of good things (129).

On Noah's Work as a Planter (*De Plantatione*)

Philo continues the discussion of Genesis 9:20 begun in the previous treatise, now focusing on the fact that Noah "planted a vineyard." He discusses God as a planter (*Plant.* 2–31) of both the universe (2–27) and humanity (28–31). After examples of good planting (73–93), Philo encourages his readers to migrate to the land of wisdom, where they can also plant (94–98). The last part of the treatise somewhat surprisingly discusses arguments by philosophers on whether a wise person will get drunk (139–77).

On Drunkenness (*De Ebrietate*)

The end of *Planting* presented the views of philosophers on whether the wise person will get drunk. This treatise now purports to give Moses' view (*Ebr.* 1). Philo claims that Moses uses strong drink as a symbol for five things: (1) aversion to discipline, (2) ignorance, (3) gluttony, (4) gladness, and (5) nakedness (cf. *Ebr.* 4, 6). But he gets through only the first three in this treatise.

His conclusions in general correspond to the opposite of drunkenness. Moses wishes us to submit to education so that we can attain knowledge (e.g., 81). We should be wisely cautious in our conclusions (205). And we should avert the unhappiness of the wicked who indulge themselves (223–24). Apparently a second treatise that completed his discussion is lost (cf. *Sobr.* 1).

On Sobriety (*De Sobrietate*)

This treatise concludes Philo's lengthy treatment of Noah's actions after the flood. In particular, it interprets Noah's coming to soberness and his blessings and curses toward Shem, Canaan, and Japheth. Philo begins with the conclusion of the preceding treatises: soberness of both soul and body is the most beneficial course (*Sobr.* 2).

The most interesting aspects of his discussion are his explanation for why Canaan was cursed instead of Ham, and his explanation of Noah's prayer for Japheth. The text curses Canaan because he represents vice in action, whereas Ham is only the potential for vice (44). Japheth's widening is the adding of bodily and external goods to the only true good: moral beauty (60–61). But Philo suspects that dwelling in the house of Shem might mean that Japheth will eventually learn that there is truly only one good (67).

On the Confusion of Tongues (*De Confusione Linguarum*)

This treatise gives us Philo's interpretation of the confusion of languages in the tower of Babel story of Genesis 11. Philo allows that the story may have literally happened (*Conf.* 190). But even if so, such a literal meaning is only "shadow" in substance (190). The "reality" is that God desires to break up and disperse vice (193–95).

We might just briefly mention three very interesting elements that appear in the course of this treatise. One relates to the last two sentences of the preceding paragraph, for *Conf.* 190 clearly applies the Platonic distinction between shadow and reality to types of interpretation. The second is Philo's discussion of the roles of God's potencies and angels in his administration of the world (168–82): God himself does not distribute punishment. Finally, *Conf.* 145–47 provides us with perhaps the clearest statement of the *logos*'s anagogical function: its role in leading someone to God.

On the Migration of Abraham (*De Migratione Abrahami*)

Migration deals with God's calling of Abraham to leave Haran for the land of Canaan. The treatise divides into two parts, the first of which largely deals with

God's command to leave and the gifts he promised to Abraham (*Mig.* 2–126). The second half then treats the going itself (127–225). Philo largely understands his migration as a movement of the mind away from body, sense-perception, and speech (e.g., 2) toward contemplation of the immortal (e.g., 36, 53).

Philo affords us a number of interesting passages in this treatise. He gives us an autobiographical snippet about himself as a writer (34–35). *Migration* 71 provides the two dimensions of *logos* as understood by the Stoics: reason and speech, unuttered and uttered word. Finally, this treatise gives us the classic text for Philo's attitude toward the literal keeping of the Jewish law (89–93). In this passage he decries those who ignore the literal keeping of the law. However, we should keep in mind that he argues for such on the basis of maintaining reputation (86).

Who Is the Heir of Divine Things? (*Quis Rerum Divinarum Heres*)

Heir is the longest treatise in the series and deals with the question of whether a person who is focused on the senses can truly inherit divine things (*Her.* 63). Philo's answer is of course a resounding no. Philo tells us in somewhat mystical language that it is the contemplative who attains to divine things (70).

The treatise has a number of interesting passages. For example, it treats the idea of the *logos* as "cutter" or divider more extensively than elsewhere. The *logos* as rationality makes logical distinctions between the various categories of reality, such as in creation (e.g., 133–40). It stands on the boundary between the created realm and the uncreated God (205–6). The course of this argument leads Philo to a number of fascinating descriptions of the universe as he understood it (e.g., 221–25, 233).

4.7.13 On Mating with the Preliminary Studies (De Congressu Quaerendae Eruditionis Gratia)

Preliminary Studies gives us the best presentation of Philo's views on education, particularly as it relates to true wisdom and virtue. In it he is expanding on the Stoic notion that the *encyclios paideia* of Greek gymnastic education constituted preliminary studies to philosophy.[24] But Philo moves beyond the Stoics in that he considers philosophy itself subordinate to true wisdom, which involves knowledge of God. Philosophy is the pursuit of wisdom, but wisdom "is the knowledge of divine and human things, as well as their causes" (*Congr.* 70). Philo develops these ideas by way of an allegorical interpretation of the Sarah/Hagar story in Genesis 16.

On Flight and Finding (De Fuga et Inventione)

This treatise gives us Philo's allegorical interpretation of Hagar's flight from Sarah (*Fug.* 2–118), her "finding" by an angel of the Lord (119–76), and the fact that the angel found her by a spring (177–213). One point of interest is the fact that

Philo is positive toward participating in politics (33–35). This anti-Cynic position is all the more fascinating because of the extremely negative position he will take just a few treatises later (*Somn.* 2.101–4).[25] Also of interest is his enumeration of God's powers, through which God acts in the world (65–66)—one of his more detailed lists.

On the Change of Names (De Mutatione Nominum)

Names discusses the change of Abram's name to Abraham, along with a host of other name changes and variations of names in the Pentateuch. Philo indicates the existence of Jewish scoffers who mock things like the addition of a single letter to someone's name as a ridiculous gift (*Mut.* 61). But he himself finds great allegorical significance in the change, namely, a change from the study of the creation (astrology) to the study of God (piety) (e.g., 70).

Names also provides interpretations of Abraham's problematic laughter and questioning of whether he could have a child at one hundred years of age (e.g., 175–76). At worst, Philo suggests, no one can be godlike for the entire length of life (185). But he also seems willing to believe that Abraham's question is a prayer fixed on the special nature of the numbers ninety-nine (Sarah's age) and one hundred (188–92).

On God (De Deo)

The treatise *On God* unfortunately has survived only in an Armenian fragment that was translated into English in 1998.[26] It presents a small portion of Philo's interpretation of Genesis 18, where the three men visit Abraham. In the extant fragment, Philo presents his standard view of God's potencies, "God" and "Lord." He also makes interesting asides on Isaiah's vision of the seraphim and on Deuteronomy 4:24: "Your Lord God is a consuming fire."

On Dreams 1–2 (De Somniis)

The two treatises *On Dreams* come last in the Allegorical Commentary as we have it. A prior treatise, unfortunately lost, dealt with dreams sent directly from God, dreams that do not involve any human thought and are absolutely clear in import. *On Dreams* 1, the first treatise we do have, then deals with a second category of dreams: dreams in which our minds work in harmony with God to reveal future events in a somewhat riddled way (*Somn.* 1.2).

This treatise has a number of fascinating discussions. Jacob's dream of a stairway to heaven naturally leads Philo to consider the space between the earth and the moon, where angels abide (1.134). We again find in this section the idea that the entire universe is filled with souls of different types (1.135). His interpretation of a second dream leads to his classic discussion of whether Genesis 21:13 speaks of two gods. Philo explains that without the word *the*, the word *god* refers to the *logos*, not to *the* God (1.228–30).

The second surviving treatise is less rich but possibly of great autobiographical value. It deals with a third kind of dreams: dreams that come of the soul's own instigation and whose truth is most obscure (*Somn.* 2.4). It primarily treats the dreams of Joseph, who symbolizes the politician. Philo's treatment is remarkable for its thinly veiled anti-Roman sentiment (e.g., 2.61–62, 91–92) and his advice to play along with the enemy when you do not have the power to mount successful opposition (2.85–89).[27] He even seems resolved to abandon his own pursuit of politics (e.g., 2.101–4).

6.8 SOME FINAL PHILOSOPHICAL TREATISES

6.8.1 *On the Eternity of the World* (*De Aeternitate Mundi*)

Of all Philo's treatises, scholars have most questioned the authenticity of this one, although the current consensus accepts Philo's authorship. The greatest problem is that the work seems to argue for the uncreatedness of the world—a highly un-Philonic belief. Philo regularly argues vehemently for the creation of the world (e.g., *Opif.* 7–12).

Any one of several suggestions may offset this sharp discrepancy. The main thrust of the treatise may be more against the Stoic idea of cyclical creation—that the world is in an eternal cycle of creation and eventual destruction—than in favor of the uncreatedness of the world. Perhaps it was one of Philo's earliest, when he was still sorting out his ideas. Probably the best explanation points out that the treatise is unfinished as we have it (*Aet.* 150). This view contends that the remainder of the treatise went on to discount the ideas for which it so vigorously argued in the first half.

If such is the case, then the treatise as we have it contributes little to our understanding of Philo's thought. Nevertheless, it provides a wealth of information for the history of philosophy. Gregory Sterling suggests it may have been used to teach such things in a school run by Philo in Alexandria.[28]

6.8.2 *On Providence* (*De Providentia*)

The original treatise consisted of two books, which exist in their entirety only in an Armenian translation.[29] The text of the first and shorter of these two is riddled with interpolations and textual difficulties. Eusebius provides us with two excerpts of the second book in Greek. The entire work was a dialogue between Philo and an Alexander, perhaps his nephew, on the topic of whether providence governed the world.

One of the issues that shows up prominently in the first book is whether God eternally creates and orders the matter of the world, whether matter coexists eternally alongside God, or whether God created the world at a particular point in time. David Winston has argued that Philo believed in both the eternal creation and ordering of matter, although the issue seems very difficult to resolve.[30]

Of the Eusebian fragments, the first responds to the question of whether the amount of matter used in creation, as well as the existence of just four elements, might contradict the idea of an ordering mind behind creation. Philo makes the claim he makes elsewhere that God used up every bit of matter in his creation. The second fragment deals with the age-old question of why bad people prosper and good people suffer if God is directing the world. Philo provides several age-old answers in turn, such as the fact that punishment is not always experienced in the moment of wickedness (*Prov.* 2.2–6), that the wicked are not truly happy (2.7–8), and that we cannot always see the good that will come of bad situations (e.g., 2.47–50).

6.8.3 *On Animals* (*De Animalia*)

This treatise has survived only in Armenian, but Abraham Terian has provided us with an English translation.[31] Also titled *Alexander* or *Whether the Animals Have Reason*, this treatise purports to be a debate between Philo and his nephew, Tiberius Alexander. Alexander argues that animals and humans are similar to each other. Philo argues that animals do not have reason, a theme that appears throughout his writings.

6.9 QUESTIONS AND ANSWERS ON GENESIS AND EXODUS

With Philo's two commentary series and all his miscellaneous treatises under your belt, you are truly on the home stretch! If you have not read it along with the Allegorical Commentary, go on now to read *Questions and Answers on Genesis*, followed by *Questions and Answers on Exodus*. Space does not allow a detailed summary of these books, which have largely survived only in Armenian. But we can whet your appetite with a few highlights.

It is interesting to compare what Philo does with certain passages in *Questions* with what he does in the Allegorical Commentary. For example, while the flaming sword outside the garden of Eden is the *logos* in *Cherubim* (*Cher.* 28), it represents heavenly ether in *QG* 1.57. On the whole, *Questions* seems to give us less developed and more diverse interpretations where such differences occur.

Between *Unchangeableness* and *Agriculture* is a sizeable gap of Genesis text, about three chapters. You may then want to pay special attention to *QG* 1.100–2.66. If we are indeed missing treatises, these paragraphs no doubt give us a hint of the kinds of things Philo said in them. *Questions* covers numerous gaps like these.

You will find several gems in *Questions*. *QG* 2.62 gives us a brief discussion of the *logos* as a second God, a topic that also appears in *Dreams* 1.228–30. *QG* 3.3 gives us an allegorical discussion of the parts of the universe based on the five animals used for sacrifice. *QG* 4.110 proceeds from the earring of Rebekah to a discussion of the *logos* in relation to the Monad, Dyad, and Decad. *QG* 4.138–46 no doubt covers material we would have found in the lost treatise *On Isaac*.

In *QE* 2.2 we have Philo's sense that circumcision of a person's flesh was not nearly so important as cutting out the desires, pleasures, and passions of the soul—an example of Philo's universalistic tendencies. *QE* 2.33 proceeds from the halving of blood in Exodus 24:6 to the fact that every created thing has a good and a bad form, such as the rational and irrational in the soul. *QE* 2.68 is a unique and extended discussion of God's powers.

Congratulations! If you have proceeded through Philo's writings as you have worked through this chapter, you have added a tremendous resource to your repertoire for several fields of study. You have conquered an essential piece of the puzzle of the ancient world, of ancient Judaism, of the history of philosophy, and of the background to the New Testament. I am sure you will agree that Philo's potential contribution to our knowledge in these areas is nothing short of immense.

Notes

1. *An Introduction to Philo Judaeus* (New York: Barnes & Noble, 1940), 30.
2. As S. Sandmel also did in his 1979 *Philo of Alexandria: An Introduction* (New York: Oxford University Press, 1979), 29–81.
3. F. H. Colson *et al.*, *Philo with an English Translation*, 10 vols. (Loeb Classical Library; Cambridge, MA: Harvard University Press, 1929–62); R. Marcus, *Philo: Supplements 1–2* (Loeb Classical Library; Cambridge, MA: Harvard University Press, 1953).
4. *Introduction to Philo*, 31.
5. Flaccus was prefect ca. 32–38 CE, beginning under the reign of Tiberius and ending with his removal during the reign of Caligula.
6. Philo's account in *Embassy* differs somewhat.
7. In *Embassy*, this installation takes place after the Jewish populace has been persecuted (*Legat.* 134).
8. It is interesting to note the value judgment of F. H. Colson at the end of his introduction to *Flaccus*. After pointing out the vindictiveness of Philo's portrayal of Flaccus's demise, Colson suggested that "this is the only one [treatise] which those who admire the beauty and spirituality so often shown both in the Commentary and the Exposition might well wish to have been left unwritten" (*Philo* [Cambridge, MA: Harvard University Press, 1941], vol. 9, 301).
9. See 2.2.1, "Philo's Three Great Commentary Series," "The Exposition of the Law."
10. P. Borgen has most explored the various "forms" Philo used to appropriate biblical material. For the category of "rewritten Bible," see his *Philo of Alexandria: An Exegete for His Time* (SNT 86; Leiden: E. J. Brill, 1997), 63–79.
11. *Introduction to Philo*, 35.
12. Goodenough considered this list the first "creed" in the history of the world (ibid., 37).
13. Ibid.
14. Paragraphs 275–76 are a conclusion, but primarily to the third section on Abraham. We can hypothesize that Philo ended the lost treatise *On Jacob* with an ending appropriate to the second triad as a whole (i.e., Abraham, Isaac, and Jacob).
15. With a concluding paragraph (*Abr.* 275–76).
16. Another interesting section, particularly to students of the New Testament, is Philo's discussion of Abraham's faith toward God (262–74).

17. Adultery here seems entirely defined in terms of the dishonor done to the husband of the woman. The dishonor to the man's wife and the defilement of the woman are distinct shames from the act of adultery.

18. And Philo does, interestingly, use the word for male rather than generic humanity, whether this comment truly excludes women or not.

19. In his *Life of Moses,* Philo, divided the Pentateuch into (1) historical material and (2) legislative material (*Mos.* 2.45–48), just as at the beginning of the Exposition of the Law, Philo divided it into (1) oracles of the creation, (2) oracles on the lives of the patriarchs, and (3) specific oracles of legislation (*Praem.* 1). The treatise *On the Decalogue* thus marks the transition in either scheme to what Philo saw as the legislative part of the law.

20. Philo relates this legislation to the seventh year (*Spec.* 2.71–109) and the fiftieth year of Jubilee (2.110–39).

21. E. R. Goodenough thought that the sections on blessings and curses were an entirely separate treatise ("Philo's Exposition of the Law and His De Vita Mosis," *HTR* 26 [1933]: 109–25).

22. *By Light, Light: The Mystic Gospel of Hellenistic Judaism* (New Haven, CT: Yale University Press, 1935).

23. See 8.1.1 for English translations of Philo's writings.

24. F. H. Colson believes it the fullest presentation we have from the ancient world of the Stoic doctrine (introduction to the treatise in volume 4 of the Loeb series, *Philo,* 452).

25. It is tempting to place this stretch of treatises around the time of the crisis in Alexandria and Philo's less-than-optimal delegation to Rome.

26. F. Siegert, "The Philonian Fragment *De Deo*: First English Translation," *SPhA* 10 (1998): 1–33. The standard edition of its Armenian text is found in F. Siegert, *Philon von Alexandrien: Über die Gottesbezeichnung "wohltätig verzehrendes Feuer" (De Deo): Rückübersetzung des Fragments aus dem Armenischen, deutsche Übersetzung und Kommentar* (WUNT 46; Tübingen: Mohr/Siebeck, 1987).

27. See also 2.43, 123–32.

28. "Philo," in *Dictionary of New Testament Background,* ed. C. A. Evans and S. E. Porter (Downers Grove, IL: InterVarsity Press, 1992), 791.

29. However, we have the classic 1822 Latin translation of Aucher, reprinted with a French translation in M. Hadas-Lebel, *De Providentia I et II: Philon d'Alexandrie* (Paris: Éditions du Cerf, 1973).

30. "Philo's Theory of Eternal Creation: *Prov.* 1.6–9," in *The Ancestral Philosophy: Hellenistic Philosophy in Second Temple Judaism: Essays of David Winston,* ed. G. E. Sterling (Providence, RI: Brown University Press, 2001), 120–22.

31. *Philonis Alexandrini De Animalibus: The Armenian Text with Introduction, Translation, Commentary* (Chico, CA: Scholars Press, 1981).

Chapter 7

Topical Index to the Philonic Corpus

We have several indexes to Philo's writings at our disposal. For example, over half the tenth volume in the Loeb series[1] consists of index, including a "Scripture Index," an "Index of Names," and several indexes relating to the footnotes of the translations. The footnote index in particular covers topics, scholars, and Greek words and phrases mentioned in the notes to this twelve-volume translation of Philo's works.[2]

You will also find a selective topical index at the rear of C. D. Yonge's one-volume English edition of Philo's works.[3] Of inestimable value to the student of Philo is the recently published *Philo Index*, primarily the work of Peder Borgen. This concordance to Philo's writings once and for all resolves the errors and omissions of previous word indexes.[4]

The topical index that follows is meant to supplement these other resources and provide a venue for further study of some of the topics mentioned in this book. It is obviously selective.

Adultery: (a) disgracing a man by sleeping with his wife (in the case of a man) or sleeping with a man who is not your husband (in the case of a woman); (b) the greatest of crimes (*Decal.* 121); (c) reasons: indulges pleasure, involves more than one person in evil, makes havoc of three families, brings uncertain status to children (*Decal.* 121–31; *Spec.* 3.65); (d) detection (*Spec.* 3.52–63); (e) cf. *Decal.* 121–31; *Spec.* 3.8–11, 72.

Afterlife: (a) for virtuous, upward in heaven (*Somn.* 1.151; *Mos.* 2.291; *Praem.* 152); (b) Roman conception: in underworld without return to life (*Legat.* 85); (c) for the wicked: Tartarus (*Praem.* 152; *Legat.* 49, 103; cf. *Somn.* 1.151; 2.133; *Spec.* 3.152–54; *Praem.* 69–70); (d) an immortal soul without a body (*Cher.* 114; *Ios.* 264; cf. *Leg.* 1.108); form like angels (*Sacr.* 5) or even better transformation (*Sacr.* 8); (e) cf. *Agr.* 100; *Her.* 276, 283; *Fug.* 59; *QG* 1.16, 86; 3.11; 4.152. See also **Immortality.**

Allegory: (a) relates to literal as soul to body (*Mig.* 93); (b) allegorists (*Mut.* 61; *Spec.* 3.178; *QG* 3.53); (c) literalists (*Conf.* 14, 190); allegory for those who cannot fathom the deeper truths (*Deus* 52, 133); (d) anti-anthropomorphic use/escape of literal meaning (*Leg.* 1.36; 2.19; 3.4, 236; *Det.* 57; *Post.* 6, 33; *Agr.* 61, 90, 97, 131, 157; *Plant.* 113; *Ebr.* 144; *Sobr.* 33; *Conf.* 98; *Congr.* 44, 54, 172; *Somn.*

> "No good man has died in my judgment, but he will live forever without old age with an immortal nature, a soul no longer bound by the necessities of a body" (*Ios.* 264).

1.52, 101–2; 164; 235); (e) cf. *Ios.* 28; *Decal.* 1; *Spec.* 1.200. See also **Allegory of the Soul.**

Allegory of the Soul: Cf. *Opif.* 157–70; *Leg.* 1.53–55, 88–89, 92–96; 2.5, 49–51; *Cher.* 57–64; *Agr.* 80, 107–8; *Her.* 52–57; *Congr.* 106; *Somn.* 2.15–16; *Praem.* 158–61.

Angels: (a) philosophers call them daemons (*Gig.* 6, 16); (b) soul-like nature (*Abr.* 113); disembodied souls (*asōmatoi psychai*), pure intelligences (*Conf.* 174; *Somn.* 1.115, 135; *Spec.* 1.66), divine "words" (*logoi*) (*Conf.* 28; *Somn.* 1.115; *QG* 3.11); (c) servants of God, mediators, ambassadors to creation (*Opif.* 72–75; *Gig.* 12–13, 16; *Conf.* 174; *Fug.* 212; *Somn.* 1.140–43; *Abr.* 115; *Virt.* 73); (d) cf. *Fug.* 203; *Mos.* 1.166; *Spec.* 1.66.

Apostasy: (a) from ancestral customs (*Mos.* 2.193; *Spec.* 4.16; *Praem.* 106, 110, 138); (b) from the one God (*Conf.* 2; *Spec.* 1.54–55; *Praem.* 162–63; *Det.* 142, 146–49).

Art: (a) definition: "system of apprehensions working together for some useful end" (*Congr.* 141); (b) some theoretical, some practical (*Leg.* 1.57).

Atheism: (a) God is the active part; matter the passive (*Opif.* 7–12, 170–72); (b) source of all iniquity (*Decal.* 91); (c) cf. *Conf.* 114; *Fug.* 114; *Abr.* 66, 75, 78, 162; *Spec.* 1.14, 330; *Legat.* 3.

Atonement: (a) patriarchs committed no intentional sins (*Abr.* 6; *Mos.* 2.59); (b) prayers can atone (*Mos.* 2.24); (c) sin intrinsic to creation, requiring prayers and sacrifices to appeal for atonement by God's grace (*Somn.* 2.299; *Mos.* 2.147; *Spec.* 1.252); (d) effectiveness of sacrifice depends on attitude, no victim even necessary (*Deus* 8; *Mos.* 2.107–8). See also **Sin, Sacrifice.**

Beauty: (a) beauty of body in well-proportioned parts; beauty of mind in harmony of thinking and virtues (*Mos.* 2.140); (b) absent where there is disorder (*Opif.* 28).

Body: (a) case for the person (*Ios.* 71); (b) region of pleasures and desires (*Congr.* 59); (c) a distraction from wisdom, a tomb, hindrance, prison (*Leg.* 1.103, 108; *Leg.* 3.22, 69–72; *Gig.* 15; *Conf.* 177; *Mig.* 9; *Her.* 68, 85; *Congr.* 96; *Fug.* 58; *Mut.* 36; *Somn.* 1.139; *Ios.* 264; *Spec.* 4.188; *Virt.* 74; *QG* 4.75).

Canon of Scripture: (a) Philo considers the end of Deuteronomy the "end of the holy words" (*Mos.* 2.290).

Causes: (a) four causes of Aristotle: formal, material, efficient, and final (*Cher.* 125–28).

Children: (a) sons and daughters belong to the house of the male parent and carry the mother with them (*Spec.* 1.130); (b) those who do not survive long enough not human (*Mos.* 1.11); (c) passions pertain to childhood (*Congr.* 81–82; adolescence normally filled with desire, vice (*Congr.* 83–84; *Mos.* 1.25); (d) stepchildren often at odds with each other (*Ios.* 232); (e) cf. *Abr.* 186–87, 195.

City, the Ancient: (a) basic components: *Opif.* 17; *Abr.* 20; *Mos.* 1.103; *Legat.* 12; (b) competitions in (*Legat.* 45); (c) theater (*Agr.* 35, 113; *Legat.* 204); (d) full of countless evils (*Decal.* 2).

Conflagration (*ekpyrōsis*): (a) *Her.* 228; *On the Eternity of the World* (esp. *Aet.* 75, 88).

Conscience (*suneidos*): (a) the faculty of the mind to know when one is doing wrong (*Ios.* 48; *Flacc.* 7); (b) cf. *Post.* 59; *Conf.* 121; *Her.* 7; *Ios.* 47, 68, 197, 215, 262; *Decal.* 91; *Spec.* 1.235; 3.54; *Virt.* 206.

Contemplation: (a) origins in the faculty of sight (*Abr.* 164–66); (b) Philo's own (*Spec.* 3.1–6); (c) Monad the basis (*Gig.* 52); (d) cf. *Leg.* 1.38; 2.58; 3.48, 71, 84; *Cher.* 41; *Sacr.* 79; *Ebr.* 51, 99, 158, 195; *Gig.* 13, 31, 60–66; *Deus* 151; *Agr.* 65; *Conf.* 95; *Her.* 46–48, 70, 249, 283; *Congr.* 133–34; *Fug.* 36–37, 63, 138, 168, 176, 195; *Somn.* 1.43, 139, 149; 2.26; *Mos.* 1.190; *Decal.* 11; *Spec.* 1.37–38, 49, 96, 269, 288, 339; 2.45, 52; 3.111, 192, 202; *Praem.* 26, 51; *On the Contemplative Life*. See also **Mysticism.**

Corporeal, Physical World: (a) copy/image/imprint/type (*mimēma, eikōn,* *charaktēr, typos, apeikonisma*) of ideal, incorporeal world (*Opif.* 16–18, 25; *Leg.* 1.45; *Mos.* 2.127); (b) world of sense by nature unstable (*Abr.* 84).

Cosmology: (a) zone above moon pure from any mixture with darkness (*Abr.* 205); ether and fixed stars at the top of the visible world (*Conf.* 5; *Spec.* 3.185–87); sun in center of planets, moon at bottom (*Her.* 221–25); sun condensed ether (*Deus* 78); moon mixed ether (*Somn.* 1.145); (b) zone below the moon (*Opif.* 32–35; *Abr.* 44); air is black and is below the moon (*Somn.* 1.134; *Spec.* 1.94); clearly mixed with air (*Abr.* 205); subject to change (*Mos.* 2.121); (c) geocentric universe (*Leg.* 1.2; *Conf.* 5; *Mos.* 1.212), with the elements earth and water (*Mos.* 2.101, 120, 241); (d) two hemispheres, one above and one below the earth (*Spec.* 1.86); sun goes over and under the earth (*Leg.* 1.2); (e) the "deep" and waters (*Abr.* 42–44); (f) each region has a status: the ether is the most holy over the earth and lower regions (*Mos.* 1.217); (g) filled with life/souls in every part (*Gig.* 7; *Plant.* 14); (h) cf. *Congr.* 104. See **Corporeal World, Creation, Heaven.**

Courage: (a) spirited element (*thymos*) resides in the chest (*Spec.* 1.146); (b) Stoic definition: *Leg.* 1.68; *Spec.* 4.145; *Virt.* 1 (knowledge of what ought to be endured); (c) cf. *Deus* 164.

Creation: (a) treatises *On the Creation* and *On the Allegorical Laws* 1 discussions of creation stories; (b) goodness of God basis (*Opif.* 21); (c) everything created simultaneously; not in six literal days (*Opif.* 13, 26–28; *Leg.* 1.2, 20); (d) only one creation, one world (*Opif.* 171–72; *Abr.* 162); (e) order out of formless matter (*Mos.* 2.267; *Spec.* 2.151); (f) all matter used up (*Det.* 154; *Plant.* 5); (g) changeable (*Leg.* 2.33; *Ios.* 134; *Decal.* 58); (h) cf. *QG* 3.3; 4.8.

Custom: (a) habits become part of a person's nature (*Abr.* 185; *Ios.* 83); (b) in time stronger than nature (*Decal.* 137); (c) keep ancestral customs (*Deus* 17; *Mig.* 89–93; *Ios.* 202–3, 254; *Spec.* 1.3; 4.149).

Death: (a) not the end of the soul; separation from body and return to God (*Conf.* 36; *Abr.* 258); (b) comes to all (*Legat.* 192); (c) not to be feared (*Ios.* 129); (d) two kinds: of a person in general and of the soul in particular (*Leg.* 1.105–8; *Praem.* 70); (e) wicked dead though alive (*Fug.* 55, 61); (f) cf. *Abr.* 230; *Ios.* 23–27; *Mos.* 1.183.

Decalogue: (a) see treatises *On the Decalogue* and *On the Special Laws*; (b) ten headings summarizing the particular laws (*Congr.* 120; *Decal.* 19, 154; *Spec.* 1.1); (c) two sets of five: duties toward God, toward humanity (*Decal.* 50–51, 110, 121, 168); (d) rewards for keeping; punishments: first five— death (*Spec.* 2.242–62).

Democracy: (a) best of constitutions, based on equality, as opposed to mob rule (*Deus* 176; *Agr.* 45; *Conf.* 108–9; *Somn.* 2.224; *Abr.* 242; *Spec.* 4.238; *Virt.* 181).

Desire (*epithymia*): (a) worst passion (*Ebr.* 6; *Decal.* 142; *Spec.* 4.80, 85, 95); (b) cf. *Leg.* 3.149; *Abr.* 160; *Mos.* 2.186; *Decal.* 142–53, 173.

Determinism: (a) God acts; humans are acted upon (*Cher.* 77); (b) mind does not choose the good by itself (fragment of the lost *Allegorical Laws* volume; *Praem.* 54); (c) cf. *Aet.* 75; *QG* 1.100; 3.13. See also **Free Will.**

Diaspora Judaism: (a) Jews in Egypt, Phoenicia, Syria, Pampylia, Cilicia, most of Asia up to Bithynia, corners of Pontus, Thessaly, Boeotia, Macedonia, Aetolia, Attica, Argos, Corinth, much of Peloponnese, Euboea, Cyprus, Crete, countries beyond Euphrates, Lybia (*Flacc.* 45); (b) not required to go to Jerusalem, not less worthy (*Mos.* 2.229–32).

Divinity: (a) category of power, sovereignty, authority, and supremacy (*Conf.* 173; *Somn.* 1.157; *Spec.* 1.12, 19; *Prob.* 43; *Legat.* 76–85); (b) Moses named god of the nation, god over Pharaoh (*Leg.* 1.40; *Sacr.* 9; *Det.* 161; *Mos.* 1.27, 154); (c) the stars as gods (*Spec.* 1.16); (d) Caligula ungodlike in nature (*physis*), being (*ousia*), and purpose (*proairesis*) (*Legat.* 114); (d) parents visible (*Decal.* 120); humanity godlike (*Spec.* 3.83). See also **God.**

Dyad: (a) image of passive matter (*Spec.* 3.180); (b) cf. *Deus* 83; *Spec.* 1.180; *QG* 4.110.

Education/Culture (*paideia*): (a) Philo's education: *Cong.* 74–76; *Spec.* 2.229–30; (b) *encyclios paideia*, see **Preliminary Studies** in general, especially *Congr.* 9–19, 148; (c) cf. *Leg.* 1.14; 3.167, 244; *Cher.* 3–8, 105; *Agr.* 9, 18, 136–41; *Ebr.* 34–35, 49, 81; *Fug.* 183, 187; *Somn.* 1.205; *Mos.* 1.23; *Spec.* 1.336; 2.229–30; *Prob.* 136, 143.

Egyptians (as Contrasted with the Greek Alexandrians): (a) Egyptian religion (*Ios.* 254; *Mos.* 2.161, 194; *Decal.* 76–80; *Spec.* 2.146; *Legat.* 139); (b) cf. *Agr.* 62; *Abr.* 107; *Ios.* 204; *Spec.* 1.2–3; *Flacc.* 78–80, 92–93.

Elements, Four (or Five): (a) four elements: fire, air, earth, water: *Opif.* 52, 146; *Det.* 8; *Plant.* 120; *Her.* 140, 152, 281; *Congr.* 117; *Somn.* 1.16–24; 2.116; *Mos.* 1.96; *Decal.* 31, 53; *Spec.* 1.208; 2.151, 255; *Contempl.* 3; *Aet.* 25, 29, 107–9; *QG* 3.3; *QE* 2.118; heaven the fourth element (*Ebr.* 106; *Somn.* 1.23); (b) ether: a fifth element? (*Conf.* 156; *Her.* 283; *Somn.* 1.21; *Abr.* 162; *QG* 3.6; 4.8; (c) some have made into gods (*Decal.* 53).

Emotion: (a) should aim at moderation of feeling (*Abr.* 257) (Aristotle); (b) joy the best of the higher emotions (*Mig.* 157; *Mut.* 1, 131; *Praem.* 31, 50).

Encyclios Paideia. See **Education.**

Epistemology: (a) mind and the objects of sense occupy two extremes, with sense-perception in the middle (Stoic: *Congr.* 141; *Somn.* 2.17; *Spec.* 1.273); (b) categories of logic: substance, quality, quantity (*Fug.* 13; *Decal.*

30–31); (c) cf. *Opif.* 151, 172; *Leg.* 1.28–30; 2.37; 3.188; *Deus* 41–44; *Conf.* 127; *Abr.* 119, 162; *Praem.* 9.

Eschatology: (a) possible expectation of a messianic figure: *Mos.* 1.290; *Praem.* 91–97; (b) belief that the world will turn to God when nation prosperous (*Mos.* 2.43–44); (c) return of Jews from exile and establishment of their nation (*Praem.* 117, 164–65, 168–72); (d) God will rid the world of covetousness (*Mos.* 2.186).

> "Knowledge is a secure and firm apprehension, unchanged by argument" (*Congr.* 141).

Ether: (a) purest, holiest substance (*Mos.* 1.217; 2.154, although cf. 2.155); (b) located in heaven (*Spec.* 3.2, 185–87; *Praem.* 36–37); (c) soul a divine fragment of ether (*Leg.* 3.161); (d) cf. *Spec.* 4.236. See also **Elements, Heaven.**

***Ex Nihilo* Creation (relevant passages):** Cf. *Opif.* 7–12, 21, 23, 171–72; *Leg.* 3.10; *Plant.* 3; *Mig.* 183; *Somn.* 2.45; *Abr.* 75, 162; *Spec.* 1.266, 328–29; 4.187; *QE* 1.1.

Faith: (a) most perfect of virtues (*Her.* 91–95; *Abr.* 270); (b) cf. *Conf.* 31; *Mig.* 46; *Fug.* 150, 154; *Abr.* 262–74; *Mos.* 1.225; *Spec.* 4.30–34; *Praem.* 27–30, 49; *Virt.* 216.

Feasts, Jewish: (a) under heading of Fourth Commandment (*Decal.* 158–64; *Spec.* 2.41–223); (b) each month has a feast day (*Decal.* 161); (c) feast of every day (*Spec.* 2.42–55); (d) Sabbath as a feast (*Spec.* 2.56–139); (e) seventh year (*Decal.* 162; *Spec.* 2.71–109); (f) year of Jubilee (*Decal.* 164; *Spec.* 2.110–39); (g) new moon (*Spec.* 2.140–44); (h) Passover (*Mos.* 2.224; *Decal.* 159; *Spec.* 2.145–49); (i) Unleavened Bread (*Decal.* 161; *Spec.* 2.150–61); (j) "Sheaf" (*Decal.* 160; *Spec.* 2.162–75); (k) Pentecost, feast of Weeks, first fruits of wheat (*Decal.* 160; *Spec.* 2.176–87); (l) feast of Trumpets, or sacred month-day, commemorates giving of law (*Decal.* 159; *Spec.* 2.188–92); (m) Day of Atonement, the "Fast" (*Mos.* 2.23–24; *Decal.* 159; *Spec.* 2.193–203; 2.194; *Legat.* 306); (n) Tabernacles (*Flacc.* 116; *Spec.* 2.204–13); (o) "Basket," not technically a feast (*Spec.* 2.215–22).

Flesh: (a) enslaver of humanity by way of passions (*Abr.* 164); (b) cf. *Deus* 56; *Agr.* 25; *Fug.* 58; *QG* 1.90.

Fortune (*tychē*): (a) most unstable of things (*Gig.* 15; *Ios.* 140; *Mos.* 1.31; *Legat.* 1); (b) cf. *Prob.* 24.

Free Will: (a) mind alone free (*Deus* 47–48); (b) cf. *Abr.* 6; *Mut.* 241. See also **Determinism.**

Friendship: (a) proverb: "The belongings of friends are held in common" (*Abr.* 235; cf. *Mos.* 1.156); (b) a second self (*QG* 1.17); (c) cf. *Ios.* 210; *Spec.* 1.68.

God: (a) God exists and has always existed, unoriginate (*Opif.* 7–12, 170–72; *Leg.* 1.51; *Gig.* 42; *Ios.* 265; *Mos.* 2.65; *Decal.* 41, 60, 64); prior to the world (*Leg.* 2.3); invisible (*Mos.*

> "The human mind would not have dared to soar up to grasp the nature of God if God himself had not drawn it up to himself" (*Leg.* 1.38).

2.65; *Spec.* 1.20; *Legat.* 318); incorruptible (*Leg.* 1.51; *Ios.* 265; *Decal.* 41); eternal (*Decal.* 41, 60, 64; *Spec.* 1.20, 28); the highest and greatest power (*Mos.* 1.111); needs no one/nothing (*Leg.* 2.2; 3.181; *Deus* 7; *Mos.* 1.111, 157; *Decal.* 41; *Spec.* 1.152, 277); simple, not composite being (*Deus* 55); (b) God is one, not many gods (*Opif.* 171–72; *Leg.* 1.51; *Mos.* 2.168; *Virt.* 35); unique (*Leg.* 2.1); God of gods (*Spec.* 1.20); nature is simple, not composite (*Leg.* 2.2; *Mut.* 184); (c) God is "he who is" (*ho ōn*) or "that which is" (*to on*) or who "truly is" (*ho ontōs ōn*) (*Leg.* 3.37–38, 181; *Det.* 160–61; *Post.* 2; *Gig.* 52; *Deus* 4, 11; *Agr.* 52, 171; *Ebr.* 43; *Conf.* 65; *Her.* 229; *Congr.* 8; *Mut.* 7; *Somn.* 2.227; *Abr.* 121; *Mos.* 1.75, 2.67, 100, 132; *Decal.* 8, 59, 81; *Spec.* 1.28, 31, 53, 65, 309, 331–32; 4.192; *Virt.* 34; *Praem.* 27; *Prob.* 43; *Legat.* 6, 347); (d) has other potencies: chiefly the creative called "God" (*theos*) and the royal called "Lord" (*kyrios*) (*Abr.* 121–22; *Mos.* 2.99; *Decal.* 176; *Spec.* 1.307; *Legat.* 6); **see also Potencies of God**; (e) Monad, the One (*Deus* 11; *Spec.* 1.66, 313, 331; *Virt.* 34, 40, 214); good in its most perfect form (*Conf.* 18–20); nature at its best (*Fug.* 172); the standard for the Monad (*Leg.* 2.3); (f) needs no name—no name can properly be used of him (*Her.* 170; *Mut.* 11; *Abr.* 51; *Mos.* 1.75); known only by revelation, as he is inscrutable (*Post.* 15; *Her.* 229; *Mut.* 7–10; *Abr.* 80; *Praem.* 43–46). *Legat.* 6); can know *that* God is (his existence) but not *what* he is (his essence) (*Deus* 62; *Fug.* 164–65; *Somn.* 1.61–67, 230; *Spec.* 1.32–50; *Praem.* 39–40); surpassing everything/"transcendent" (*Opif.* 8: better than virtue, better than knowledge, better than the good itself and the beautiful itself; *Decal.* 52; better than the Monad, than the One, *Praem.* 40; better than the good, purer than the One, older than the Monad, *Contempl.* 2); nothing is higher than God (*Abr.* 58); Moses sees what he can (*Fug.* 41); (g) "First Cause" (*Leg.* 1.20; 3.7; 2.46–47; *Conf.* 124; *Fug.* 161–65; *Somn.* 1.92; *Decal.* 155), the oldest cause (*Spec.* 1.31); source/maker of all things (*Leg.* 3.29; *Her.* 36; *Decal.* 41, 52, 64; *Spec.* 1.20, 30; *Legat.* 3); created through his potencies, since he could not touch chaotic, formless matter (*Conf.* 179; *Spec.* 1.328–29); only truly active, truly free force (*Cher.* 77; *Somn.* 2.253); cause only of good things (*Deus* 87, 107; *Conf.* 180; *Abr.* 143); all things come into being by God's power, but only the most excellent things both by his power and his agency (*Leg.* 1.41); punishes through potencies (*Leg.* 3.177–78; *Conf.* 180–82; *Fug.* 66, 79; *Abr.* 133; *Decal.* 178); (h) does not exist in a place: he is his own place; world could not contain him (*Leg.* 1.44); world is his city (*Somn.* 2.248); unseen (*Spec.*

1.20); perceived by the understanding alone (*Spec.* 1.20); everywhere present (*Leg.* 3.4; *Post.* 6, 14; *Conf.* 136); his Spirit cannot stay too long in a human soul (*Gig.* 19, 28); divine Spirit is wisdom (*Gig.* 23); (i) mind of the universe (*Opif.* 8); the soul of the universe (*Leg.* 1.91); archetype and pattern of the laws (*Spec.* 1.279); model of a model (*Somn.* 1.75); (j) everything subject to God (*Mos.* 1.201); king of kings, God of gods (*Congr.* 116; *Decal.* 41, 155; *Spec.* 1.307), ruler of the world-city (*Decal.* 53), pilot/charioteer who steers everything (*Somn.* 1.157; *Decal.* 53, 60); the good shepherd (*Agr.* 44, 49–51); the monarch of the world (*Spec.* 1.12); (k) cares for the creation (*Opif.* 171–72) and humanity (*Abr.* 137; *Flacc.* 102); shields the wronged (*Deus* 76; *Abr.* 96; *Mos.* 1.101); champion of the just (*Abr.* 232; *Legat.* 336); loves to give and gives good things to all (*Leg.* 1.34; *Mos.* 2.61; *Spec.* 2.180); watches over all things with justice (*Legat.* 336); compassionate (*Flacc.* 102); gracious (*Leg.* 3.78; *Spec.* 1.43); patron (*Leg.* 3.31); God of providence (*Ebr.* 199; *Conf.* 114–15; *Ios.* 236; *Mos.* 1.12, 67; *Decal.* 58; *Spec.* 1.209; 3.121; *Aet.* 47; treatise *On Providence*); suggests good decisions (*Legat.* 245); makes his will easy (*Mos.* 1.19); his goodness holds everything together (*Deus* 108; *Mos.* 2.132–33, 238); father (*Ios.* 265); graciousness extends to remorseful (*Spec.* 1.242), although not absolute (*Spec.* 2.23, 253); sets pardon before punishment (*Spec.* 2.196); savior (*Ios.* 194; *Spec.* 1.272); author of salvation (*Cher.* 130; *Spec.* 1.252); good (*Opif.* 21; *Sacr.* 53; *Post.* 21); gives only good things (*Agr.* 129, 173; *QG* 3.3); source of all virtue (*Virt.* 55); source of life (*Fug.* 197–98); only absolutely sinless (*Fug.* 157; *Virt.* 177); cannot be the cause of evil (*Opif.* 75); prince of peace (*Decal.* 178); he himself is the good (*Spec.* 2.53); (l) helps the Jews and their nation, defending them against those who might do them wrong (*Flacc.* 116, 170, 191); (m) foreknows (*Opif.* 45); all-knowing (*Opif.* 149; *Leg.* 3.88; *Deus* 29, 72; *Her.* 15; *Fug.* 136; *Mos.* 2.217); in eternal now (*Deus* 32); cannot be deceived (*Mos.* 1.283); sees and hears everything (*Cher.* 17; *Ios.* 265; *Decal.* 90; *Virt.* 57, 172); alone can scan the soul (*Abr.* 104; *Spec.* 3.52); his wisdom is holy (*Fug.* 196, 202); (n) cannot suffer injury (*Abr.* 127); is without fear or passion (*Deus* 52; *Abr.* 202); cannot change (*Leg.* 1.51; 2.33, 89; *Cher.* 19; *Deus*; *Conf.* 96; *Somn.* 2.221) or change his mind (*Mos.* 1.283); without error (*Conf.* 115); his word is his deed (*Mos.* 1.283; 2.61; *Decal.* 47) (o) all things possible for God (*Abr.* 175; *Ios.* 244; *Mos.* 174; *Virt.* 26); (p) rejoicing most closely associated with God (*Cher.* 86; *Abr.* 202; *Spec.* 2.54–55); alone partakes of perfect happiness and blessedness (*Abr.* 202; *Spec.* 2.53); (q) never rests, never stops making (*Leg.* 1.5–6; *Cher.* 87–90); father of those things coming into existence (*Leg.* 1.18); (r) could sooner change into a man than a man into God (*Legat.* 118); (s) does not have physicality such as mouth, tongue, or windpipe (*Decal.* 32); (t) argument from design (*Leg.* 3.98–99; *Deus* 30; *Praem.* 42). See also **Divinity, Powers**.

Godliness (*eusebeia*): (a) highest and greatest of virtues (*Abr.* 60; but see *Abr.* 27; *Spec.* 4.135, 147; *Praem.* 53); (b) cf. *Opif.* 155, 172; *Det.* 21; *Plant.* 77; *Fug.* 150; *Somn.* 2.186; *Abr.* 114, 208, 235; *Mos.* 2.66; *Decal.* 52, 119; *Spec.* 1.100, 257–345.

> "Nothing is more effortless than godliness" (*Abr.* 171).

Golden Mean. See Moderation.

Good, the: (a) moral beauty the only good (so Plato: *Ebr.* 200; *Sobr.* 60, 62; *Conf.* 185; *Somn.* 2.9); (b) against Aristotle's three goods (external, bodily, soul): *Det.* 7–9; *Ebr.* 200; *Sobr.* 67; *Fug.* 19, 148; *Somn.* 2.9; *Virt.* 15, 187; but cf. *Her.* 285–86; *QG* 3.16; (c) against Epicurus's pleasure as prime good (*Fug.* 148).

Good Life (*to eu zēn*). See Happiness.

Government: bad forms of government: oligarchy, mob rule (*Agr.* 45–48; *Decal.* 155; *Virt.* 181). See also **Democracy.**

Happiness (*eudaimonia*): (a) Platonic: the goal of happiness to become like God (*Fug.* 63; *Decal.* 73, 81;

> "Happiness is the exercise and enjoyment of virtue" (*Det.* 60).

Spec. 1.31, 345; 4.73; *Virt.* 168; *Praem.* 30); (b) Stoic: to live in accordance with nature (*Praem.* 11; *Prob.* 160); (c) rejected Aristotle's three goods for happiness: *Det.* 7; *Fug.* 19, 148; *Somn.* 2.9; *Virt.* 15, 187; but cf. *Her.* 285–86; *QG* 3.16; also need for food, *Congr.* 33; appropriate laws and commandments, *Decal.* 17; (d) good life to serve God: *Virt.* 221; cf. *Deus* 118; *Agr.* 25; *Spec.* 1.339; 2.229; (e) knowledge the source; ignorance the source of unhappiness (*Legat.* 69; *Praem.* 81); (f) balance of three parts of the soul (*Virt.* 13); (g) two best lives: practical and contemplative (*Leg.* 1.57–58; *Mig.* 47; *Fug.* 36; *Mos.* 1.48; *Decal.* 101; *Spec.* 2.64; *Praem.* 11; see also the treatise *On the Contemplative Life*); contemplative the better (*Contempl.* 67); Essenes reflect the active, practical life of virtue (*Contempl.* 1, cf. *Prob.* 75–91; *Hypoth.* 11.1–18), Therapeutae the contemplative, theoretical (*Contempl.* 1, 21–90); (h) absolute happiness impossible, *Mut.* 36; (h) cf. *Sacr.* 47; *Post.* 185; *Agr.* 157; *Abr.* 201–4; *Mos.* 2.212; *QG* 3.4.

Heaven: (a) best of created things (*Opif.* 27; *Congr.* 50; *Praem.* 1; *QG* 4.87); position of dignity among objects of sense (*Opif.* 37); purest portion of the universe (along with air; *Opif.* 55; *Spec.* 1.34; *Mos.* 1.113, *Decal.* 155; *Spec.* 4.235), palace of highest sanctity (*Mos.* 2.194); (b) location of the "visible and perceptible gods" (*Opif.* 27); (c) world within the world (*Abr.* 159); like the soul in the body (*Abr.* 272); (d) two spheres: outermost (fixed stars), innermost (planets) (*Cher.* 21–24); (e) heaven known to thought alone, like the heaven of heaven (*Spec.* 1.302), where things discerned by the mind are located (*Leg.* 1.1); (f) cf. *Opif.* 36, 112; *Ios.* 146; *Decal.* 57, 104; *Spec.* 1.89.

High Priest: (a) Moses the most perfect one (*Mos.* 2.66–187); (b) vestures of Jewish high priest had representations of the universe and its parts (*Mos.* 2.117, 143; *Spec.* 1.82–97); he takes the universe with him into the sanctuary (*Mos.* 2.133); (c) prays for the whole human race and also all of nature (*Spec.* 1.97); (d) cf. *Spec.* 1.113, 230.

Homosexual Sex: (a) Sodom and Gomorrah (*Abr.* 135); (b) Caligula engaged in it with boys at times (*Legat.* 14); (c) cf. *Spec.* 1.325; 2.50; 3.37–42.

Hope: (a) dearest possession of the human soul (*Abr.* 8), the first step toward blessing (*Abr.* 7); the best of nourishments (*Ios.* 113); (b) cf. *Abr.* 7–16.

Hospitality: (a) law to show respect to strangers (*Abr.* 94); (b) cf. *Abr.* 107–18.

Household: (a) fifth "word" of the ten words deals with relations of old to young, rulers to subjects, benefactors to benefited, slaves to masters (*Decal.* 165); (b) husbands teach wives the law; fathers teach children; masters teach slaves (*Hypoth.* 7.14).

Human, Ideal: (a) man of Genesis 1:27 (*Opif.* 25), a heavenly prototype (*Leg.* 1.31–32); (b) created "according to the image of God [= the *logos*]" (*Opif.* 25, 69; *Leg.* 1.31; 2.4; *Spec.* 3.84, 207); image and likeness in terms of the human mind (*Opif.* 69); rational spirit in us formed according to the archetypal idea of the divine image (*Spec.* 1.171); cf. *Fug.* 71; (c) both male *and* female (*Opif.* 76, 134).

Human, Molded, Physical: (a) creation of molded man in Genesis 2:7 (*Opif.* 134–35; *Leg.* 2.4), a different man from the one created according to the image of God in Genesis 1:27 (double creation scheme), earthly as opposed to the heavenly man of Genesis 1:27 (*Leg.* 1.31–32; *Plant.* 44; *QG* 1.4); (b) borderline between mortal and immortal nature (*Opif.* 135).

Humans: (a) best of living creations (*Opif.* 68, 136; *Somn.* 1.108; *Decal.* 134; *Spec.* 2.84, 173; *Praem.* 1); (b) king of all creatures under the moon (*Opif.* 84); driver, pilot of all things (*Opif.* 88); (c) purpose: to complete the world (*Somn.* 2.116); (d) physical body a sacred temple for the rational soul (*Opif.* 137); (e) Adam the best, those after increasingly less (*Opif.* 136–50); (f) should know him- or herself (*Spec.* 1.10, 44, 263).

Idolatry: (a) against the Jewish religion (*Legat.* 290); (b) condemnation: *Mos.* 2.161–73, 205; *Spec.* 1.21–27.

Immortality: (a) for virtuous, afterlife is upward in heaven (*Gig.* 14; *Mos.* 2.291; *Spec.* 4.112); given to the soul that offers sacrifice with a pure and just heart (or even if no victim is even brought [*Mos.* 2.108]; for Moses, resolution of soul and body into a single entity *Mos.* 2.288) or disuniting of elements (*Virt.* 205), although his body is buried (*Mos.* 2.291); (b) incorporeal (*Gig.* 14); (c) cf. *Leg.* 2.57; *Conf.* 149; *Her.* 239; *Fug.* 55–57; *Somn.* 1.181, 218; *Spec.* 1.303, 345; 2.124; 4.14; *Virt.* 9, 14, 67, 76; *Praem.* 110; *Aet.* 46; *Legat.* 371; *QG* 1.85. See also **Afterlife.**

Impressions (*phantasiai*): (a) "imprint made on soul" (*Deus* 43); (b) first impressions bound to be poor reflections of reality (*Mos.* 1.230); (c) cf. *Leg.* 1.30; *QG* 3.3.

Incorporeal World of Ideas: pattern/archetype/ideal (*paradeigma, archetypos, noētē idea*), discerned by mind or soul, that is the template behind the world (*Opif.* 16; *Mos.* 2.127); (b) cf. *Opif.* 16–28; *Her.* 280; *Mos.* 2.74; *Spec.* 1.327–29; *QG* 2.4; *QE* 2.57.

Inspiration: (a) inspiration of a prophet, dictation theory (*Mos.* 2.246–91; *Spec.* 4.49); (b) translators of the Septuagint inspired (*Mos.* 2.37); (c) Philo's (*Cher.* 27; *Spec.* 3.1; *QG* 4.140); (d) cf. *Deus* 4, 139; *Conf.* 44; *Mig.* 34–35; *Her.* 46, 64, 259–65; *Somn.* 2.172; *Mos.* 1.210; 277.

> "The world discerned by the mind is nothing other than the word of God already in the act of making the world" (*Opif.* 24).

Israel: (a) nation dearest to God (*Abr.* 98); destined to be victorious over its opponents in war (*Mos.* 1.217); national zeal (*Mos.* 1.303–4; 2.43–44); (b) priests on behalf of humanity (*Abr.* 56, 98; *Mos.* 1.149); (c) the nations would adopt the Jewish law if the nation were only more prosperous (*Mos.* 2.43–44); (d) cf. *Mos.* 1.186; *Legat.* 4. See also **Jewish Identity.**

Jewish Identity: (a) importance of Jerusalem and its temple (*Legat.* 156, 212, 216, 312); (b) special privileges in empire (*Legat.* 156, 311); (c) importance of customs, keeping law (*Deus* 17; *Mig.* 89–94; *Ios.* 202–3, 254; *Spec.* 1.3; 4.149; *Legat.* 361–62); (d) cf. *Mos.* 1.241.

Jewish Law: (a) most excellent, truly from God; (b) revered by nations (*Mos.* 2.12–44); nations would adopt if nation were prosperous (*Mos.* 2.43–44); (c) have remained unchanged (*Mos.* 2.14–16); (d) story of Septuagint (*Mos.* 2.25–44).

Joy: (a) two kinds: unmixed, which pertains to God alone; the mixed, for the wise person (*Spec.* 2.55); (b) best of the higher emotions (*Mig.* 157; *Mut.* 1, 131; *Praem.* 31, 50).

Justice (*dikē; dikaiosunē*): (a) chief of the virtues (*Abr.* 27; but see *Abr.* 60); wisdom, courage, and self-control working in harmony (*Leg.* 1.72); (b) cf.

Congr. 90; *Abr.* 27–46; *Ios.* 170; *Decal.* 95; *Spec.* 3.19; 4.231; *Praem.* 22; *Flacc.* 104, 107, 146.

Kings: imitate the divine nature (*Abr.* 144); (b) shepherds of their people (*Ios.* 2–3; *Mos.* 1.61–62; *Legat.* 44); (c) best if philosophers (*Mos.* 2.2); (d) *Flacc.* 4; *Legat.* 51, 69.

Law: (a) creation is in accordance with (*Opif.* 3; *Spec.* 2.13); (b) lives of the patriarchs embody it/are originals (*archetypoi*) of specific laws, which are like copies (*eikones*) (*Abr.* 3); (c) must include two provisions: honors for the good and punishment for evil; (d) cf. *Legat.* 7, 241.

> "Some say, not off the mark, that states only progress toward wellness when the kings philosophize or the philosophers rule" (*Mos.* 2.2).

Logic. See **Epistemology**.

Logos **(Divine Reason, Word):** (a) basic definitions, thought and word (Stoic: *Mig.* 71; *QE* 2.110–11); (b) first creation, firstborn, eldest son, angel (*Leg.* 2.86; 3.175; *Sacr.* 119; *Agr.* 51; *Conf.* 62, 146–47; *Her.* 205–6; *QE* 2.117; (c) shadow/image of God (*Leg.* 3.96; *Somn.* 1.239), wisdom of God (*Leg.* 1.65; *Fug.* 97, 137), second god (*Leg.* 3.81; *Somn.* 1.228; *QG* 2.62; 3.34); (d) directs universe, governs, shepherds, steers, charioteer of world (*Leg.* 3.118, 128, 137; *Mig.* 6; *Agr.* 51; *Somn.* 1.241; *QG* 4.110); holds everything together (*Cher.* 27–28; *Plant.* 9; *Her.* 188; *Fug.* 112; *Mos.* 2.133), seeks justice, surveys everything (*Leg.* 3.171, 177–78; *Ios.* 174), surveys all things (*Leg.* 3.171); (e) ideal archetype/location of the ideas (*Opif.* 20, 25; *Fug.* 12; *Somn.* 2.45; *QG* 1.4), wears world (*Fug.* 110); (f) agent, instrument of creation (*Leg.* 1.19–21; *Cher.* 127; *Sacr.* 8; *Deus* 57; *Plant.* 18; *Her.* 135–40; *Spec.* 1.81); divider or cutter (*Her.* 119–32); image of God according to whose image the ideal man was made (*Opif.* 25, 69; *Leg.* 1.31; *Det.* 83; *Conf.* 41; *Plant.* 20; *Spec.* 3.84, 207); (g) anagogical function, priest/high priest (*Leg.* 3.82, 207–8; *Cher.* 17; *Sacr.* 51; *Gig.* 52; *Ebr.* 65; *Conf.* 97, 145–47; *Mig.* 102; *Her.* 185; *Somn.* 1.215; *QE* 2.68); (h) as angel: *Cher.* 35; *Agr.* 51. See also ***Logos* Seeds**.

***Logos* Seeds:** cf. *Leg.* 3.150; *QE* 2.90.

Man. See **Human**.

Marriage: (a) purpose the birth of children (*Abr.* 248); (b) betrothal: cf. *Agr.* 52; (c) monogamy presumed (*Congr.* 34; *Abr.* 253); (d) intermarriage a bond between unconnected households (*Legat.* 72).

Mind: (a) God, the mind of the universe (*Opif.* 8); (b) ruler of the human body and soul (*Opif.* 30, 53, 69; *Leg.* 1.39–40; 2.6; *Fug.* 182; *Somn.* 1.77; 2.207; *Abr.* 57; *Mos.* 2.82; *Spec.* 1.18; *Prob.* 146); (c) heavenly element, soul of the soul (*Opif.* 66; *Gig.* 60; *Deus* 46; *Plant.* 18; *Congr.* 97; *Somn.* 1.34, 146;

Spec. 3.207); copy (*ekmageion*), fragment (*apospasma*), ray (*apaugasma*) of divine nature (*Opif.* 146); a likeness (*apeikonisma*) and copy (*mimēma*) of the eternal and happy idea (*idea*) (*Decal.* 134); copy of *logos* (*Praem.* 163); (d) able to soar to heaven to contemplate the incorporeal patterns (*Opif.* 71; *Deus* 45); (e) cf. *Opif.* 73; *Virt.* 188; *Legat.* 21.

Moderation: (a) moderation of passions for the person progressing in virtue (*Leg.* 3.132–34, 144; *Virt.* 195); (b) golden mean (*Deus* 164); (c) cf. *Ios.* 26, 205, 221; *Mos.* 1.160.

Monad: (a) incorporeal image (*asōmatos eikōn*) of God the first cause (*Spec.* 2.176; 3.180); God the standard for, older than the Monad (*Leg.* 2.3; *Praem.* 40); (b) source of other numbers (*Her.* 190); (c) basis for contemplation (*Gig.* 52); (d) cf. *Deus* 82; *Spec.* 1.180; *QG* 4.110. See also **God.**

Moses: (a) *De Vita Mosis* treats Moses as king (esp. 1.148–334), legislator (2.8–65), high priest (2.66–186), and prophet (2.187–291); (b) greatest, most perfect person (*Mos.* 1.1); spirit the purest of spirits (*Mos.* 2.40); holiest of all humans ever born (*Mos.* 2.192); (c) consummate philosopher (*Opif.* 8); (d) Greek philosophers took their best ideas from him (*Leg.* 1.108; *Her.* 214; *Prob.* 57; *Aet.* 18–19); (e) cf. *Mos.* 1.158, 162.

Mysteries/"Mystical" Passages: (a) distinction between major and minor (*Cher.* 48–49; *Sacr.* 62; *Mos.* 1.62; *QG* 4.110); inappropriate to participate in them (*Spec.* 1.319–23); (b) translators of Septuagint like prophets and priests of the mysteries (*Mos.* 2.40); (c) imagery: *Leg.* 3.3, 27, 100, 173; *Cher.* 12, 31, 48–49; *Ebr.* 129; *Sobr.* 20; *Deus* 61; *Her.* 249; *Fug.* 85; *Somn.* 2.78; *Mos.* 1.27; 2.71, 153, 201; *Decal.* 35, 41; *Spec.* 1.207; *Virt.* 178; *Praem.* 27, 30, 36–37, 62, 121; *Prob.* 14; *Legat.* 5, 366; *QG* 4.8. See also **Contemplation.**

Nature/Natural Law: (a) world in harmony with the law (*Opif.* 3); universal in scope (*Agr.* 43); (b) governs human and divine with justice (*Spec.* 2.231), has foreknowledge of things (*Leg.* 1.28); (c) cf. *Spec.* 2.42; 4.46, 232.

Number: (a) subsequent to creation (*Leg.* 2.3); (b) one: pertains to incorporeal world, represented in Genesis by day one (*Opif.* 35); see also **Monad;** (c) two: image (*eikōn*) of matter (*Leg.* 1.3); see also **Dyad;** (d) three: cf. *Leg.* 1.3; *Abr.* 121–30); (e) four: cf. *Opif.* 47–52; *Plant.* 117–25; *Abr.* 12–14; (f) five: number of the senses: sight, hearing, taste, smell, touch (*Opif.* 62); (g) six: perfect number; cf. *Opif.* 13–14; *Leg.* 1.3–4; (h) seven: cf. *Opif.* 89–128; *Leg.* 1.5–18; *Decal.* 102–5; *Spec.* 2.56; seventh day the festival of creation (*Opif.* 89); motherless, ever-virgin, birthday of world (*Mos.* 210; *Decal.* 102; *Spec.* 2.56); seven planets (*Leg.* 1.8); seven months of pregnancy before birth (*Leg.* 1.9); stages of human growth (in seven-year blocks, according to Solon): teeth, fertility, beard, strength, marriage, understanding, improvement of mind and reason, perfection of mind and reason, taming of the passions, end of life (*Opif.* 103–4; cf. *Leg.* 1.10); seven periods of life: little boy, boy, lad, young man, man, elderly man, old man (*Opif.* 105); seven zones of heaven: arctic, antarctic, summer solstice, winter solstice, equinox, zodiac, and Milky Way (*Opif.* 112); seven parts to the unreasoning soul: the five senses, faculty of speech, and generation, all controlled by the understanding (*Opif.* 117; *Leg.* 1.11–12, but cf. *Abr.* 28–30); seven visible parts of a body, seven inside parts (*Opif.* 119; *Leg.* 1.12); first cubic number, marking the transition from conceptual to solid (*Spec.* 2.212); (i) ten: cf. *Congr.* 89–110; *Decal.* 20–31; number of the *logos* (*Abr.* 244); contains every kind of number, ratio, and progression (*Decal.* 23), as well as shape (*Decal.* 24); number of the categories (*Decal.* 30).

Paideia. See **Education.**

Passions (*pathē*): (a) Stoic definition: irrational and unnatural movement of soul (*Spec.* 4.79); (b) four passions: pleasure (*ēdonē*), desire (*epithymia*), fear (*phobos*), and grief (*lypē*) (*Leg.* 2.8, 99, 102; 3.113, 139, 250; *Det.* 119; *Agr.* 83; *Her.* 269–70; *Congr.* 92; *Abr.* 236; *Decal.* 143–46; *Spec.* 2.30; 4.113; *Praem.* 71; *Prob.* 18, 159); (c) best extirpated from soul (*Leg.* 3.25, 129–32; *Agr.* 10, 17; *Somn.* 2.270; *Spec.* 4.55; *Prob.* 17, 107); the person progressing toward virtue moderates (*Leg.* 3.132–34, 144; *Virt.* 195); (d) generally negative: cf. *Leg.* 2.50–52, 90, 106; 3.113; *Congr.* 60; *Abr.* 164; *Ios.* 5; *Spec.* 2.30, 46; 4.79; *Praem.* 17, 159; *Legat.* 114; *QG* 2.25, 39; but cf. *Leg.* 2.5.

Peace: (a) gift no human can bestow (*Mos.* 1.304); (b) comes from right government (*Legat.* 68); (c) better than war (*Spec.* 4.221); in peace prepare for war (*Virt.* 153).

Pederasty: cf. *Decal.* 168; *Spec.* 2.50; 3.37–42; *Contempl.* 61; *QG* 4.38.

Perfection: (a) as completion (*Fug.* 115, 170–72); (b) distinction between relative and absolute (*Abr.* 36); (c) cf. *Deus* 13, 26; *Sacr.* 7–8, 83; *Agr.* 42, 158–68; *Plant.* 82, 93–94; *Ebr.* 51; *Conf.* 72; *Mig.* 73; *Her.* 121; *Congr.* 138; *Mut.* 270; *Somn.* 1.131, 213; 2.234; *QG* 4.133.

Philosophy: (a) definitions: the pursuit of wisdom (*Congr.* 79); to seek to know all reality accurately (*Conf.* 97; *Congr.* 144); (b) servant of wisdom (*Congr.* 79); (c) three branches: logic, ethics, physics (*Leg.* 1.57; *Agr.* 14–16; *Mut.* 75–76; *Virt.* 8; *Prob.* 80); (d) cf. *Opif.* 54; *Leg.* 3.72; *Post.* 101–2; *Abr.* 163; *Spec.* 3.185–91; *QG* 4.167).

> "Philosophy is the pursuit of wisdom" (*Congr.* 79).

Piety. See **Godliness.**

Pleasure (*ēdonē*): (a) origins explained (*Decal.* 143); (b) negative: *Opif.* 152; *Leg.* 3.61–64, 68; 109–12; *Deus* 143; *Spec.* 3.8; (c) best removed (*Post.* 164; *Spec.* 1.9).

Politician (*politicus*): (a) an addition to life according to nature (*Ios.* 31); (b) three characteristics: shepherding, household management, self-control (*Ios.* 54); (c) positive: *Fug.* 33–35 (anti-Cynic), 126; cf. *On Joseph*; (d) negative: *On Dreams*.

Polity (*politeia*): (a) the ordering of the state should mirror the well-ordered household (*Ios.* 38; cf. *Fug.* 36); (b) attitudes toward Romans: *Somn.* 2.43; *Flaccus*, *Embassy*; (c) cf. *Leg.* 3.3; *Det.* 134; *Somn.* 2.154; *Ios.* 31, 32, 38. See also **Democracy, World-City.**

Potencies or Powers of God (*dynameis*): (a) most comprehensive enumerations: *Fug.* 94–105; *QE* 2.68; (b) two chief: creative power "God" (*theos*) and royal one "Lord" (*kyrios*) (*Sacr.* 59; *Plant.* 85–86; *Conf.* 137; *Her.* 165; *Mut.* 15–38; *Somn.* 1.163, 185; *Abr.* 121–22; *Mos.* 2.99; *Decal.* 176; *Spec.* 1.307; *Legat.* 6; *QG* 1.57; 2.75; 3.39; 4.2, 8); (c) also beneficent, punitive (*Her.* 312); other powers (*Sacr.* 131–32; *Mut.* 14; *QE* 1.23; 2.68); numberless (*Conf.* 171); (d) unknowable in essence (*Mut.* 15; *Spec.* 1.45–50); (e) created world, judges through them (*Leg.* 3.177–78; *Conf.* 172; *Spec.* 1.328–29); angels serve them (*Spec.* 1.66); (f) cf. *Leg.* 3.73; *Cher.* 27–31; *Deus* 109–10; *Somn.* 2.254; *Spec.* 1.45.

Prayer and Supplication: (a) path to God's mercy (*Abr.* 6); (b) cf. *Deus* 156; *Agr.* 100; *Legat.* 336.

Prophecy: (a) discovers what the mind and reasoning cannot grasp (*Mos.* 2.6, 187; *Spec.* 4.49); (b) three kinds of divine oracles (*Mos.*

> "Prayer is a petition for good things" (*Agr.* 100).

2.188–91): those spoken directly by God (cf. lost first treatise *On Dreams*), those given in answer to a question (cf. the existing *On Dreams* 1), those understood through the faculty of an individual (cf. *On Dreams* 2); (c) cf. *Somn.* 1.2; *Spec.* 1.65, 315–18.

Proselytism: cf. *Mos.* 1.147; *Spec.* 1.51–52, 310; *Praem.* 152; *Legat.* 211; *QE* 2.2.

Reason, Divine. See *Logos*.

Repentance: (a) on road to perfection (*Abr.* 17–26); (b) cf. *Leg.* 3.213; *Fug.* 157–60; *Spec.* 1.102–3, 187; *Praem.* 15–16.

Sabbath: (a) days of training in the "ancestral philosophy" (*Mos.* 2.215–16; *Decal.* 97–101; *Spec.* 2.62; *Legat.* 156); (b) cf. *Somn.* 2.123; *Mos.* 1.205–7; 2.21–22; 70, 209–20, 263–69; *Decal.* 96–105; *Spec.* 2.65–70; *Contempl.* 30–33; *Prob.* 81; *Hypoth.* 7.10–20. See also **Synagogue.**

Sacrifices: (a) appropriate intent necessary (*Plant.* 108, 164; *Mos.* 2.106–8, 162, 279; *Spec.* 1.215); (b) result in immortality—even if no victim is brought

(*Mos.* 2.106–8, 162); (c) two purposes: give thanks for blessings or ask for pardon and forgiveness (*Spec.* 1.67, 195, 283–84); (d) when offered: daily sacrifice—one lamb at dawn, one at dusk (*Spec.* 1.169, 171); daily for the emperor (*Legat.* 157); (e) three types (*Spec.* 1.194–97): whole burnt offering (*Spec.* 1.196, 198–211); health or preservation offering (*Spec.* 1.196, 212–25); sin offering, for remission of sins (*Spec.* 1.190, 196, 226–33); (f) animals (three kinds—ox, sheep, goat): *Spec.* 1.162–93; 2.35; (g) cf. *Spec.* 1.168, 190, 271, 277, 287, 290; 2.35; *Legat.* 156.

Self-Control: (a) (*enkrateia*) rewarded by strength and health (*Legat.* 14); lack (*akrasia*) leads to sickness and disease, almost death; (b) cf. *Leg.* 1.69; *Somn.* 1.124; *Contempl.* 34.

Senses (*aisthēsis*): (a) necessary, potentially helpful (*Leg.* 2.5; *Congr.* 21, 96; *Fug.* 45), but prone to error (*Ios.* 142; *Legat.* 2); neither good nor bad (*Leg.* 3.67); (b) instruments of pleasure (*Abr.* 147); cf. *Opif.* 139; *Leg.* 1.24, 39; *Congr.* 21; *Decal.* 147; (c) five: sight, the best, noblest of the senses (*Opif.* 53, 120; *Deus* 45; *Fug.* 208; *Abr.* 57; *Mos.* 1.124; *Contempl.* 10), most closely associated with the soul (*Abr.* 150–59); hearing, inferior to sight but link with philosophy (*Abr.* 150, 160); three most animal—taste, smell, and touch (*Abr.* 149, 160); See also **Allegory of the Soul.**

Sex: (a) only for procreation (*Ios.* 43; *Mos.* 1.28; 2.68–69; *Spec.* 3.34–36; *Praem.* 108); (b) hindrance to the soul's purity and ability to prophesy (*Mos.* 2.69); (c) Jewish men and women mate as virgins (*Ios.* 43; cf. *Spec.* 3.65; (d) illicit sex: adultery (*Spec.* 3.8–11); with mothers (*Spec.* 3.12–19); with stepmothers (*Spec.* 3.20–21); with sisters (*Spec.* 3.22–25); other relations (*Spec.* 3.26–28); bestiality (*Spec.* 3.43–45); prostitution (*Spec.* 3.51). See also **Homosexual Sex, Pederasty.**

Sin: (a) deliberate sin the basis of culpability (*Decal.* 141); (b) culpable for unintentional sins? (*Leg.* 1.35; cf. *Spec.* 1.238); different sacrificial atonement for voluntary and involuntary sin (*Spec.* 1.227); basic distinction: *Post.* 11; *Deus* 128, 134; *Agr.* 176–80; *Spec.* 2.196; *QG* 4.63; (c) intrinsic to creation (*Mos.* 2.147); all persons sin (*Deus* 75; *Spec.* 1.252; but cf. *Abr.* 6; *Mos.* 2.59); (d) sacrifices effective on basis of attitude, no victim even necessary (*Mos.* 2.107–8); (e) cf. *Deus* 84; *Spec.* 4.181. See also **Atonement.**

> "Pardon is given to one who does wrong due to ignorance of the better course of action, but the one who does wrong knowingly has no defense" (*Flacc.* 7).

Slavery: (a) no person is naturally a slave, especially a good person (Stoic idea) (*Spec.* 2.69; cf. *Spec.* 3.137–43; *That Every Good Person Is Free*); (b) sometimes necessary (*Spec.* 2.123); (c) cf. *Congr.* 175; *Virt.* 111; *Praem.* 137; *Prob.* 79; *Contempl.* 70; *Legat.* 119.

Sophists: cf. *Opif.* 157–66; *Leg.* 1.74; 3.232; *Det.* 35–40; *Post.* 101, 150; *Gig.* 39; *Agr.* 136–45, 159–64; *Conf.* 39; *Mig.* 82; *Congr.* 52–53, 67; *Fug.* 209; *Ios.* 125; *Contempl.* 4; *QG* 4.95.

Soul: (a) Stoic: eight parts to the soul, one part rational, seven parts irrational (*Leg.* 1.11; *Det.* 167–68; *Agr.* 30; *QG* 1.75, 77; 3.4; 4.110); rational part: mind, the dominant element (*Leg.* 1.39; *Det.* 80; *Congr.* 26; *Abr.* 57; *Spec.* 1.333); spirit the "soul's soul" (*Her.* 55; *Spec.* 4.123), a fragment or ray of the divine (*Leg.* 3.161; *Spec.* 4.123); irrational part: the five senses, organs of speech and generation (*Leg.* 1.11, 24; *Congr.* 21; *Spec.* 1.333); blood the substance of the irrational part (*Det.* 79–82; *Spec.* 4.122); cf. *Leg.* 2.2, 6; (b) Platonic: soul consists of three parts—reasoning part, spirited part, desiring part (*Leg.* 1.70; 3.115; *Conf.* 21; *Her.* 225; *Spec.* 4.92–93); soul fashioned after the image (*eikōn*) of the One who is; image of God is the *logos*, through which the whole world was made (*Spec.* 1.81); incorporeal (*Somn.* 1.30); (c) soul in the body is like the mind in the soul or heaven in the world or God in heaven (*Her.* 233; *Abr.* 272); can soar to behold the uncreated and divine (*Legat.* 5); has prophetic potential (*Flacc.* 186); temple (*Somn.* 1.215); (d) death not the end, separation from body and return to God (*Abr.* 258), immortal (*Spec.* 1.81); (e) soul of infant neither good nor bad (*Leg.* 2.53); (f) souls fill the universe, roam the sky (*Conf.* 176; *Somn.* 1.135). See also **Mind.**

Spirit (*pneuma*): (a) connotes strength and vigor and power (*Leg.* 1.42); (b) relates to day one of creation in Genesis (*Opif.* 30); (c) generates thoughts (*Spec.* 1.6); (d) formed according to the archetypal idea of the divine image (*Spec.* 1.171); (e) substance of the rational part of soul, soul's soul (*Her.* 55; *Spec.* 4.123).

Stars: (a) visible (have bodies) but divine, rational natures (*Opif.* 73, 144), made up of pure substance (*Decal.* 64); but cf. mind in its purest form (*Gig.* 7–8; *Plant.* 12; *Somn.* 1.23, 135); (b) serve the purpose of aiding human sight (*Abr.* 158).

Synagogue (*synagōgion*): schools of self-control and righteousness (*Legat.* 312), virtue (*Spec.* 2.62); see *Spec.* 2.88.

***Telos,* or Goal of Life.** See **Happiness.**

Temple, Cosmic: (a) cosmic: universe the truest temple of God, with angels as priests (*Plant.* 50; *Her.* 75; *Somn.* 1.215; *Spec.* 1.66); (b) soul: *Her.* 75; *Somn.* 1.215.

Temple, Jerusalem: (a) description (*Spec.* 1.67–79); (b) one God, so one temple (*Spec.* 1.67); (c) greatest Jewish zeal toward (*Legat.* 212); (d) attempted desecration by Caligula by setting up a colossal statue of himself (*Legat.* 184–348); (e) cf. *Spec.* 1.69, 77–78; *Legat.* 156, 212, 216, 312.

Ten Commandments, or Ten Words. See **Decalogue.**

Time: (a) began simultaneously with world or after (*Opif.* 26; *Sacr.* 65; *Aet.* 53); came to exist through the (creation of) the world (*Leg.* 1.2; *Deus* 31); (b) cf. *Ios.* 10.

Truth: cf. *Ios.* 68, 95; *Mos.* 2.177; *Decal.* 7, 138; *Prob.* 158; *Flacc.* 99.

Virgins: (a) Philo's definition (*Spec.* 1.107); (b) minds easily influenced to virtue and ready to be taught (*Spec.* 1.105); (c) belong in the innermost part of the house (*Spec.* 3.169). See also **Women.**

Virtue (*aretē*): (a) virtue the art of all life (*Leg.* 1.57); (b) a gift of God for the mortal race (*Leg.* 1.45; *Virt.* 55); (c) the dominant virtues are prudence (*phronēsis*), temperance (*sōphrosunē*), justice (*dikaiosunē*), and courage (*andreia*) (cf.

> "Virtue is the art of all life" (*Leg.* 1.57).

Leg. 1.63; *Cher.* 6, 96; *Sacr.* 37, 54, 84; *Deus* 79; *Agr.* 18; *Ebr.* 23; *Sobr.* 38; *Somn.* 2.243; *Abr.* 219; *Mos.* 2.185, 216; *Prob.* 67; *QG* 1.12); (d) other virtues (*Leg.* 1.66; *Cher.* 96; *Praem.* 160; *Virt.* 51; cf. treatise *On Virtues*); (e) opposed to pleasure (e.g., *Ios.* 153); (f) Abraham—virtue by teaching; Isaac—by nature; Jacob—by practice (*Leg.* 3.18; *Sac.* 7; *Deus* 4; *Congr.* 31, 35–36, 46, 69–70; *Fug.* 166; *Mut.* 12; *Somn.* 1.160, 167; 2.10; *Abr.* 52–53; *Mos.* 1.76; *Praem.* 27, 31–46, 58–59); (g) cf. *Congr.* 9–19, 53; *Virt.* 10. See also **Courage, Godliness, Justice, Self-Control, Wisdom.**

War: cf. *Conf.* 43, 46; *Abr.* 225.

Wisdom: (a) definition: the knowledge of divine and human things, as well as their causes (*Congr.* 79; cf. *Deus* 143; *QG* 3.43); (b) origins in sight (*Abr.* 163); (c) heavenly wisdom's allegorical names: "beginning," "image," "vision of God" (*Leg.* 1.43; cf. *Her.* 53, 112, 182, 297–99, 314); instrument of creation (*Det.* 54; *Ebr.* 30–33; *Fug.* 109), masculine (*Fug.* 51); cf. *Det.* 115; *Mig.* 40; *QG* 1.8; (d) earthly wisdom a copy (*mimēsis*) of heavenly wisdom as an archetype (*archetypos*) (*Leg.* 1.43; cf. *Somn.* 2.12); (e) cf. *Leg.* 1.66–67; *Abr.* 57; *Decal.* 98–100.

Women: (a) belong in the private domain of the house, passive role, less complete, serve husbands, as opposed to men who belong to the public domain, active role, more complete (*Leg.* 3.40; *Det.* 172; *Ebr.* 59; *Abr.* 102–3, 135–36, 150; *Mos.* 1.8; *Spec.* 1.200–201; 2.124; 3.169–77; 4.223; *Hypoth.* 7.3); (b) judgments weaker than those of men; are limited to the senses, with exceptions (*Prob.* 117; *Legat.* 320; *QG* 3.3); (c) gender distinctions apply only to humans (*Agr.* 139); (d) women of innocence veil their heads (*Spec.* 3.56, 60); (e) cf. *Opif.*

> "Wisdom is the knowledge of divine and human things, as well as their causes" (*Congr.* 79).

151–52, 165; *Congr.* 180; *Fug.* 51, 128, 167; *Somn.* 2.9; *Mos.* 1.14; 2.236; *Spec.* 2.124–25, 207; 3.32–36; *Virt.* 19–21; *Contempl.* 33, 69; *Hypoth.* 11.14–17; *Flacc.* 89; *Legat.* 39. See also **Virgins.**

Word. See *Logos.*

World: (a) partitioned into earth and sea, air and heaven (*Flacc.* 123); (b) world a city (*polis*) with heavenly bodies as rulers and creations beneath the moon as subjects (*Mig.* 59; *Spec.* 1.13; *Mos.* 2.51); ruled by law (*Ios.* 29); Adam first citizen (*Opif.* 143–44); Abraham contemplated it (*Abr.* 61); Moses world citizen (*Mos.* 1.157); true statesman citizen of the world (e.g., Joseph; *Ios.* 69); associates of wisdom its citizens (*Spec.* 2.45); cf. *Somn.* 1.39, 243; (c) God's son (*Mos.* 2.134); (d) governed by providence (*Praem.* 23, 42). See also **Cosmology.**

World of Ideas. See **Incorporeal World of Ideas.**

Notes

1. The standard translation for English speakers, made by F. H. Colson et al., *Philo with an English Translation*, 10 vols. (Loeb Classical Library: Cambridge, MA: Harvard University Press, 1929–62).
2. The notes do not cover the two supplements to the series that translate the Armenian text of Questions and Answers on Genesis and Exodus, which appeared separately from the other ten volumes; R. Marcus, trans. *Philo: Supplements 1–2* (Loeb Classical Library: Cambridge, MA: Harvard University Press, 1953). The second of these supplements includes numerous fragments of Philo's writings.
3. *The Works of Philo: Complete and Unabridged*, new updated version (Peabody, MA: Hendrickson, 1993).
4. P. Borgen, K. Fuglseth, and R. Skarsten, *The Philo Index: A Complete Greek Word Index to the Writings of Philo of Alexandria* (Grand Rapids: Wm. B. Eerdmans, 2000).

Glossary

allegorical interpretation: Interpretation that ascribes hidden, symbolic meanings to various elements in a text that are not the meanings of the words in their normal or plain sense.

anagogical: Leading the human soul upward to the realm of the divine.

apocalyptic: Relating to the revelation of events in the heavenly realm to those on earth, usually in relation to some approaching transformation or judgment of the earthly realm at a specific point in time.

archetype (*archetypos*): Term Plato used for the realities in the world of ideas that stood behind the shadowy representations of them in the visible world.

Aristeas, Letter of: Pseudonymous work from the second century BCE that presents a fictional account of the Pentateuch's translation into Greek.

Aristobulus: Jewish thinker from Alexandria in the mid–second century BCE who incorporated Greek philosophy into his interpretation of Scripture and Jewish practice.

bios: An ancient biography

copy (*mimēma*): Term Plato used for the visible things in the world of sense, which were far less real than their ideal counterparts.

corporeal: Embodied, with a body (not necessarily a physical one).

covenantal nomism: The notion that normative Jewish practice is based on a solemn agreement or covenant between God and Israel as found in the Jewish law (the Pentateuch).

creatio aeterna: The notion that God has created the world for all of eternity past.

creatio ex nihilo: The notion that God created the universe from no prior existing materials.

creatio simultanea: The idea that creation took place at the point when God created time.

determinism: The belief that the course of unfolding events is already determined, destined, or fated, often accompanied by the idea that some directive force is operative behind those events.

Dyad: In Pythagorean and Platonic thought, the passive of two supreme principles, also known as Limitlessness. Middle Platonic thinkers placed it below a single, transcendent principle.

Encyclios paideia: The general education expected of a cultured individual, a course of study involving such subjects as grammar, arithmetic, rhetoric, dialectic, geometry, music, and astronomy.

epistemology: The field of philosophy devoted to the question of how we know what we know (logic, the ancient term).

eschatology: The field that questions whether history is moving toward a climactic moment, often the end of the world ("study of last things").

essence: That without which something would not be what it is.

Eusebius: Church historian (ca. 263–339 CE) who facilitated the use of Philo's writings in defending the intellectual respectability of the Jewish Scriptures or Old Testament.

forms (*idea*): Term Plato used for the realities in the world of ideas that stood behind the shadowy representations of them in the visible world.

gymnasium: The center of Greek culture for the elite of society in the Hellenistic Age. Here male youths received both physical and intellectual training, leading to their passage into manhood.

haggadah: The interpretation and appropriation of biblical stories.

halakhah: Jewish ethics and practice; Jewish teaching on how to live.

hypostasis: A distinct entity or personality, even if also a subordinate and closely related one.

ideas: For Plato, the realities behind the visible world of sense-perception. The physical things around us are only shadowy copies and images of the real, ideal patterns we understand with our minds.

image (*eikōn*): Term Plato used for the visible things in the world of sense, which were far less real than their ideal counterparts.

incorporeal: Not embodied.

interpolation: A later insertion into a text.

Jews, Diaspora: Jews who lived outside of Palestine; Jews who had "dispersed."

Jews, Hellenistic: Jews for whom Greek was a first language.

lacuna: A lost portion of text.

logic: In the ancient world, the field of philosophy devoted to the question of how we know what we know.

logos: Reason or word. In the Stoic system, the divine reason that directed and permeated the world. In Middle Platonism, the middle term between God and the world, which is both a copy of God and (as container of the world of ideas) a pattern for the world of sense.

metaphysics: The study of the world and of the nature of reality.

Middle Platonism: The form Platonism took on in the period between the first century BCE and the end of the second century CE. Platonists in this period placed Plato's ideas in an intermediate position between a transcendent, supreme principle of which it was a copy and the world of sense that was a copy of it. Platonism in this period was highly eclectic, particularly in its combination of Platonism with Stoic and Pythagorean philosophy.

Mishnah: A collection of Jewish oral traditions on the meaning of the law and how to keep it, dating to about the year 200 CE.

Monad: Another name for the One; in Pythagorean and Platonic thought, the active of two supreme principles, also known as Limit. Middle Platonic thinkers could use it both in this sense and of a single, supreme, transcendent principle beyond it.

monism: The belief that everything that exists consists of the same type of "stuff," whatever it might be (e.g., material, ideal).

monotheism: Belief in a single God in the most literal sense of that word.

negative theology/*via negativa*: The idea that God is known not by what he is but by what he is not. Knowledge of God is thus often conceived in mystical terms.

Neo-Pythagoreanism: The revival of interest in the teachings of Pythagoras that took place in some circles in the period from the first century BCE to the second century CE.

Origen: The one (ca. 185–254 CE) we have most to thank for the survival of the Philonic corpus. His interest in Philo came mostly from the use of allegorical methods to interpret the Bible.

paideia: Greek education.

particularism, Jewish: An emphasis on the sole legitimacy of the Jewish way of life over and against other races and influences.

pattern (*paradeigma*): Term Plato used for the realities in the world of ideas that stood behind the shadowy representations of them in the visible world.

physics: In the ancient world, the study of the world and of the nature of reality (i.e., metaphysics).

politeuma: A smaller political unit within a city, usually a particular ethnic group allowed limited authority to self-govern according to its own customs. Sometimes such a body was directed by an *ethnarch* (a single ethnic leader), as the Alexandrian Jews were until the time of the emperor Augustus. After

Augustus, the Jews had this limited self-governance by way of a *gerousia* (a council of elders).

proselyte: A convert from one religion to another.

providence: For the Stoics, another word for the *logos,* or rational, directive force behind what happens in the world.

pseudonymity: The practice of writing under the authority of another name, usually an authority figure from the past.

resurrection: Rising from the dead, often understood by Jews in bodily terms.

senses: The faculties of a person that see, hear, touch, smell, and taste—that perceive the physical, visible world around us.

Septuagint: Properly, the Greek translation of the Pentateuch made in Alexandria in the third century BCE. Scholars also regularly use the term in reference to the translation of the entire Jewish Scriptures prevalent at the time of Christ.

shadow (*skia*): Term Plato used for the visible things in the world of sense, which were far less real than their ideal counterparts.

Stoicism: Founded by Zeno of Citium around 300 BCE in Athens, Stoicism emphasized the rational structure and direction of the universe, urging a life in accord with nature and the elimination of the passions.

transcendent: Beyond everything else that exists.

universalism, Jewish: The belief that non-Jewish races and religions are equally valid to the Jewish equivalents, that a person can have legitimate status before God outside of Jewish practices and beliefs.

Wisdom of Solomon: A book of wisdom reputed to come from Solomon, likely written in Alexandria either the first century before or after Christ. It reflects Platonic influence at various points.

world of ideas: The world of all the Platonic ideals and forms taken together.

world of senses: The world of all the shadowy copies of the ideas, perceived by our senses.

Bibliography

8.1 TEXTS/COLLECTIONS OF PHILO'S WORKS

8.1.1 The Whole Corpus

Colson, F. H. et al. *Philo with an English Translation*. 10 vols. Loeb Classical Library. Cambridge, MA: Harvard University Press, 1929–62.

Marcus, R., trans. *Philo: Supplements 1–2*. Vol. 1, *Questions and Answers on Genesis*. Vol. 2, *Questions and Answers on Exodus*. 2 vols. Loeb Classical Library. Cambridge, MA: Harvard University Press, 1953.

The Works of Philo: Complete and Unabridged. Translated by C. D. Yonge. New updated version. Peabody, MA: Hendrickson, 1993.

8.1.2 Individual Treatises and Fragments

Hadas-Lebel, M. *De Providentia I et II: Philon d'Alexandrie*. Paris: Éditions du Cerf, 1973.

Harris, J. R. *Fragments of Philo Judaeus*. Cambridge: Cambridge University Press, 1886.

Siegert, F. "The Philonian Fragment *De Deo*: First English Translation." *SPhA* 10 (1998): 1–33.

Smallwood, E. Mary. *Philonis Alexandrini Legatio ad Gaium: Edited with an Introduction Translation and Commentary*. Leiden: E. J. Brill, 1961.

Terian, A. *Philonis Alexandrini De Animalibus: The Armenian Text with Introduction, Translation, and Commentary.* Chico, CA: Scholars Press, 1981.

8.2 BIBLIOGRAPHIES OF PHILO STUDIES

Goodhart, H. L., and E. R. Goodenough. "A General Bibliography of Philo Judaeus." In E. R. Goodenough, *The Politics of Philo Judaeus: Practice and Theory,* 125–32. New Haven, CT: Yale University Press, 1938.
Radice, R., and D. T. Runia. *Philo of Alexandria: An Annotated Bibliography 1937–1986* 2d ed. VChrS 8. Leiden: E. J. Brill, 1992.
Runia, D. T. *Philo of Alexandria: An Annotated Bibliography 1987–96* VChrS 57. Leiden: E. J. Brill, 2000 [continued yearly in the *Studia Philonica Annual*].

8.3 RECENT COMMENTARIES ON PHILO'S WORKS

Hadas-Lebel, M. *De Providentia I et II: Philon d'Alexandrie.* Paris: Éditions du Cerf, 1973.
Runia, D. T. *On the Creation of the Cosmos according to Moses.* Leiden: E. J. Brill, 2001.
Siegert, F. *Philon von Alexandrien: Über die Gottesbezeichnung "wohltätig verzehrendes Feuer" (De Deo): Rückübersetzung des Fragments aus dem Armenischen, deutsche Übersetzung und Kommentar.* WUNT 46. Tübingen: Mohr/Siebeck, 1987.
Terian, A. *Philonis Alexandrini De Animalibus: The Armenian Text with Introduction, Translation, and Commentary.* Chico, CA: Scholars Press, 1981.
van der Horst, P. *Philo's Flaccus: The First Pogrom.* Leiden: E. J. Brill, 2003.
Winston, D. *Philo of Alexandria: The Contemplative Life, the Giants and Selections.* New York: Paulist Press, 1981.
Winston, D., and J. Dillon, eds. *Two Treatises of Philo of Alexandria: A Commentary on* De Gigantibus *and* Quod Deus Sit Immutabilis. Chico, CA: Brown Judaic Studies, 1983.

8.4 BOOKS AND ARTICLES ON PHILO

Attridge, H. A. *The Epistle to the Hebrews.* Philadelphia: Fortress Press, 1989.
Bamberger, B. J. "Philo and the Aggadah." *HUCA* 48 (1977): 153–85.
Barclay, J. M. G. *Jews in the Mediterranean Diaspora: From Alexander to Trajan (323 BCE–117 CE).* Berkeley: University of California Press, 1996.
Barrett, C. K. "The Eschatology of the Epistle to the Hebrews." In *The Background of the New Testament and Its Eschatology*, ed. D. Daube and W. D. Davies, 363–93. Cambridge: Cambridge University Press, 1956.
Birnbaum, E. *The Place of Judaism in Philo's Thought: Israel, Jews, and Proselytes.* Atlanta: Scholars Press, 1996.
———. "Allegorical Interpretation and Jewish Identity among Alexandrian Jewish Writers." In *Neotestamentica et Philonica: Studies in Honor of Peder Borgen*, ed. D. E. Aune, T. Seland, and J. H. Ulrichsen, 307–29. Leiden: E. J. Brill, 2003.
Borgen, P. *Bread from Heaven: An Exegetical Study of the Concept of Manna in the Gospel of John and the Writings of Philo.* SNT 10. Leiden: E. J. Brill, 1965.
———. *Philo, John, and Paul: New Perspectives on Judaism and Early Christianity.* Atlanta: Scholars Press, 1987.

———. "There Shall Come Forth a Man": Reflections on Messianic Ideas in Philo." In *The Messiah: Developments in Earliest Judaism and Christianity*, 341–61. Minneapolis: Fortress Press, 1992.

———. *Philo of Alexandria: An Exegete for His Time*. Leiden: E. J. Brill, 1997.

Borgen, P. and R. Skarsten. "Quaestiones et Solutiones: Some Observations on the Form of Philo's Exegesis." *SPhilo* 4 (1976–77): 1–15.

Borgen, P., K. Fuglseth, and R. Skarsten. *The Philo Index: A Complete Greek Word Index to the Writings of Philo of Alexandria*. Grand Rapids: Wm. B. Eerdmans, 2000.

Brandenberger, E. *Fleisch und Geist: Paulus und die dualistische Weisheit*. WMANT 29. Neukirchen-Vluyn: Neukirchener Verlag, 1968.

Braun, F.-M. *Jean le théologien*, Etudes bibliques. Vol. 2: *Les grandes traditions d'Israël et l'accord des écritures selon le quatrième évangile*. Paris: Gabalda, 1964.

Bréhier, É. *Les Idées philosophiques et religieuses de Philon d'Alexandrie*. 3d ed. Paris: Gabalda, 1950.

Cazeaux, J. *La trame et la chain: ou les structures littéraires et l'exégèse dans cinq des traits de Philon d'Alexandrie*. ALGHJ 15. Leiden: E. J. Brill, 1983.

Chadwick, H. "St. Paul and Philo of Alexandria." *Bulletin of the John Rylands Library* 48 (1966): 287–88.

Cohen, N. G. *Philo Judaeus: His Universe of Discourse*. BEATAJ 24. Frankfurt am Main: Peter Lang, 1995.

Collins, J. J. *Between Athens and Jerusalem: Jewish Identity in the Hellenistic Diaspora*. 2d ed. Grand Rapids: Wm. B. Eerdmans, 2000.

DeMaris, R. E. *The Colossian Controversy: Wisdom in Dispute at Colossae*. SNTSMS 96. Sheffield: JSOT, 1994.

Dey, L. K. K. *The Intermediary World and Patterns of Perfection in Philo and Hebrews*. SBLDS 25. Missoula, MT: Scholars Press, 1975.

Dillon, J. *The Middle Platonists: 80 B.C. to A.D. 220*. Rev. ed. Ithaca, NY: Cornell University Press, 1977.

Dodd, C. H. *The Interpretation of the Fourth Gospel*. Cambridge: Cambridge University Press, 1953.

Dodds, E. R. "The Parmenides of Plato and the Origin of the Neoplatonic 'One.'" *CQ* 22 (1928): 132 n. 1.

Drummond, J. *Philo Judaeus: The Jewish-Alexandrian Philosophy in Its Development and Completion*. 2 vols. London, 1888.

Dunn, J. D. G. *Christology in the Making: An Inquiry into the Origins of the Doctrine of the Incarnation*. London: SCM, 1980.

Eisele, W. *Ein unerschütterliches Reich: Die mittelplatonische Umformung des Parusiegedankens im Hebräerbrief*. BZNW 116. Berlin: Walter de Gruyter, 2003.

Feld, H. "Der Hebräerbrief: Literarische Form, religionsgeschichtlicher Hintergrund, theologische Fragen." In *ANRW* II 25.4 (1987): 3522–601.

Feldman, L. H. *Jew and Gentile in the Ancient World: Attitudes and Interactions from Alexander to Justinian*. Princeton, NJ: Princeton University Press, 1993.

Festugière, A. J. *La révélation d'Hermès trismégiste*. Paris: Gabalda, 1945–54.

Frick, Peter, *Divine Providence in Philo of Alexandria*. WUNT 77. Tübingen: Mohr/Siebeck, 1999.

Glucker, J. *Antiochus and the Late Academy*. Göttingen: Vandenhoeck & Ruprecht, 1978.

Goodenough, E. R. "Philo's Exposition of the Law and His De Vita Mosis." *HTR* 26 (1933): 109–25.

———. *By Light, Light: The Mystic Gospel of Hellenistic Judaism*. New Haven, CT: Yale University Press, 1935.

———. *The Politics of Philo Judaeus: Practice and Theory*. New Haven, CT: Yale University Press, 1938.

———. *An Introdution to Philo Judaeus.* 1940. Reprint, Oxford: Oxford University Press, 1979.

Goulet, R. *La philosophie de Moïse: essai de reconstitution d'un commentaire philosophique préphilonien du Pentateuque.* Paris: Université de Paris, 1987.

Grabbe, L. L. "Philo and the Aggada: A Response to B. J. Bamberger." *SPhA* 3 (1991): 153–66.

Hamerton-Kelly, R. G. "Sources and Traditions in Philo of Alexandria: Prolegomena to an Analysis of His Writings." *SPhilo* 1 (1972): 3–26.

Hay, D. M. "References to Other Exegetes." In *Both Literal and Allegorical: Studies in Philo of Alexandria's Questions and Answers on Genesis and Exodus,* 81–97. Atlanta: Scholars Press, 1991.

———, ed. *Both Literal and Allegorical: Studies in Philo of Alexandria's* Questions and Answers on Genesis and Exodus. Atlanta: Scholars Press, 1991.

Heinemann, I. *Philons griechische und jüdische Bildung.* 1929. Reprint, Hildesheim: Gg Olms, 1962.

Hengel, M. *Judaism and Hellenism.* 2 vols. Philadelphia: Fortress Press, 1974.

Hilgert, E. "The *Quaestiones*: Texts and Translations." In *Both Literal and Allegorical: Studies in Philo of Alexandria's* Questions and Answers on Genesis and Exodus, ed. D M. Hay, 1–15. Atlanta: Scholars Press, 1991.

Horsley, R. "*Pneumatikos* vs. *Psychikos*: Distinctions of Spiritual Status among the Corinthians." *HTR* 69 (1976): 269–88.

Hurst, L. D. *The Epistle to the Hebrews: Its Background of Thought.* SNTSMS 65. Cambridge: Cambridge University Press, 1990.

Jonas, H. *Gnosis und spätantiker Geist: Von der Mythologie zur mystischen Philosophie.* Göttingen: Vandenhoeck & Ruprecht, 1954.

Kasher, A. *The Jewish in Hellenistic and Roman Egypt.* Tübingen: Mohr/Siebeck, 1985.

Leonhardt, Jutta. *Jewish Worship in Philo of Alexandria.* TSAJ 84. Tübingen: Mohr/Siebeck, 2001.

Long, A. A. *Hellenistic Philosophy: Stoics, Epicureans, Sceptics.* Berkeley: University of California Press, 1986.

Mack, B. "Exegetical Traditions in Alexandrian Judaism: A Program for the Analysis of the Philonic Corpus." *SPhilo* 3 (1974–75): 71–112.

———. "Philo Judaeus and Exegetical Traditions in Alexandria." *ANRW* 21.1 (1984): 227–71.

———. "Wisdom and Apocalyptic in Philo." *SPhA* 3 (1991): 21–39.

MacRae, G. W. "Heavenly Temple and Eschatology in the Letter to the Hebrews." *Semeia* 12 (1978): 179–99.

Massebieau, M. L. "Le classement des oeuvres de Philon," *Bibliothèque de l'École des Hautes Études: Sciences religieuses* 1 (1889): 1–91.

Mendelson, A. *Secular Education in Philo of Alexandria* (Cinncinati: Hebrew Union, 1982).

———. *Philo's Jewish Identity.* Atlanta: Scholars Press, 1988.

Nikiprowetzky, V. *Le commentaire de l'ecriture chez Philon d'Alexandrie.* Leiden: E. J. Brill, 1977.

———. "L'éxègese de Philon d'Alexandrie dans le *De Gigantibus* et le *Quod Deus sit Immutabilis.*" In *Two Treatises of Philo of Alexandria: A Commentary on* De Gigantibus *and* Quod Deus Sit Immutabilis, ed. D. Winston and J. Dillon, 5–75. Atlanta: Scholars Press, 1983.

Pearson, B. *The Pneumatikos-Psychikos Terminology in 1 Corinthians: A Study in the Theology of the Corinthian Opponents of Paul and Its Relation to Gnosticism.* SBLDS 12. Missoula, MT: Scholars Press, 1973.

Radice, R. *Platonismo e creazionismo in Filone di Alessandria.* Milan: Vita e Pensiero, 1989.

Reydams-Schils, G. J. *Demiurge and Providence: Stoic and Platonist Readings of Plato's 'Timaeus.'* Monothéismes et Philosophie. Turnhout: Brepols Publishers, 1999.

Ritter, B. *Philo und die* Halacha. Leipzig, 1879.

Rochais, G. "La formation du prologue (Jn 1:1–18)." *ScEs* 37 (1985): 173–82.

Royse, J. R. "The Original Structure of Philo's *Quaestiones.*" *SPhilo* 4 (1976–77): 48–63.

———. "Philo's Division of His Works into Books." In *In the Spirit of Faith: Studies in Philo and Early Christianity in Honor of David Hay*, SPhA 8 (2001): 59–85.

Runia, D. T. "Further Observations on the Structure of Philo's Allegorical Treatises." In *Exegesis and Philosophy: Studies on Philo of Alexandria*, 114–20. 1985. Reprint, Aldershot: Variorum, 1990.

———. *Philo of Alexandria and the* Timaeus *of Plato*. PhilAnt 44. Leiden: E. J. Brill, 1986.

———. *Exegesis and Philosophy: Studies on Philo of Alexandria*. Aldershot: Variorum, 1990.

———. "Secondary Texts in Philo's *Quaestiones.*" In *Both Literal and Allegorical: Studies in Philo of Alexandria's* Questions and Answers on Genesis and Exodus, ed. D. M. Hay, 47–79. Atlanta: Scholars Press, 1991.

———. *Philo in Early Christian Literature: A Survey*. Minneapolis: Fortress Press, 1993.

Sandbach, F. H. *The Stoics*. Bristol: Chatto & Windus, 1975.

Sandmel, S. *Philo of Alexandria: An Introduction*. Oxford: Oxford University Press, 1979.

Sanders, E. P. *Paul and Palestinian Judaism: A Comparison of Patterns of Religion*. Philadelphia: Fortress Press, 1977.

———. *Paul, the Law, and the Jewish People*. Philadelphia: Fortress Press, 1983.

Schenck, K. L. "Keeping His Appointment: Creation and Enthronement in the Epistle to the Hebrews." *JSNT* 66 (1997): 91–117.

———. "A Celebration of the Enthroned Son: The Catena of Hebrews 1." *JBL* 120 (2001): 469–85.

———. "*Philo and the Epistle to the Hebrews*: Ronald Williamson's Study after Thirty Years." *SPhA* 14 (2002): 112–35.

———. *Understanding the Book of Hebrews: The Story behind the Sermon*. Louisville, KY: Westminster/John Knox Press, 2003.

Schürer, E. *Geschichte des Jüdischen Volkes im Zeitalter Jesu Christi*. Vol 3. 4th ed. Leipzig: Hinrichs, 1909.

Segal, A. F. *The Two Powers in Heaven: Early Rabbinic Reports about Christianity and Gnosticism*. SJLA 25. Leiden: E. J. Brill, 1977.

———. *The Other Judaisms of Late Antiquity*. Atlanta: Scholars Press, 1987.

Sellin, G. *Die Streit um die Auferstehung der Toten: Eine religionsgeschichtliche und exegetische Untersuchung von 1 Korinther 15*. FRLANT 138. Göttingen: Vandenhoeck & Ruprecht, 1986.

Sly, D. *Philo's Perception of Women*. Atlanta: Scholars Press, 1990.

———. *Philo's Alexandria*. London: Routledge, 1996.

Sowers, S. G. *The Hermeneutics of Philo and Hebrews*. Richmond: John Knox Press, 1965.

Spicq, Ç. *L'épître aux Hébreux*. 2 vols. Paris: Gabalda, 1952.

Sterling, G. E. "Philo's *Quaestiones*: Prolegomena or Afterthought." In *Both Literal and Allegorical: Studies in Philo of Alexandria's* Questions and Answers on Genesis and Exodus, ed. D. M. Hay, 99–123. Atlanta: Scholars Press, 1991.

———. "*Creatio Temporalis, Aeterna, vel Continua*? An Analysis of the Thought of Philo of Alexandria." *SPhA* 4 (1992): 15–41.

———. "Philo." In *Dictionary of New Testament Background*, ed. C. A. Evans and S. E. Porter, 789–93. Downers Grove, IL: InterVarsity Press, 1992.

———. "'Wisdom among the Perfect': Creation Traditions in Alexandrian Judaism and Corinthian Christianity." *NovT* 37 (1995): 355–84.

———. "A Philosophy according to the Elements of the Cosmos: Colossian Christianity and Philo of Alexandria." In *Philon d'Alexandrie et le langage de la philosophie*, ed. C. Lévy, 349–73. Monothéismes et Philosophie. Turnhout: Brepols Publishers, 1998.

————. "Prepositional Metaphysics in Jewish Wisdom Speculation and Early Christian Liturgical Texts." In *Wisdom and* Logos: *Studies in Jewish Thought in Honor of David Winston. SPhA* 9 (1997): 219–38.

————. "Recherché or Representative? What Is the Relationship between Philo's Treatises and Greek-speaking Judaism?" *SPhA* 11 (1999): 1–30.

————. "Ontology versus Eschatology: Tensions between Author and Community." In *In the Spirit of Faith: Studies in Philo and Early Christianity in Honor of David Hay,* ed. D. T. Runia and G. E. Sterling. *SPhA* 13 (2001): 208–10.

————. *The Jewish Plato: Philo of Alexandria, Greek-speaking Judaism, and Christian Origins.* Peabody, MA: Hendrickson, forthcoming.

Tcherikover, V. *Hellenistic Civilization and the Jews.* 1958. Reprint, Peabody, MA: Hendrickson, 1999.

Terian, A. "The Priority of *Quaestiones* among Philo's Exegetical Commentaries." In *Both Literal and Allegorical: Studies in Philo of Alexandria's* Questions and Answers on Genesis and Exodus, ed. D. M. Hay, 29–46. Atlanta: Scholars Press, 1991.

————. "Back to Creation: The Beginning of Philo's Third Grand Commentary." In *Wisdom and Logos: Studies in Jewish Thought in Honor of David Winston*, ed. D. T. Runia and G. E. Sterling. *SPhA* 9 (1997): 19–36.

Theiler, W. *Die Vorbereitung des Neuplatonismus.* Berlin: Weidmann, 1930.

————. "Philo von Alexandria und der hellenisierte *Timaeus.*" In *Philomathes: Studies and Essays in the Humanities in Honour of Philip Merlan*, ed. R. B. Palmer and R. G. Hammerton-Kelly, 25–35. The Hague: Martinus Nijhoff, 1971.

Tobin, T. *The Creation of Man: Philo and the History of Interpretation.* CBQMS 14. Washington, DC: Catholic Biblical Association, 1983.

————. "The Prologue of John and Hellenistic Jewish Speculation." *CBQ* 52 (1990): 252–69.

————. "Philo and the Sibyl." In *Wisdom and Logos: Studies in Jewish Thought in Honor of David Winston*, ed. D. T. Runia and G. E. Sterling. *SPhA* 9 (1997): 84–103.

Walter, N. *Der Thoraausleger Aristobulus.* TU 86. Berlin: Akademie, 1964.

Wan, Sze-kar. "Philo's *Quaestiones et Solutions in Genesim et in Exodum*: A Synoptic Approach." Th.D. diss., Harvard University, 1992.

Williamson, R. *Philo and the Epistle to the Hebrews.* ALGHJ 4. Leiden: E. J. Brill, 1970.

Winston, D. *The Wisdom of Solomon: A New Translation with Introduction and Commentary.* New York: Doubleday, 1979.

————. *Philo of Alexandria: The Contemplative Life, the Giants and Selections.* New York: Paulist Press, 1981.

————. "Was Philo a Mystic?" In *Studies in Jewish Mysticism*, ed. J. Dan and F. Talmage, 29–35. Cambridge, MA: Harvard University Press, 1982.

————. *Logos and Mystical Theology in Philo of Alexandria.* Cincinnati: Hebrew Union, 1985.

————. "Response to Runia and Sterling." *SPhA* 5 (1993): 141–46.

————. "Philo's Mysticism." *SPhA* 8 (1996): 74–82.

————. "Freedom and Determinism in Philo of Alexandria." In *The Ancestral Philosophy: Hellenistic Philosophy in Second Temple Judaism: Essays of David Winston,* 135–50. Providence, RI: Brown University Press, 2001.

————. "Philo's Theory of Eternal Creation: Prov. 1.6–9." In *The Ancestral Philosophy: Hellenistic Philosophy in Second Temple Judaism: Essays of David Winston,* 117–27. Providence, RI: Brown University Press, 2001.

Winter, B. W. *Philo and Paul among the Sophists: Alexandrian and Corinthian Responses to a Julio-Claudian Movement.* Grand Rapids: Wm. B. Eerdmans, 1997.

Wolfson, H. *Philo: Foundations of Religious Philosophy in Judaism, Christianity, and Islam.* 2 vols. (Cambridge, MA: Harvard University Press, 1947).

General Index

Source Index

155

Scholar's Index